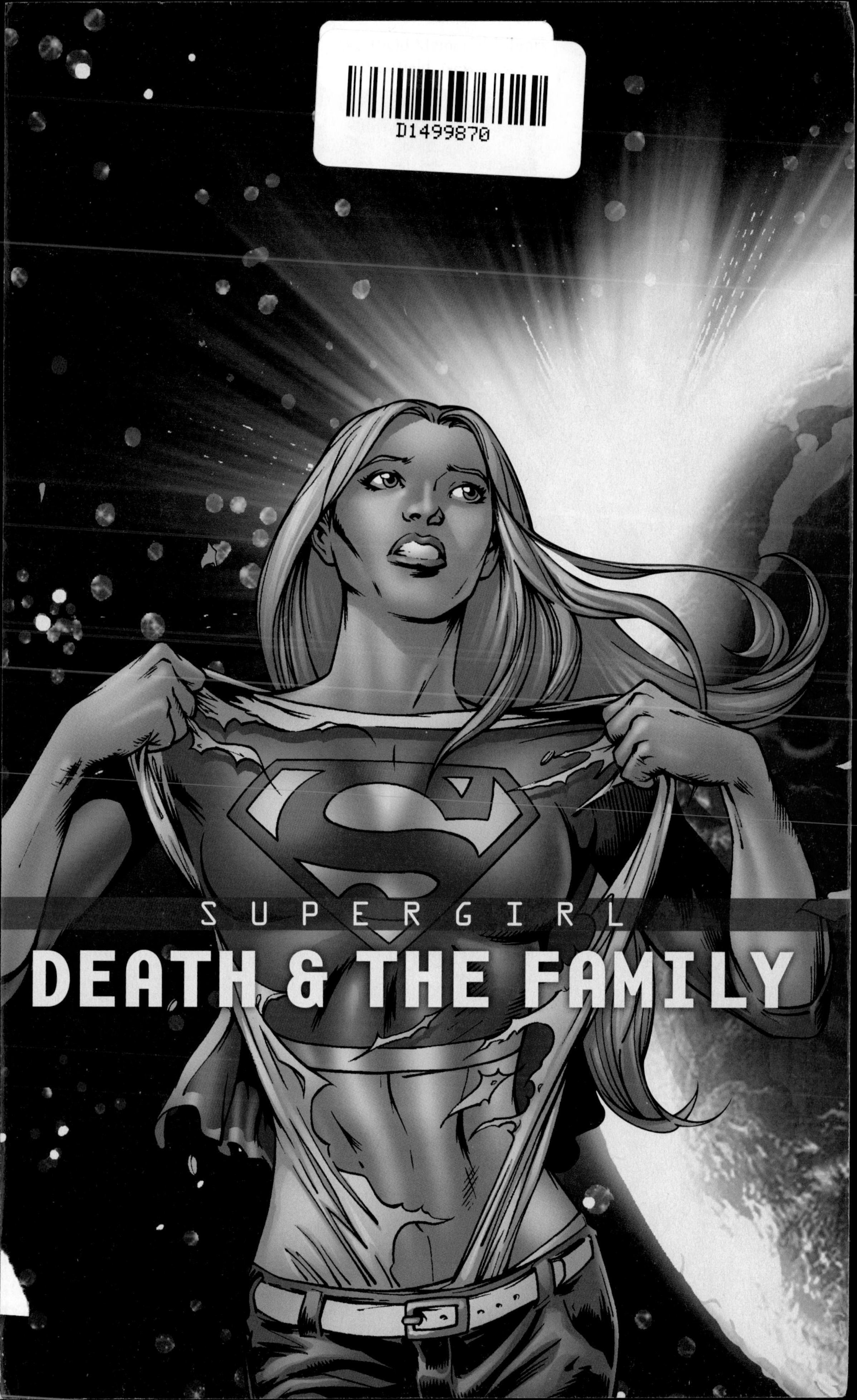
SUPERGIRL
DEATH & THE FAMILY

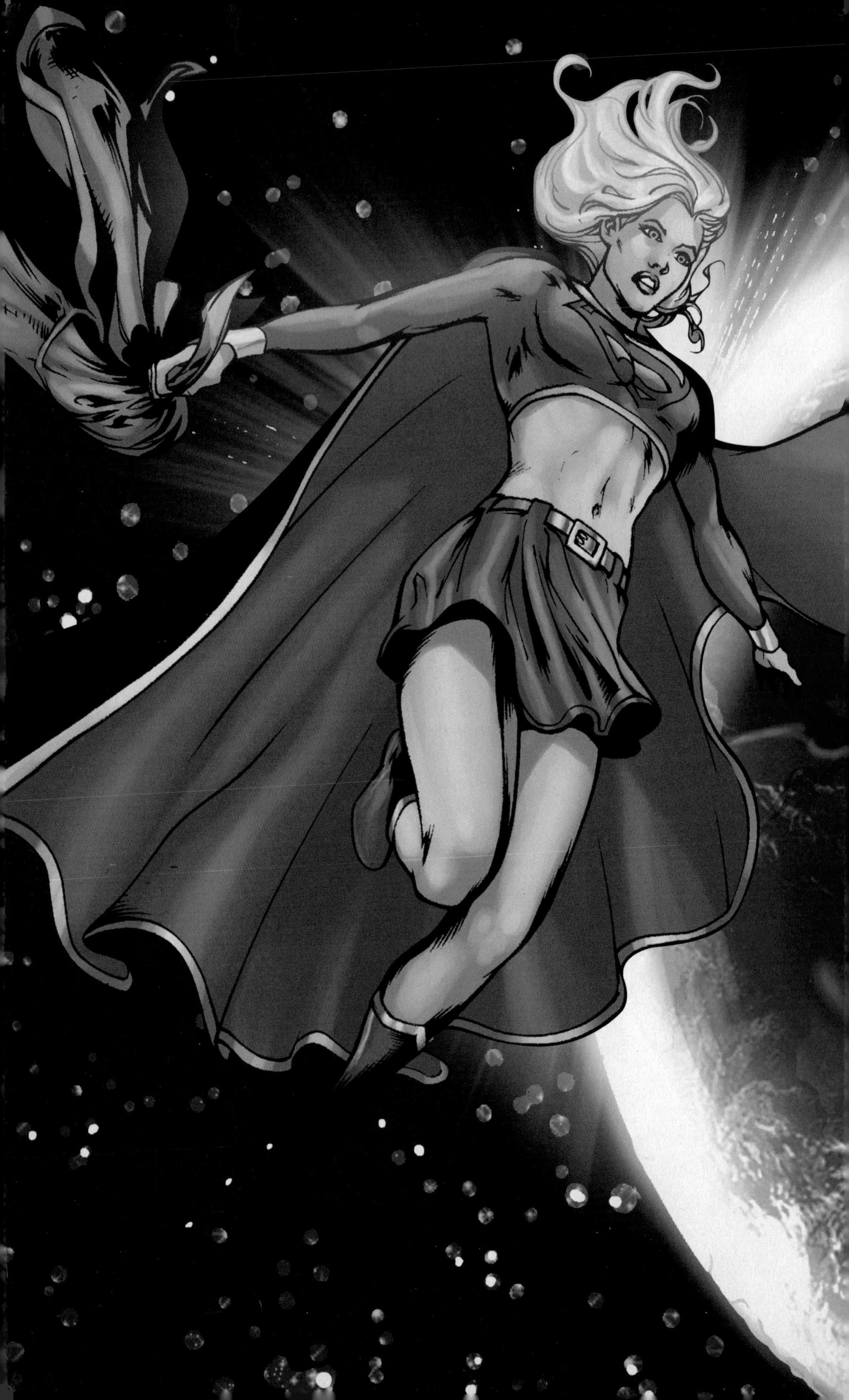

SUPERGIRL
DEATH
& THE FAMILY

STERLING GATES
WITH
JAKE BLACK & HELEN SLATER
WRITERS

FERNANDO DAGNINO JAMAL IGLE
MATT CAMP CLIFF CHIANG
PENCILLERS

RAÚL FERNANDEZ MATT CAMP
JON SIBAL MARK MCKENNA
CLIFF CHIANG
INKERS

BLOND NEI RUFFINO ULISES ARREOLA
PETE PANTAZIS DAVE MCCAIG
COLORISTS

TRAVIS LANHAM
JARED K. FLETCHER
LETTERERS

RENATO GUEDES
COVER

MATT IDELSON EDITOR-ORIGINAL SERIES
WIL MOSS ASSISTANT EDITOR-ORIGINAL SERIES
BOB HARRAS GROUP EDITOR-COLLECTED EDITIONS
BOB JOY EDITOR
ROBBIN BROSTERMAN DESIGN DIRECTOR-BOOKS

DC COMICS
DIANE NELSON PRESIDENT
DAN DIDIO AND **JIM LEE** CO-PUBLISHERS
GEOFF JOHNS CHIEF CREATIVE OFFICER
PATRICK CALDON EVP-FINANCE AND ADMINISTRATION
JOHN ROOD EVP-SALES, MARKETING AND BUSINESS DEVELOPMENT
AMY GENKINS SVP-BUSINESS AND LEGAL AFFAIRS
STEVE ROTTERDAM SVP-SALES AND MARKETING
JOHN CUNNINGHAM VP-MARKETING
TERRI CUNNINGHAM VP-MANAGING EDITOR
ALISON GILL VP-MANUFACTURING
DAVID HYDE VP-PUBLICITY
SUE POHJA VP-BOOK TRADE SALES
ALYSSE SOLL VP-ADVERTISING AND CUSTOM PUBLISHING
BOB WAYNE VP-SALES
MARK CHIARELLO ART DIRECTOR

SUPERGIRL: DEATH & THE FAMILY
PUBLISHED BY DC COMICS. COVER, TEXT AND COMPILATION COPYRIGHT
© 2010 DC COMICS. ALL RIGHTS RESERVED.

ORIGINALLY PUBLISHED IN SINGLE MAGAZINE FORM IN SUPERGIRL 48-50,
SUPERGIRL ANNUAL 1. COPYRIGHT © 2009, 2010 DC COMICS. ALL RIGHTS
RESERVED. ALL CHARACTERS, THEIR DISTINCTIVE LIKENESSES AND RELATED
ELEMENTS FEATURED IN THIS PUBLICATION ARE TRADEMARKS OF DC COMICS.
THE STORIES, CHARACTERS AND INCIDENTS FEATURED IN THIS PUBLICATION
ARE ENTIRELY FICTIONAL. DC COMICS DOES NOT READ OR ACCEPT UNSOLICITED
SUBMISSIONS OF IDEAS, STORIES OR ARTWORK.

DC COMICS, 1700 BROADWAY, NEW YORK, NY 10019
A WARNER BROS. ENTERTAINMENT COMPANY
PRINTED BY QUAD/GRAPHICS, DUBUQUE, IA, USA.
8/18/10. FIRST PRINTING.
ISBN: 978-1-4012-2913-9

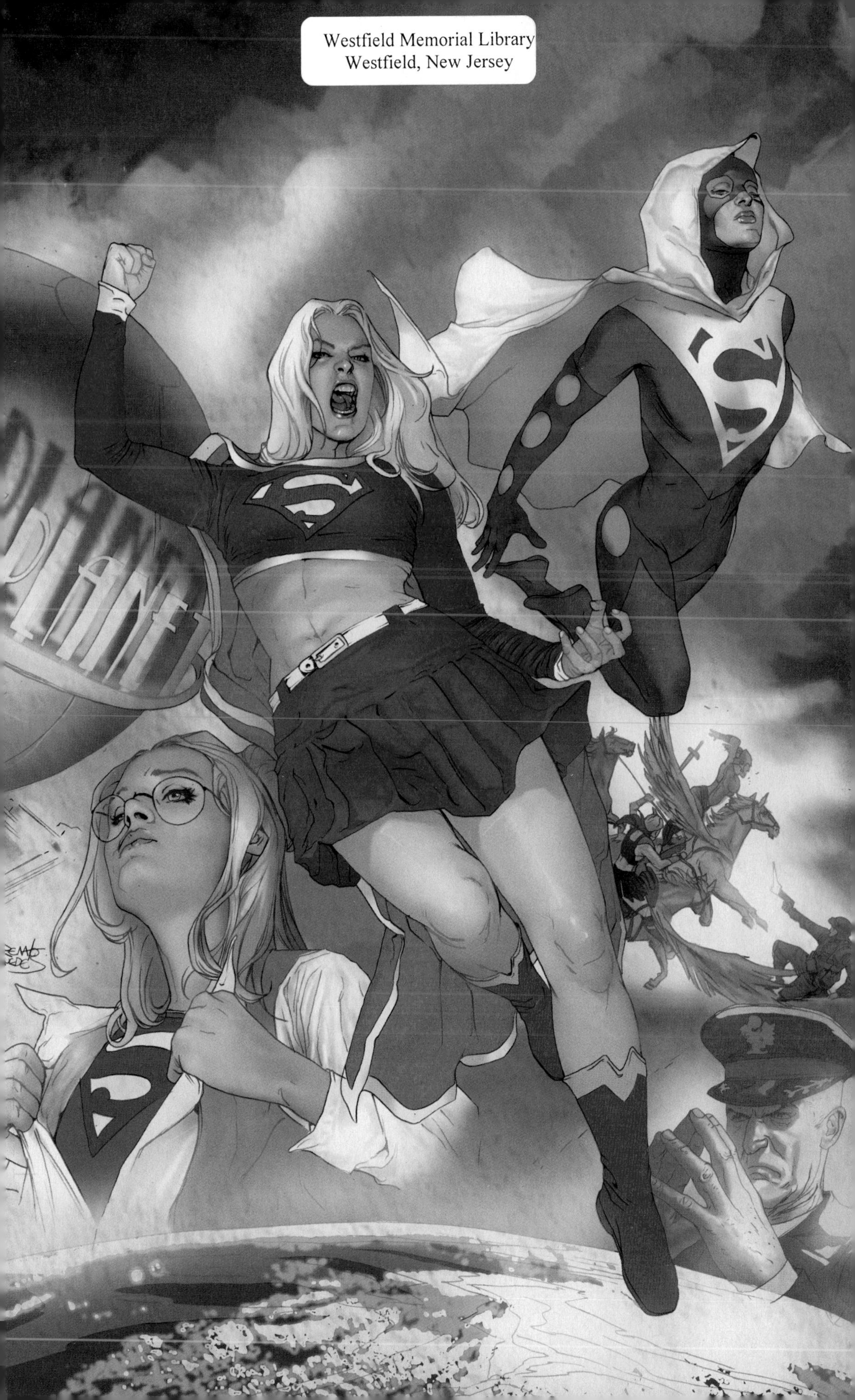

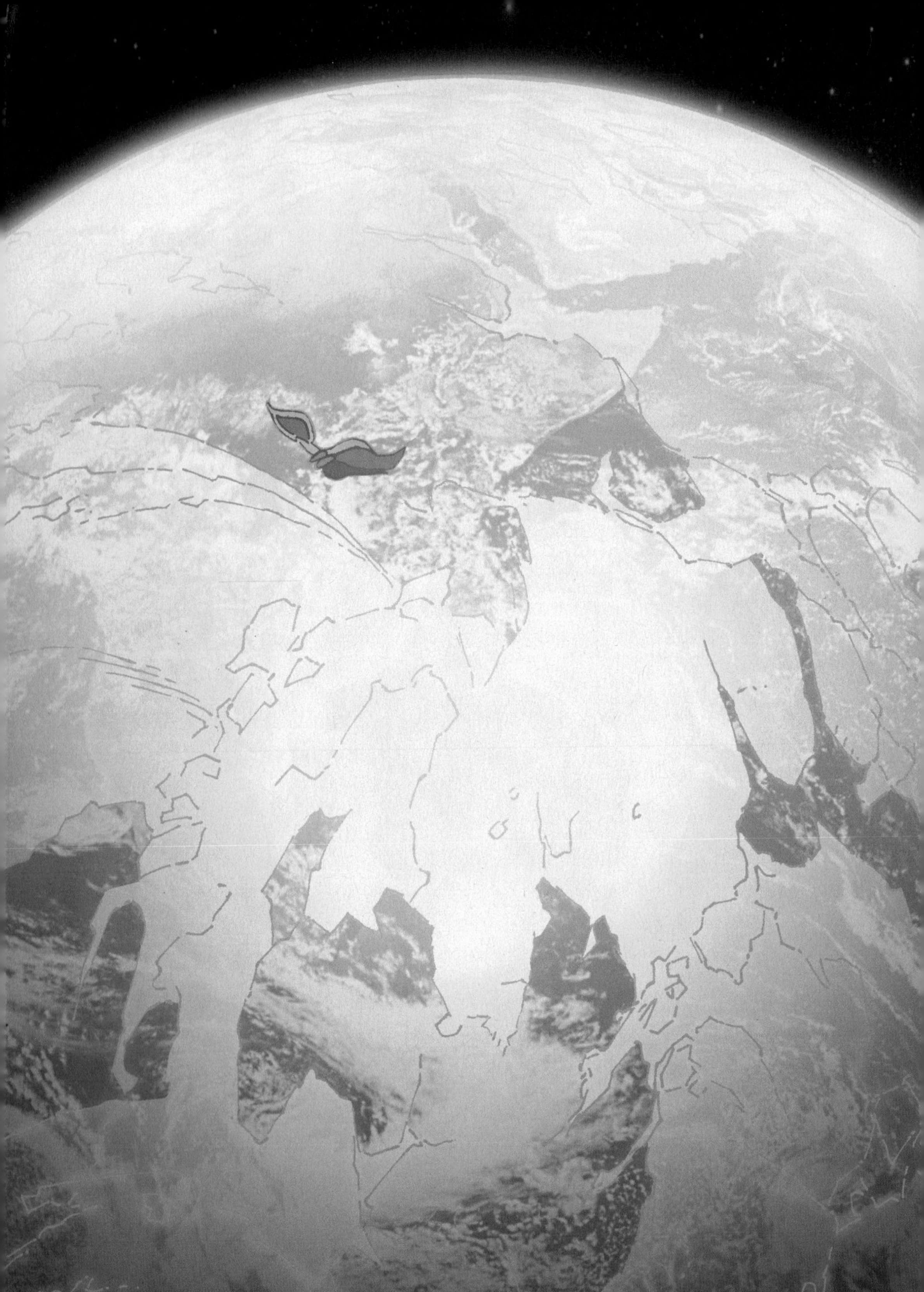

SECRET IDENTITIES

STERLING GATES WRITER **FERNANDO DAGNINO** PENCILLER
RAÚL FERNANDEZ INKER

COVER BY **RENATO GUEDES**

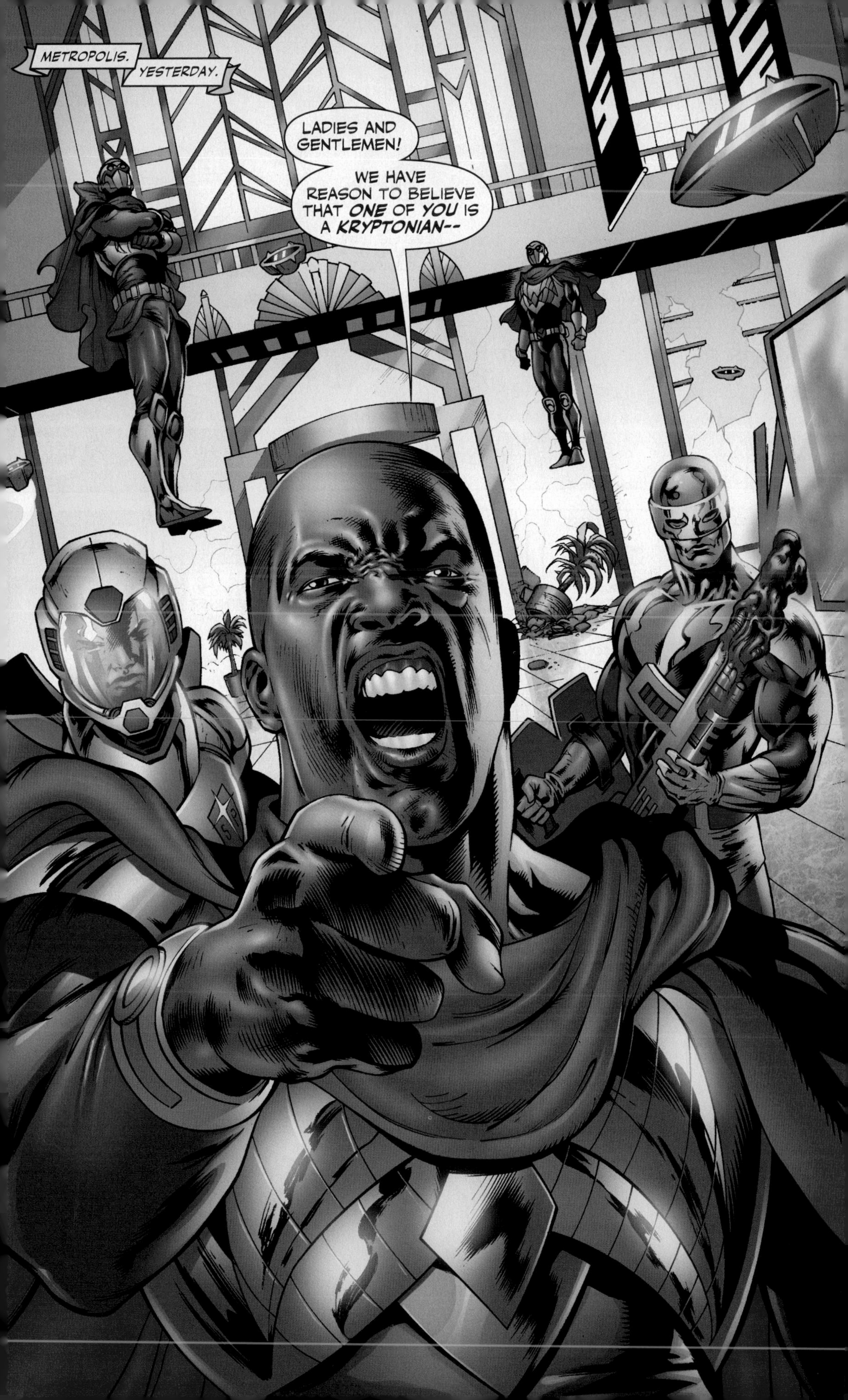
METROPOLIS.
YESTERDAY.
LADIES AND GENTLEMEN!
WE HAVE REASON TO BELIEVE THAT ONE OF YOU IS A KRYPTONIAN--

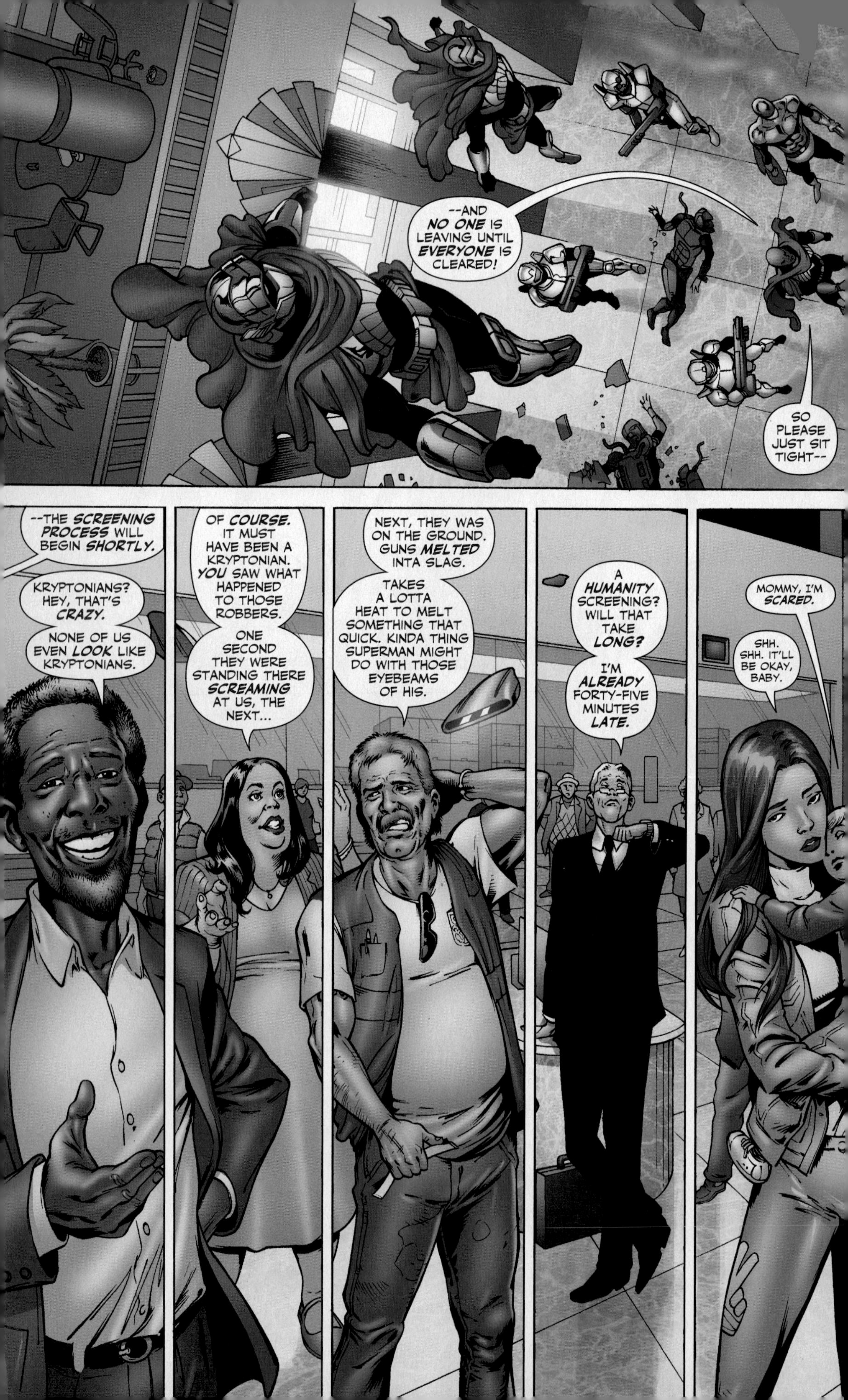
--AND NO ONE IS LEAVING UNTIL EVERYONE IS CLEARED!
SO PLEASE JUST SIT TIGHT--
--THE SCREENING PROCESS WILL BEGIN SHORTLY.
KRYPTONIANS? HEY, THAT'S CRAZY.
NONE OF US EVEN LOOK LIKE KRYPTONIANS.
OF COURSE. IT MUST HAVE BEEN A KRYPTONIAN. YOU SAW WHAT HAPPENED TO THOSE ROBBERS.
ONE SECOND THEY WERE STANDING THERE SCREAMING AT US, THE NEXT...
NEXT, THEY WAS ON THE GROUND. GUNS MELTED INTA SLAG.
TAKES A LOTTA HEAT TO MELT SOMETHING THAT QUICK. KINDA THING SUPERMAN MIGHT DO WITH THOSE EYEBEAMS OF HIS.
A HUMANITY SCREENING? WILL THAT TAKE LONG?
I'M ALREADY FORTY-FIVE MINUTES LATE.
MOMMY, I'M SCARED.
SHH. SHH. IT'LL BE OKAY, BABY.

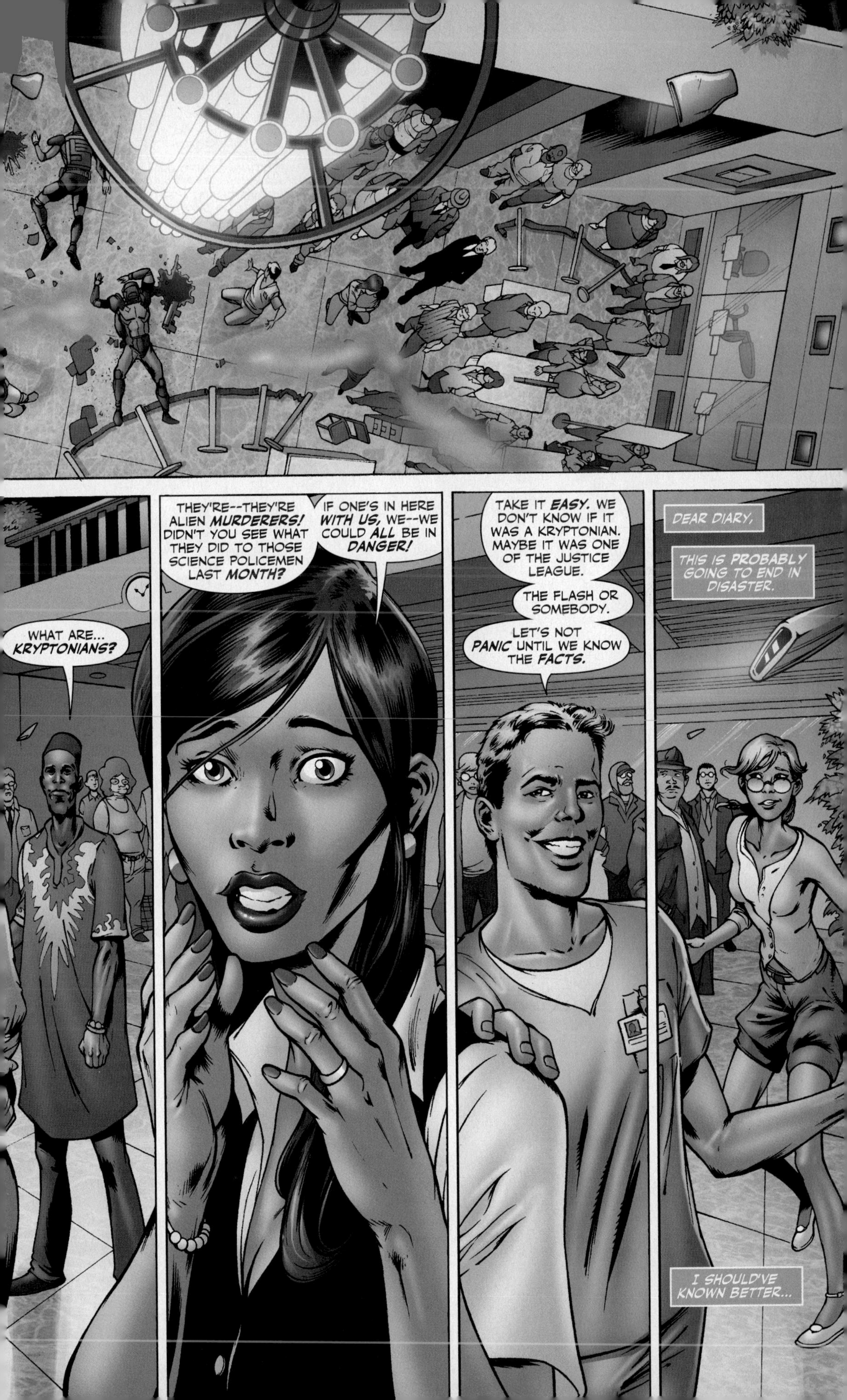
WHAT ARE... KRYPTONIANS?
THEY'RE--THEY'RE ALIEN MURDERERS! DIDN'T YOU SEE WHAT THEY DID TO THOSE SCIENCE POLICEMEN LAST MONTH?
IF ONE'S IN HERE WITH US, WE--WE COULD ALL BE IN DANGER!
TAKE IT EASY. WE DON'T KNOW IF IT WAS A KRYPTONIAN. MAYBE IT WAS ONE OF THE JUSTICE LEAGUE.
THE FLASH OR SOMEBODY.
LET'S NOT PANIC UNTIL WE KNOW THE FACTS.
DEAR DIARY,
THIS IS PROBABLY GOING TO END IN DISASTER.
I SHOULD'VE KNOWN BETTER...

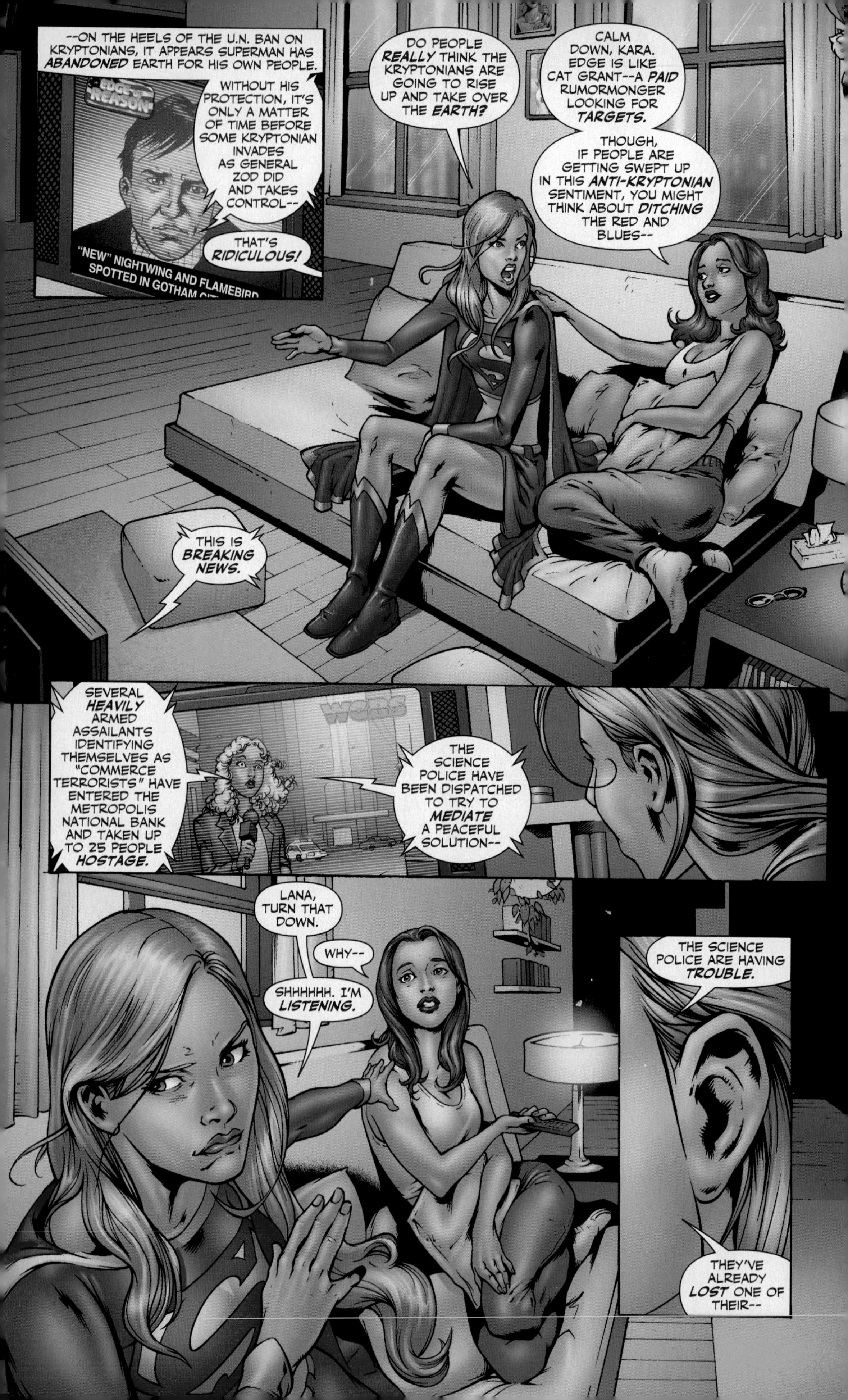
--ON THE HEELS OF THE U.N. BAN ON KRYPTONIANS, IT APPEARS SUPERMAN HAS ABANDONED EARTH FOR HIS OWN PEOPLE.
WITHOUT HIS PROTECTION, IT'S ONLY A MATTER OF TIME BEFORE SOME KRYPTONIAN INVADES AS GENERAL ZOD DID AND TAKES CONTROL--
THAT'S RIDICULOUS!
EDGE OF REASON
"NEW" NIGHTWING AND FLAMEBIRD SPOTTED IN GOTHAM CIT
DO PEOPLE REALLY THINK THE KRYPTONIANS ARE GOING TO RISE UP AND TAKE OVER THE EARTH?
CALM DOWN, KARA. EDGE IS LIKE CAT GRANT--A PAID RUMORMONGER LOOKING FOR TARGETS.
THOUGH, IF PEOPLE ARE GETTING SWEPT UP IN THIS ANTI-KRYPTONIAN SENTIMENT, YOU MIGHT THINK ABOUT DITCHING THE RED AND BLUES--
THIS IS BREAKING NEWS.
SEVERAL HEAVILY ARMED ASSAILANTS IDENTIFYING THEMSELVES AS "COMMERCE TERRORISTS" HAVE ENTERED THE METROPOLIS NATIONAL BANK AND TAKEN UP TO 25 PEOPLE HOSTAGE.
WGBS
THE SCIENCE POLICE HAVE BEEN DISPATCHED TO TRY TO MEDIATE A PEACEFUL SOLUTION--
LANA, TURN THAT DOWN.
WHY--
SHHHHHH. I'M LISTENING.
THE SCIENCE POLICE ARE HAVING TROUBLE.
THEY'VE ALREADY LOST ONE OF THEIR--

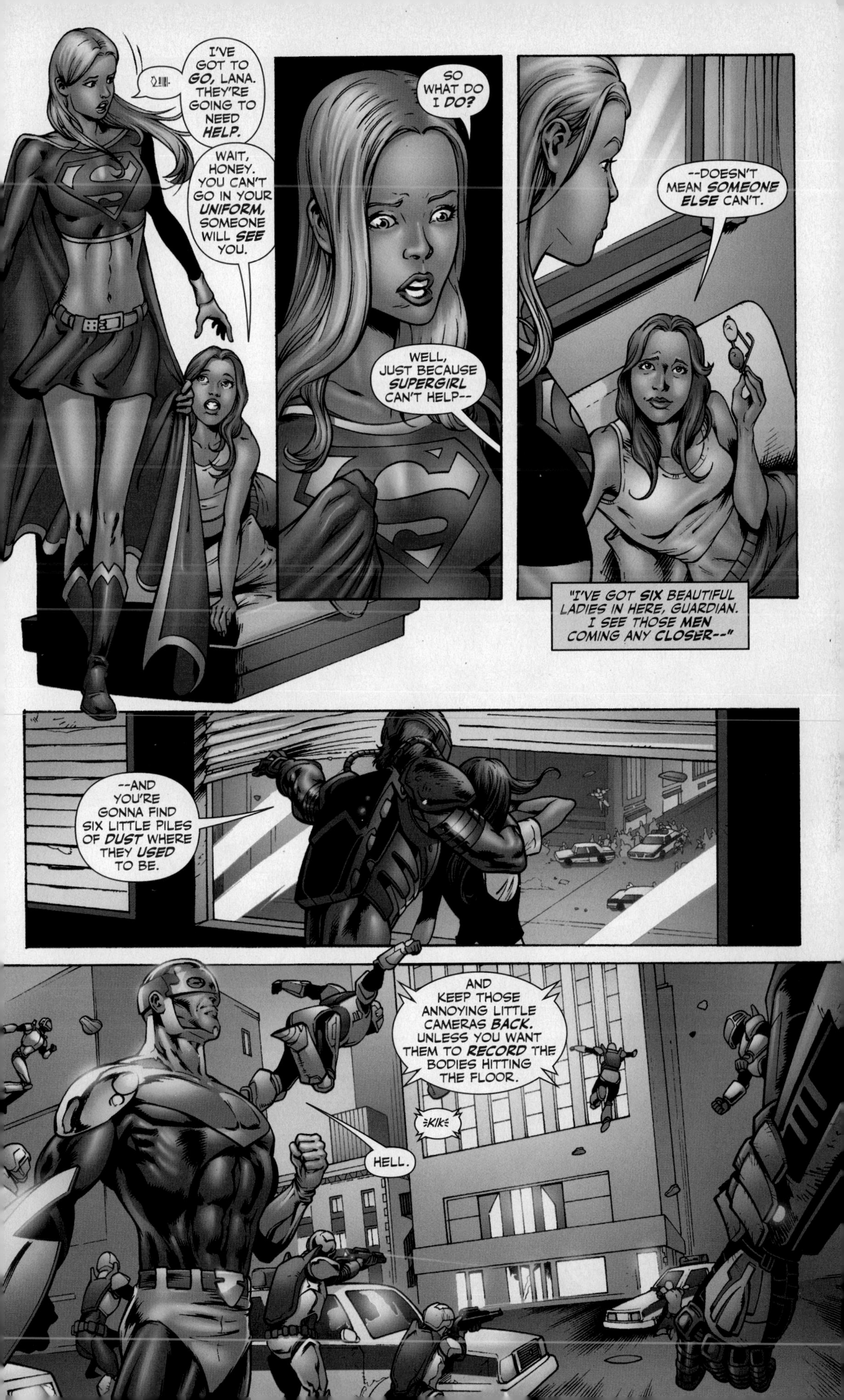

I'VE GOT TO GO, LANA. THEY'RE GOING TO NEED HELP.
WAIT, HONEY. YOU CAN'T GO IN YOUR UNIFORM, SOMEONE WILL SEE YOU.
SO WHAT DO I DO?
WELL, JUST BECAUSE SUPERGIRL CAN'T HELP--
--DOESN'T MEAN SOMEONE ELSE CAN'T.
"I'VE GOT SIX BEAUTIFUL LADIES IN HERE, GUARDIAN. I SEE THOSE MEN COMING ANY CLOSER--"
--AND YOU'RE GONNA FIND SIX LITTLE PILES OF DUST WHERE THEY USED TO BE.
AND KEEP THOSE ANNOYING LITTLE CAMERAS BACK. UNLESS YOU WANT THEM TO RECORD THE BODIES HITTING THE FLOOR.
KIK
HELL.

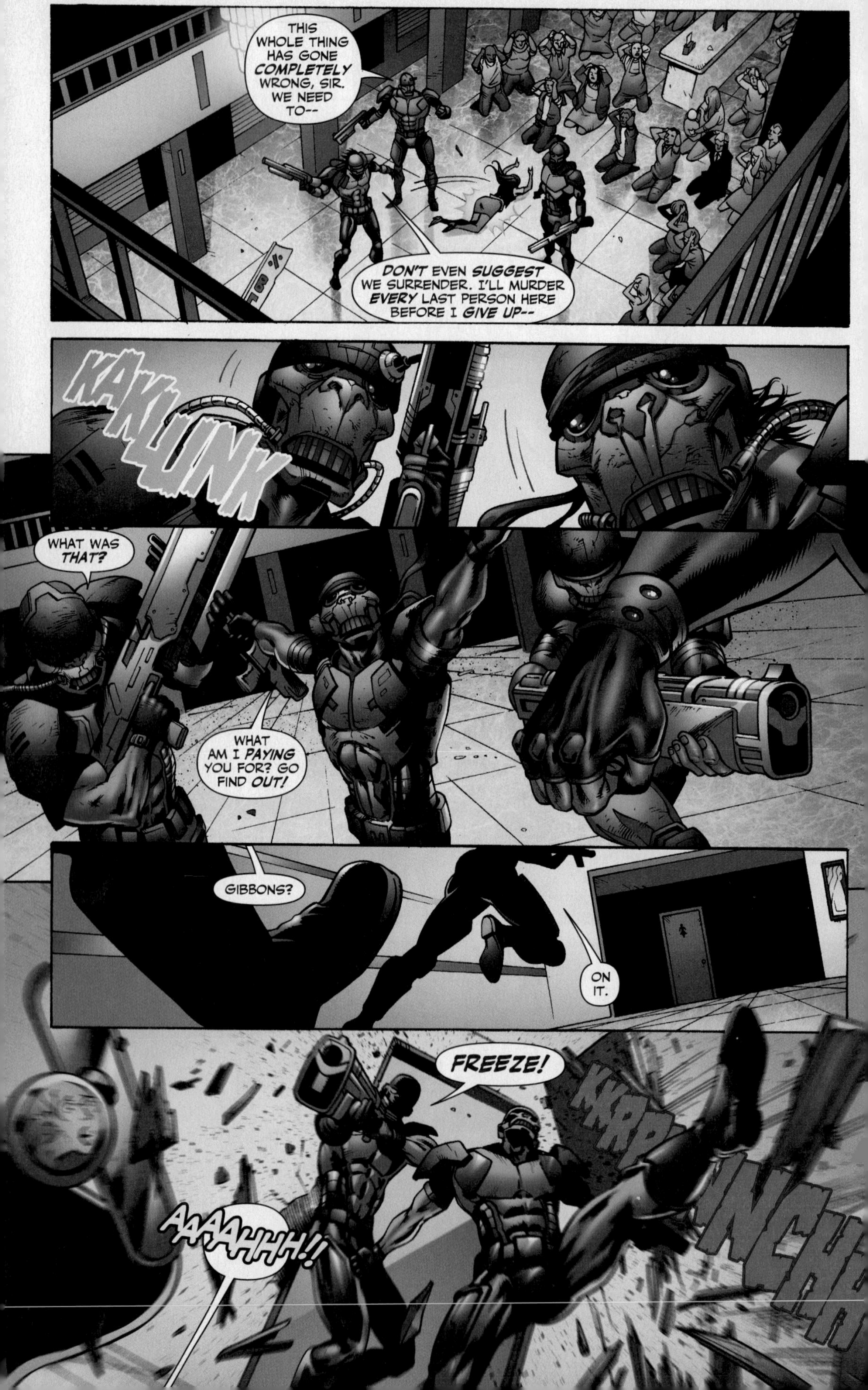
THIS WHOLE THING HAS GONE COMPLETELY WRONG, SIR. WE NEED TO--
DON'T EVEN SUGGEST WE SURRENDER. I'LL MURDER EVERY LAST PERSON HERE BEFORE I GIVE UP--
KAKLUNK
WHAT WAS THAT?
WHAT AM I PAYING YOU FOR? GO FIND OUT!
GIBBONS?
ON IT.
FREEZE!
AAAAHHH!!

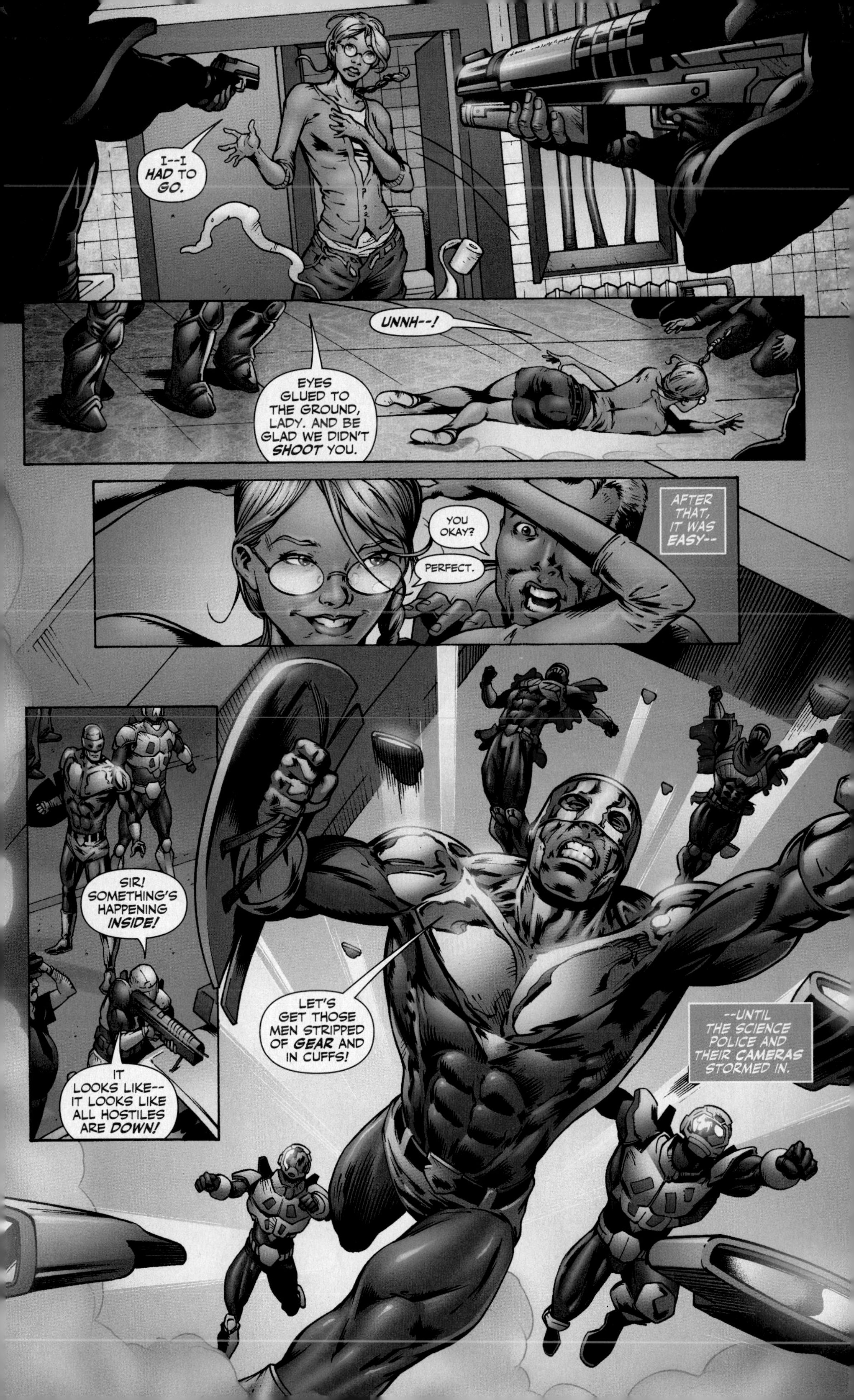

I--I HAD TO GO.
UNNH--!
EYES GLUED TO THE GROUND, LADY. AND BE GLAD WE DIDN'T SHOOT YOU.
AFTER THAT, IT WAS EASY--
YOU OKAY?
PERFECT.
SIR! SOMETHING'S HAPPENING INSIDE!
IT LOOKS LIKE-- IT LOOKS LIKE ALL HOSTILES ARE DOWN!
LET'S GET THOSE MEN STRIPPED OF GEAR AND IN CUFFS!
--UNTIL THE SCIENCE POLICE AND THEIR CAMERAS STORMED IN.

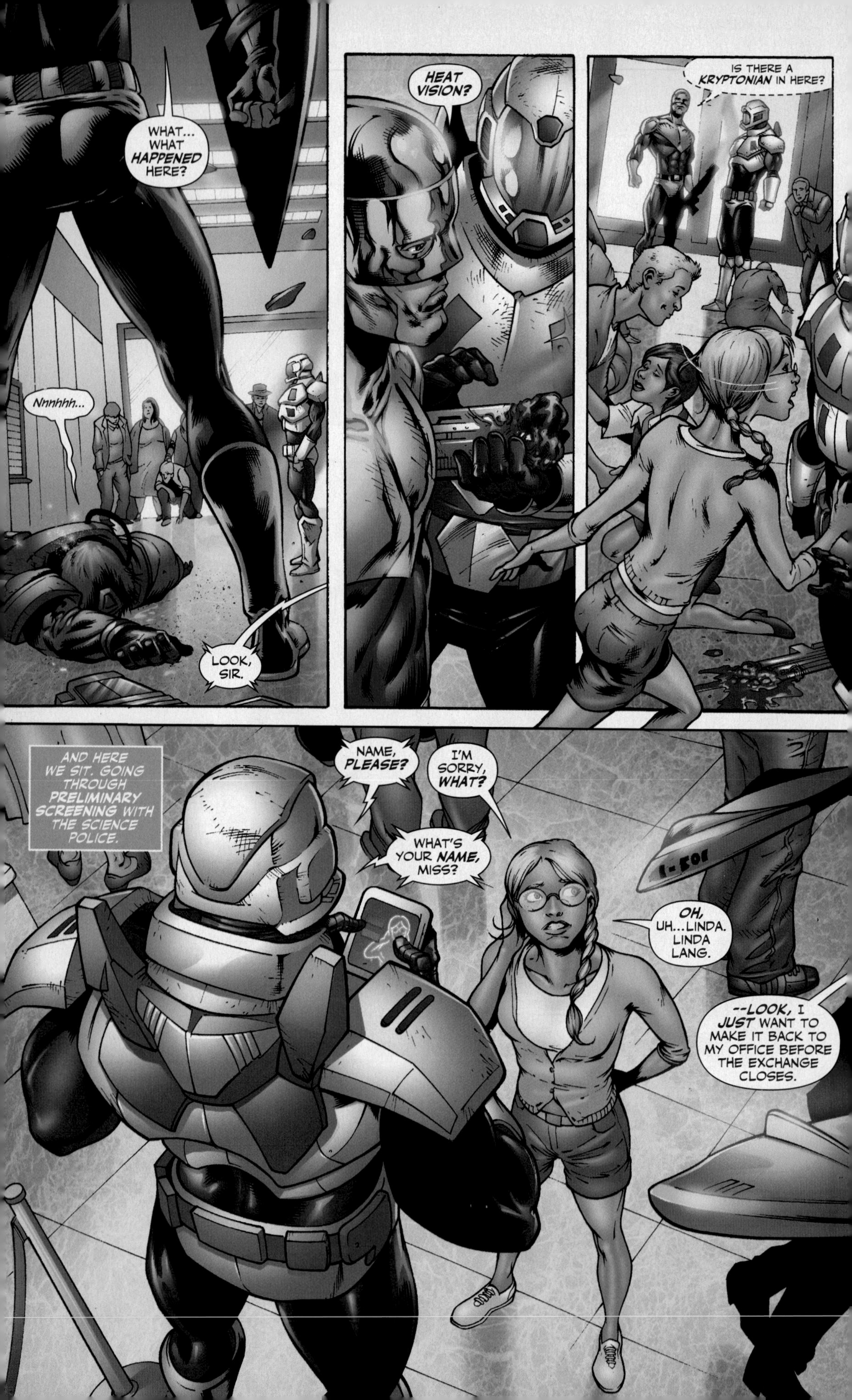
WHAT... WHAT HAPPENED HERE?
Nnnhhh...
LOOK, SIR.
HEAT VISION?
IS THERE A KRYPTONIAN IN HERE?
AND HERE WE SIT. GOING THROUGH PRELIMINARY SCREENING WITH THE SCIENCE POLICE.
NAME, PLEASE?
I'M SORRY, WHAT?
WHAT'S YOUR NAME, MISS?
OH, UH...LINDA. LINDA LANG.
--LOOK, I JUST WANT TO MAKE IT BACK TO MY OFFICE BEFORE THE EXCHANGE CLOSES.

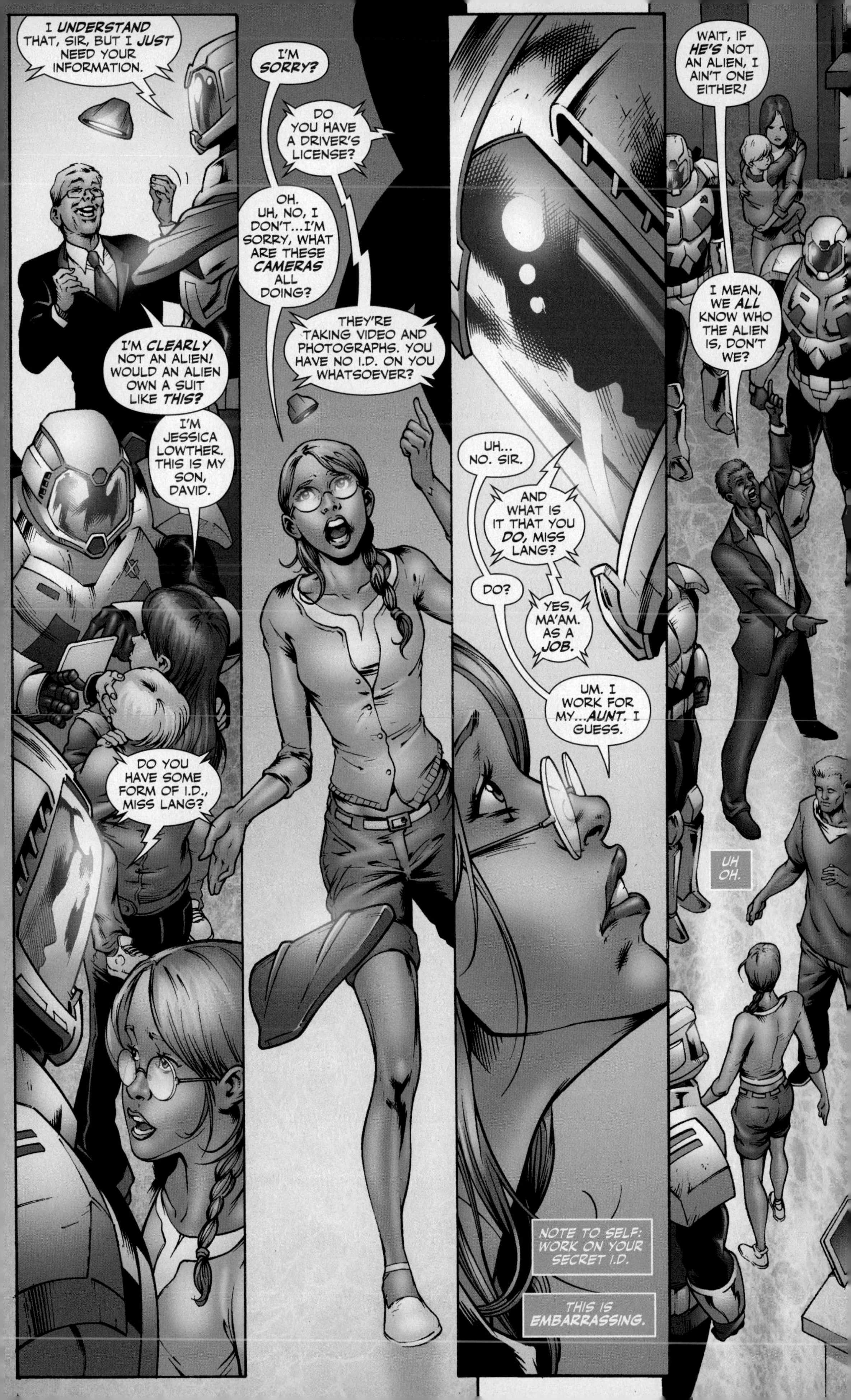
I UNDERSTAND THAT, SIR, BUT I JUST NEED YOUR INFORMATION.
I'M CLEARLY NOT AN ALIEN! WOULD AN ALIEN OWN A SUIT LIKE THIS?
I'M JESSICA LOWTHER. THIS IS MY SON, DAVID.
DO YOU HAVE SOME FORM OF I.D., MISS LANG?
I'M SORRY?
DO YOU HAVE A DRIVER'S LICENSE?
OH. UH, NO, I DON'T...I'M SORRY, WHAT ARE THESE CAMERAS ALL DOING?
THEY'RE TAKING VIDEO AND PHOTOGRAPHS. YOU HAVE NO I.D. ON YOU WHATSOEVER?
UH... NO. SIR.
AND WHAT IS IT THAT YOU DO, MISS LANG?
DO?
YES, MA'AM. AS A JOB.
UM. I WORK FOR MY...AUNT. I GUESS.
NOTE TO SELF: WORK ON YOUR SECRET I.D.
THIS IS EMBARRASSING.
WAIT, IF HE'S NOT AN ALIEN, I AIN'T ONE EITHER!
I MEAN, WE ALL KNOW WHO THE ALIEN IS, DON'T WE?
UH OH.

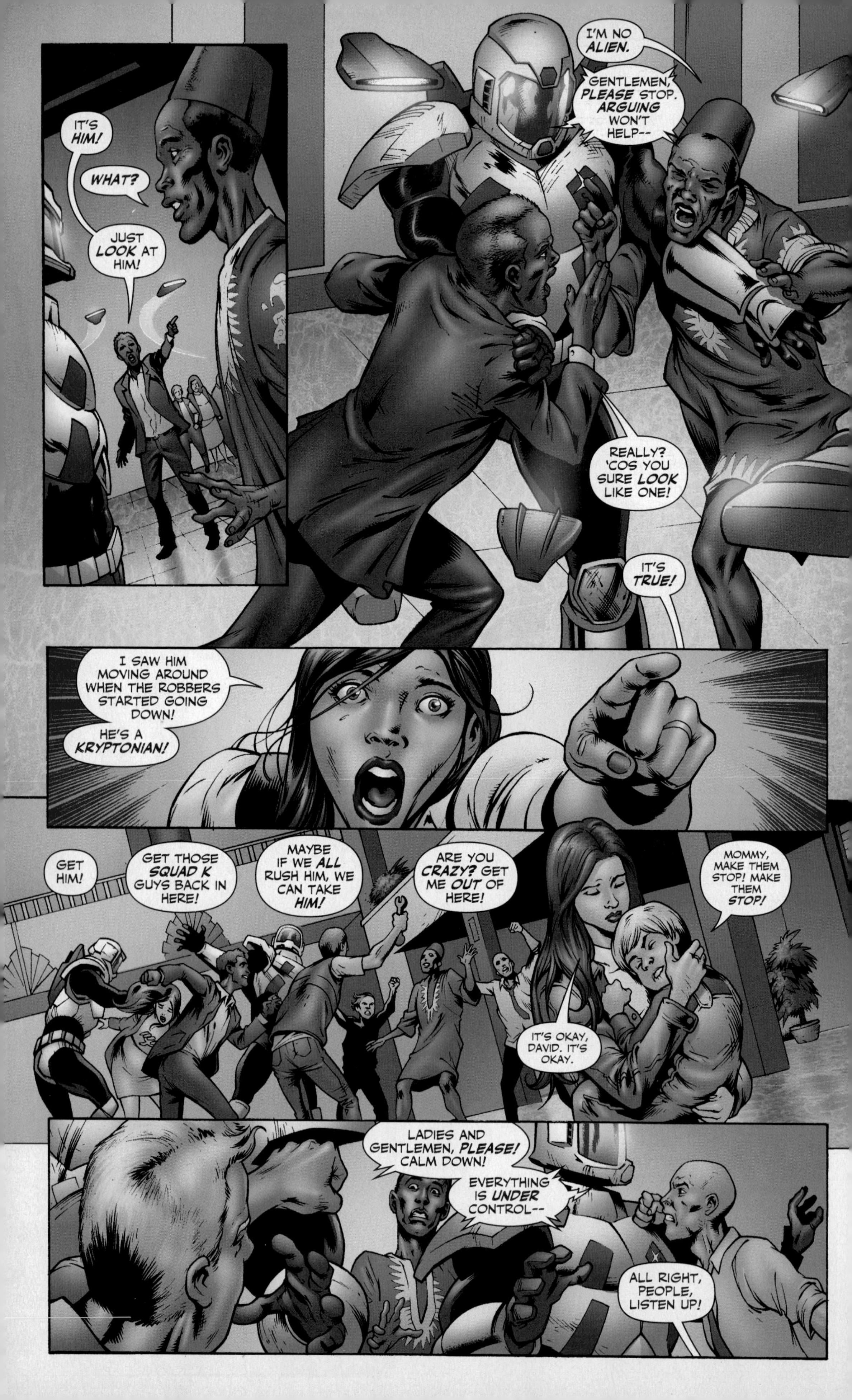
IT'S HIM!
WHAT?
JUST LOOK AT HIM!
I'M NO ALIEN.
GENTLEMEN, PLEASE STOP. ARGUING WON'T HELP--
REALLY? 'COS YOU SURE LOOK LIKE ONE!
IT'S TRUE!
I SAW HIM MOVING AROUND WHEN THE ROBBERS STARTED GOING DOWN!
HE'S A KRYPTONIAN!
GET HIM!
GET THOSE SQUAD K GUYS BACK IN HERE!
MAYBE IF WE ALL RUSH HIM, WE CAN TAKE HIM!
ARE YOU CRAZY? GET ME OUT OF HERE!
MOMMY, MAKE THEM STOP! MAKE THEM STOP!
IT'S OKAY, DAVID. IT'S OKAY.
LADIES AND GENTLEMEN, PLEASE! CALM DOWN!
EVERYTHING IS UNDER CONTROL--
ALL RIGHT, PEOPLE, LISTEN UP!

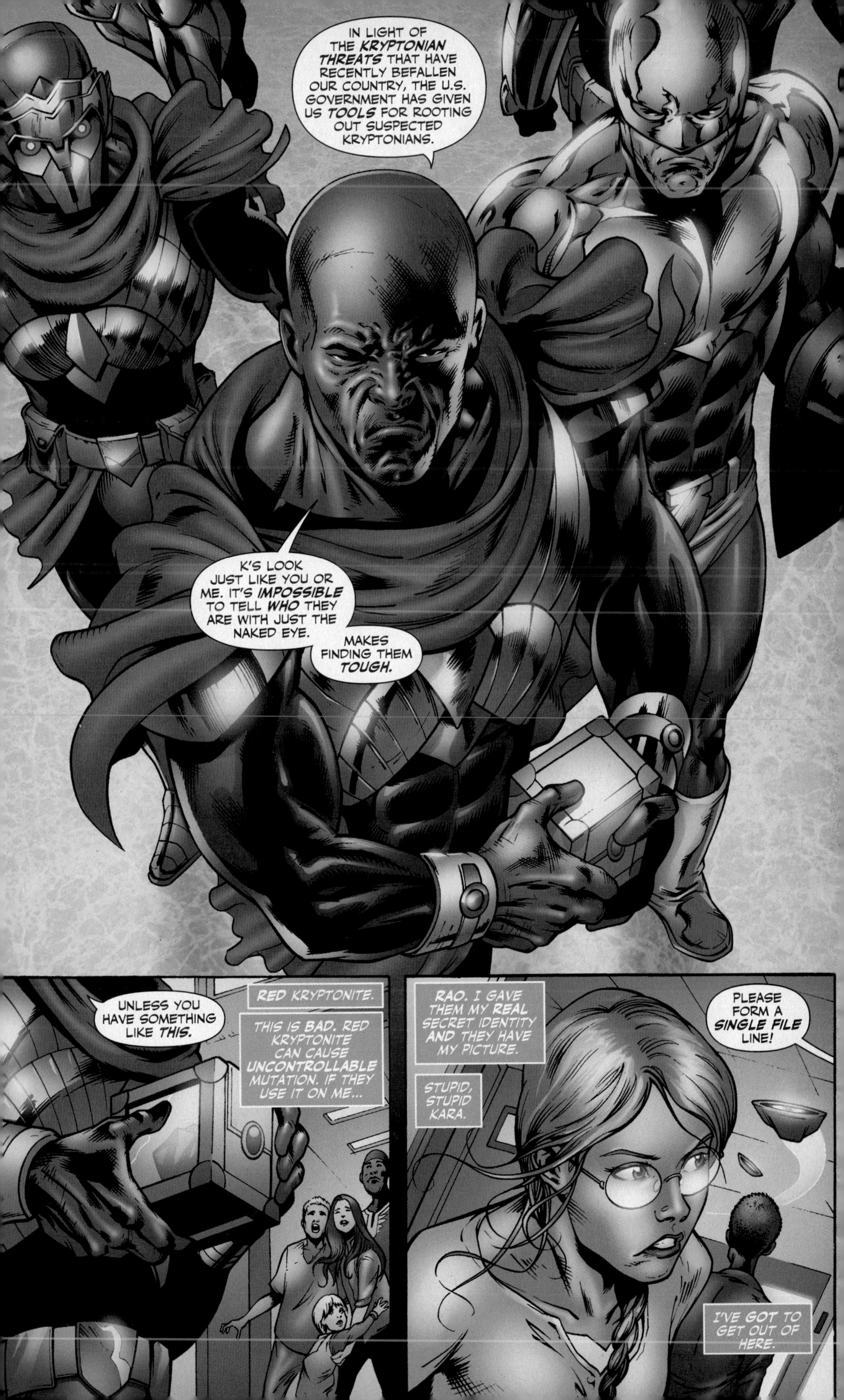
IN LIGHT OF THE KRYPTONIAN THREATS THAT HAVE RECENTLY BEFALLEN OUR COUNTRY, THE U.S. GOVERNMENT HAS GIVEN US TOOLS FOR ROOTING OUT SUSPECTED KRYPTONIANS.
K'S LOOK JUST LIKE YOU OR ME. IT'S IMPOSSIBLE TO TELL WHO THEY ARE WITH JUST THE NAKED EYE.
MAKES FINDING THEM TOUGH.
UNLESS YOU HAVE SOMETHING LIKE THIS.
RED KRYPTONITE.
THIS IS BAD. RED KRYPTONITE CAN CAUSE UNCONTROLLABLE MUTATION. IF THEY USE IT ON ME...
RAO. I GAVE THEM MY REAL SECRET IDENTITY AND THEY HAVE MY PICTURE.
STUPID, STUPID KARA.
PLEASE FORM A SINGLE FILE LINE!
I'VE GOT TO GET OUT OF HERE.

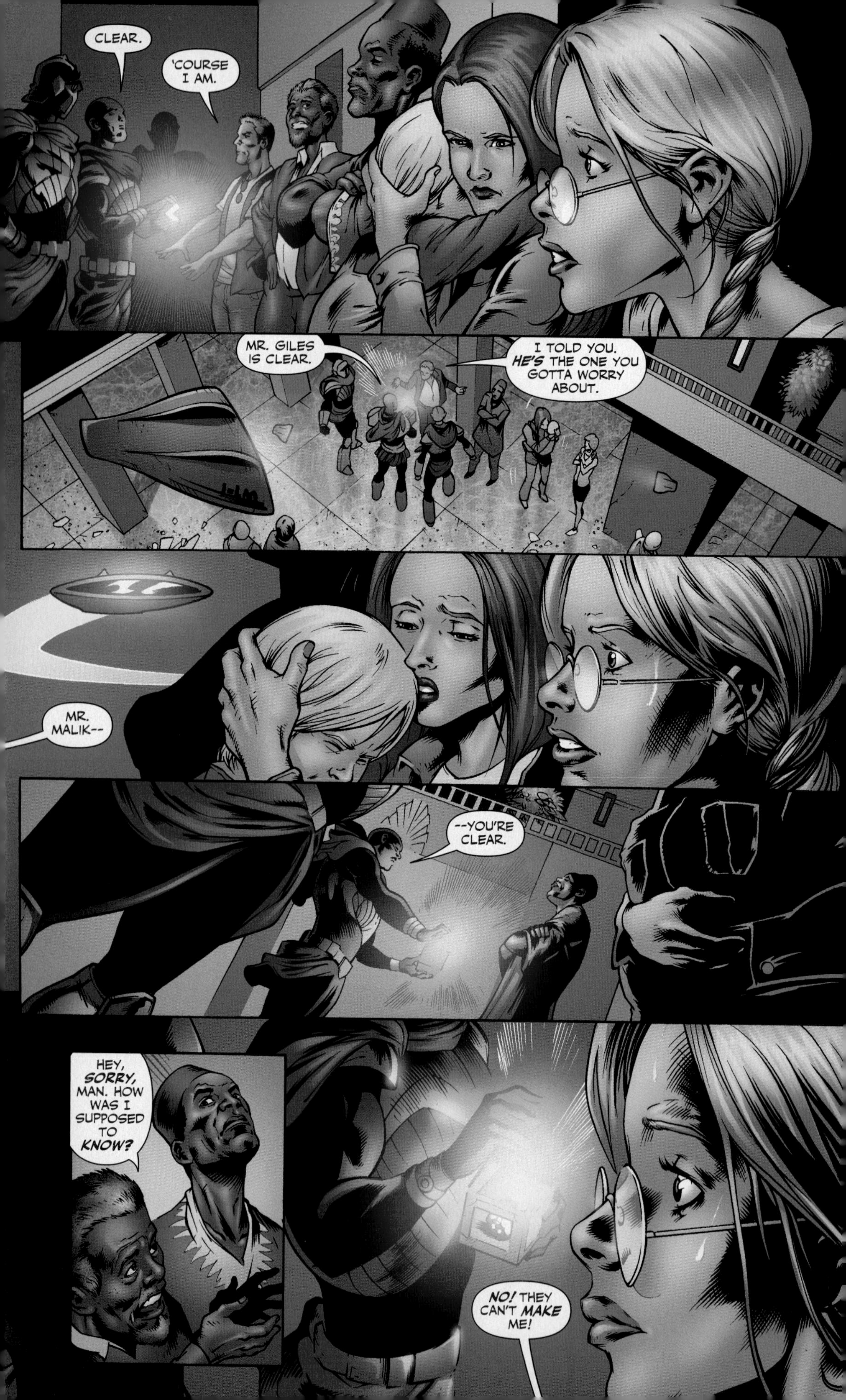
CLEAR.
'COURSE I AM.
MR. GILES IS CLEAR.
I TOLD YOU. HE'S THE ONE YOU GOTTA WORRY ABOUT.
MR. MALIK--
--YOU'RE CLEAR.
HEY, SORRY, MAN. HOW WAS I SUPPOSED TO KNOW?
NO! THEY CAN'T MAKE ME!

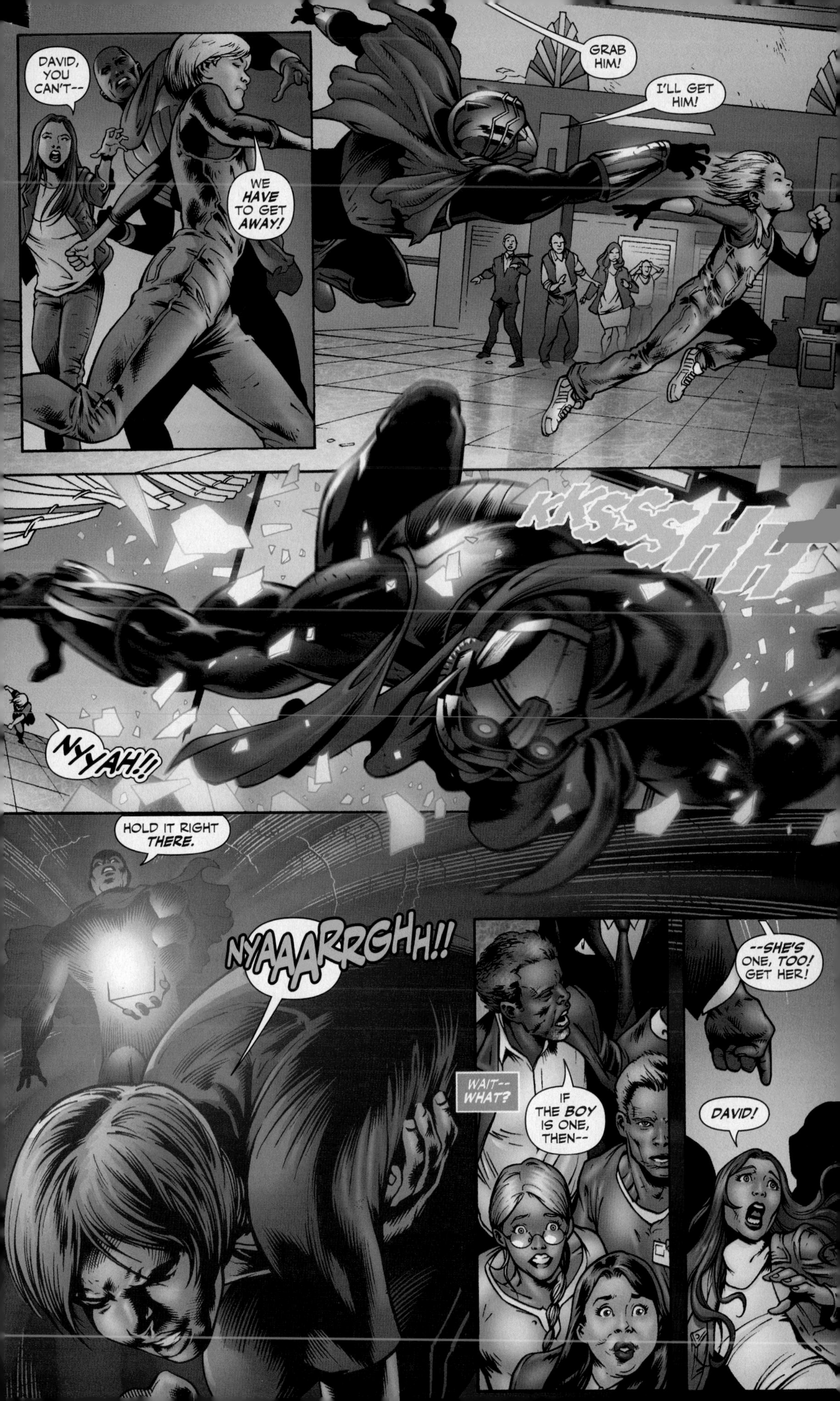

DAVID, YOU CAN'T--
WE HAVE TO GET AWAY!
GRAB HIM!
I'LL GET HIM!
KKSSSHH
NYYAH!!
HOLD IT RIGHT THERE.
NYAAARRGHH!!
WAIT-- WHAT?
IF THE BOY IS ONE, THEN--
--SHE'S ONE, TOO! GET HER!
DAVID!

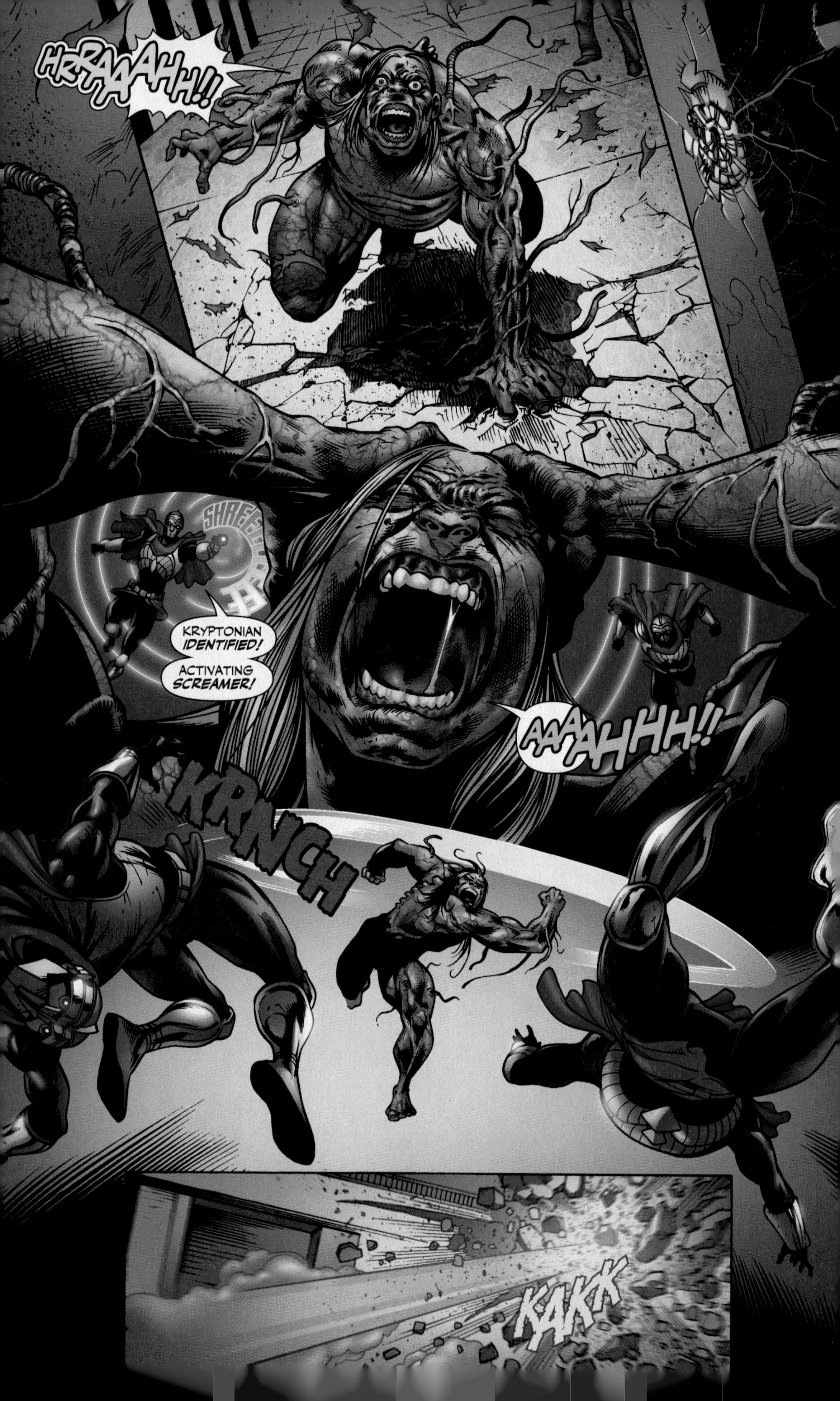

HRRAAAHH!!
SHREEEEEEE
KRYPTONIAN IDENTIFIED!
ACTIVATING SCREAMER!
AAAAHHH!!
KRNCH
KAKK

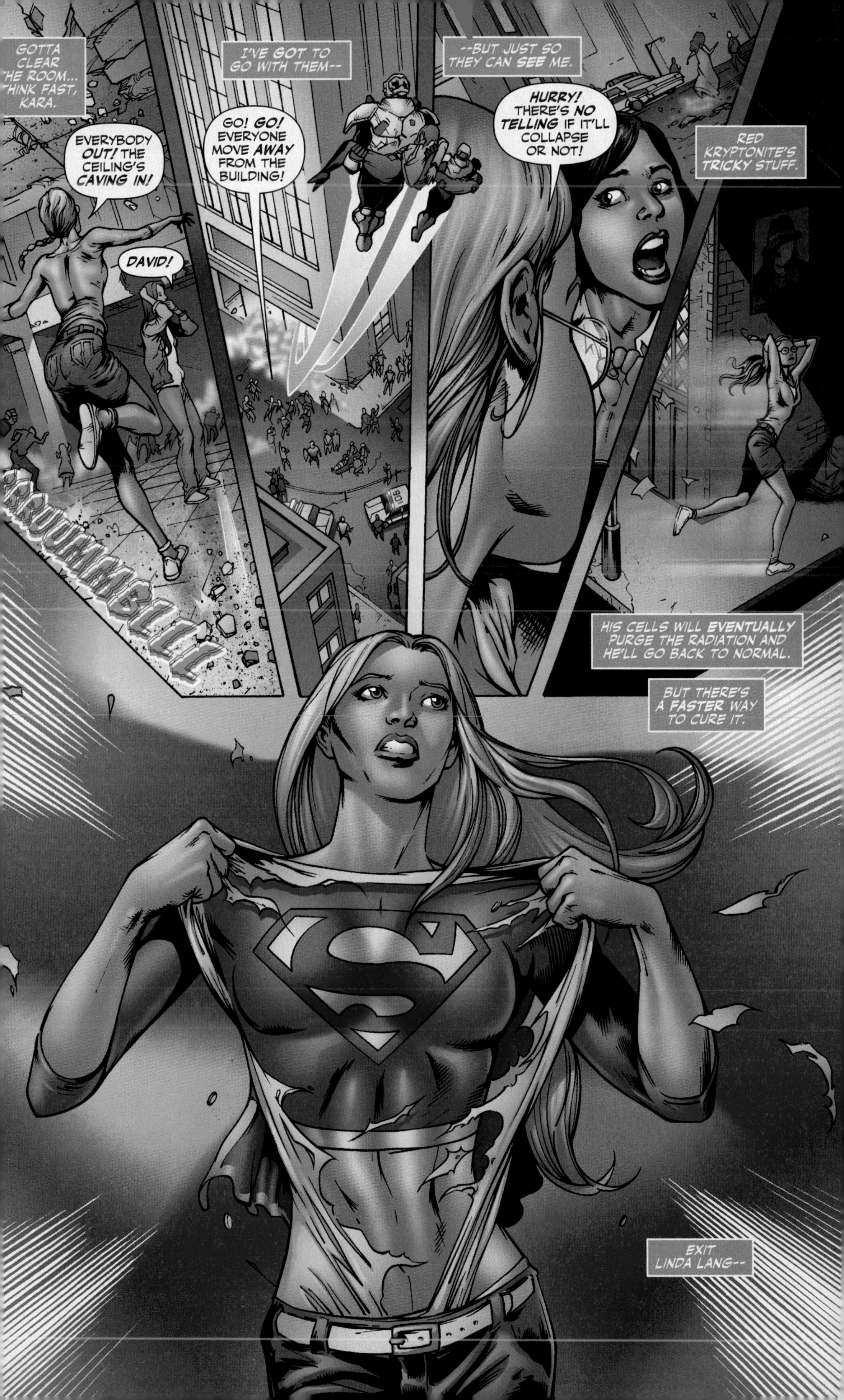
GOTTA CLEAR THE ROOM... THINK FAST, KARA.
EVERYBODY OUT! THE CEILING'S CAVING IN!
DAVID!
I'VE GOT TO GO WITH THEM--
GO! GO! EVERYONE MOVE AWAY FROM THE BUILDING!
--BUT JUST SO THEY CAN SEE ME.
HURRY! THERE'S NO TELLING IF IT'LL COLLAPSE OR NOT!
RED KRYPTONITE'S TRICKY STUFF.
HIS CELLS WILL EVENTUALLY PURGE THE RADIATION AND HE'LL GO BACK TO NORMAL.
BUT THERE'S A FASTER WAY TO CURE IT.
EXIT LINDA LANG--

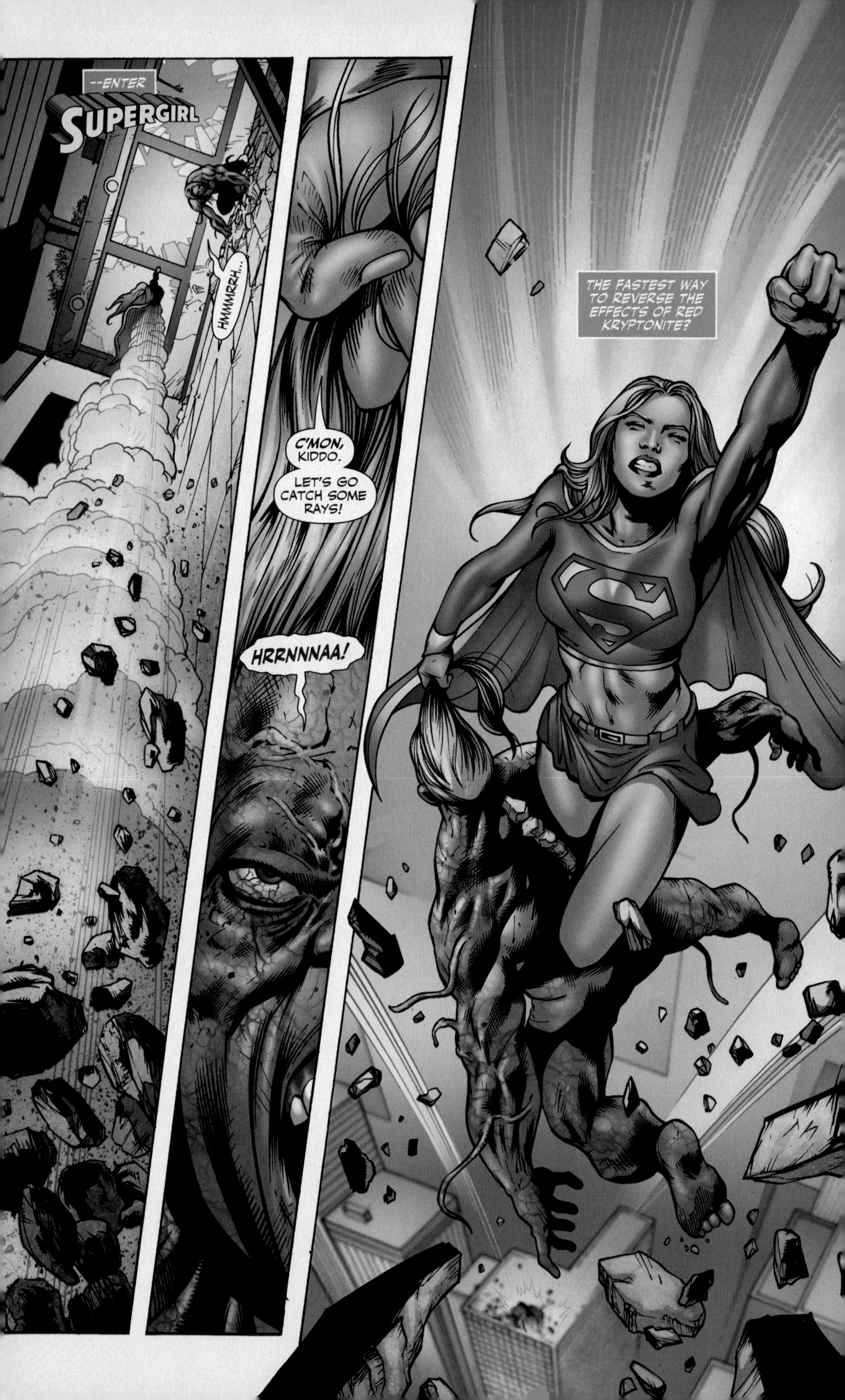
--ENTER
SUPERGIRL
HMMMRRH...
C'MON, KIDDO.
LET'S GO CATCH SOME RAYS!
HRRNNNAA!
THE FASTEST WAY TO REVERSE THE EFFECTS OF RED KRYPTONITE?

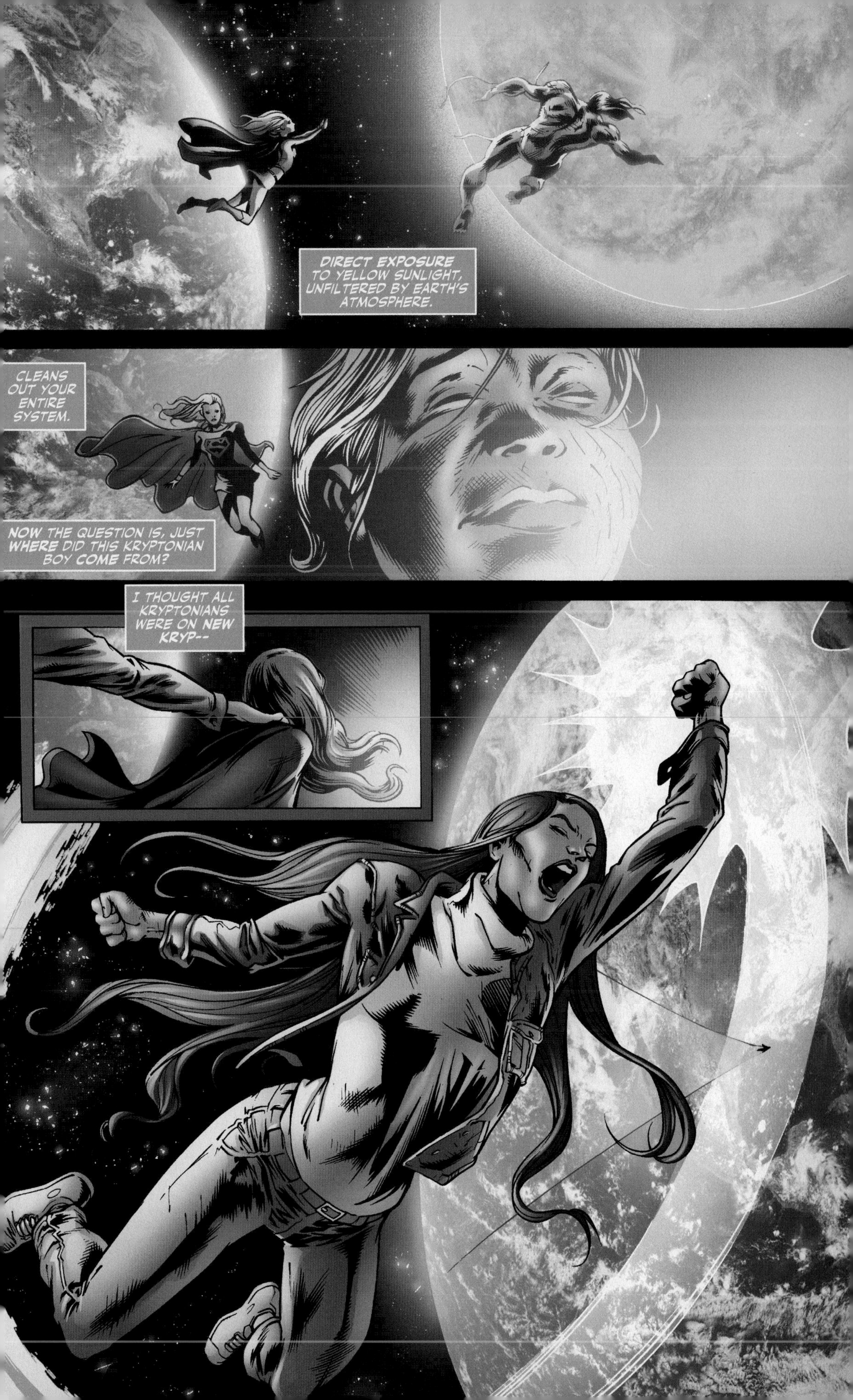
DIRECT EXPOSURE TO YELLOW SUNLIGHT, UNFILTERED BY EARTH'S ATMOSPHERE.
CLEANS OUT YOUR ENTIRE SYSTEM.
NOW THE QUESTION IS, JUST WHERE DID THIS KRYPTONIAN BOY COME FROM?
I THOUGHT ALL KRYPTONIANS WERE ON NEW KRYP--

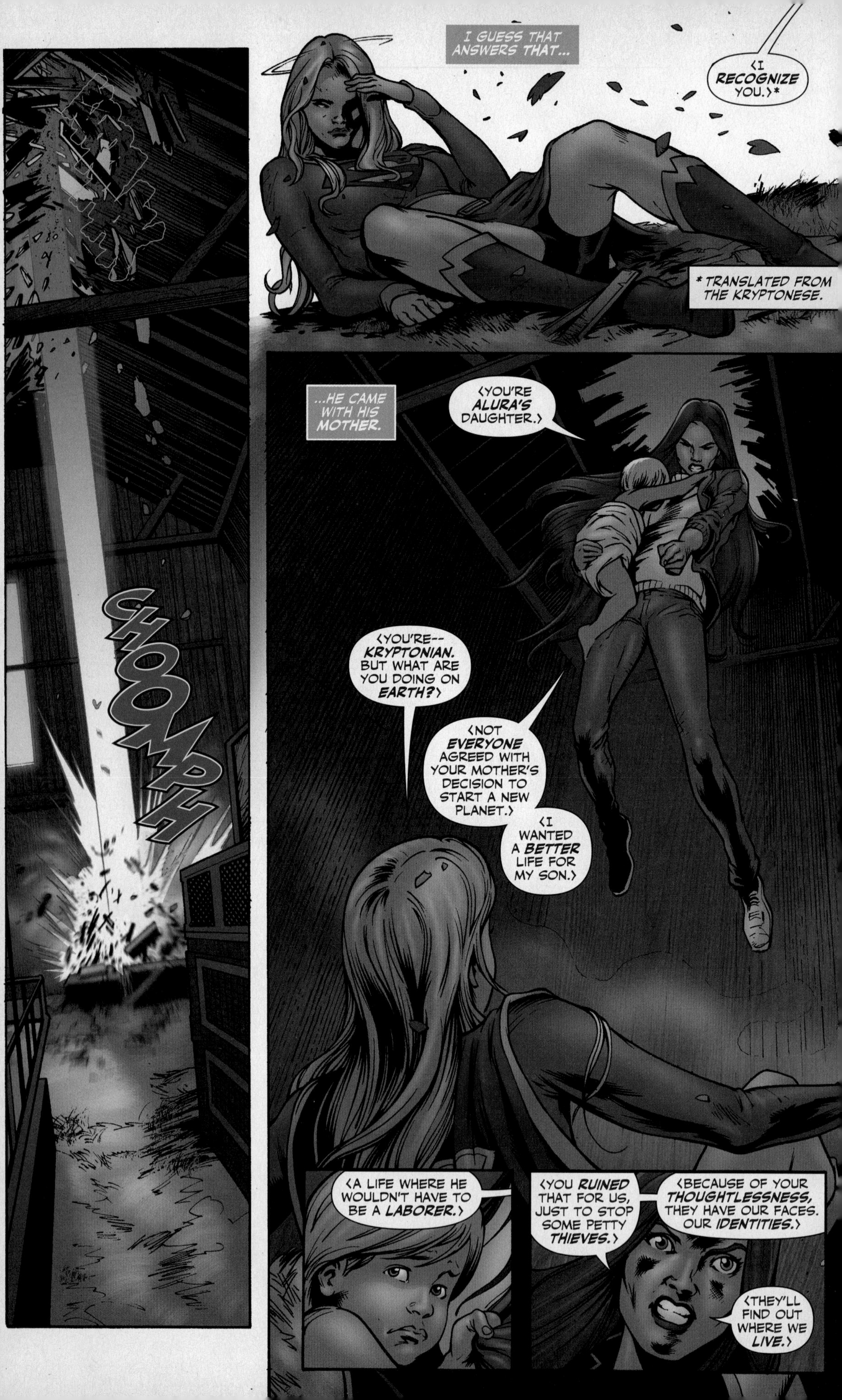
CHOOMPH
I GUESS THAT ANSWERS THAT...
<I RECOGNIZE YOU.>*
* TRANSLATED FROM THE KRYPTONESE.
...HE CAME WITH HIS MOTHER.
<YOU'RE ALURA'S DAUGHTER.>
<YOU'RE-- KRYPTONIAN. BUT WHAT ARE YOU DOING ON EARTH?>
<NOT EVERYONE AGREED WITH YOUR MOTHER'S DECISION TO START A NEW PLANET.>
<I WANTED A BETTER LIFE FOR MY SON.>
<A LIFE WHERE HE WOULDN'T HAVE TO BE A LABORER.>
<YOU RUINED THAT FOR US, JUST TO STOP SOME PETTY THIEVES.>
<BECAUSE OF YOUR THOUGHTLESSNESS, THEY HAVE OUR FACES. OUR IDENTITIES.>
<THEY'LL FIND OUT WHERE WE LIVE.>

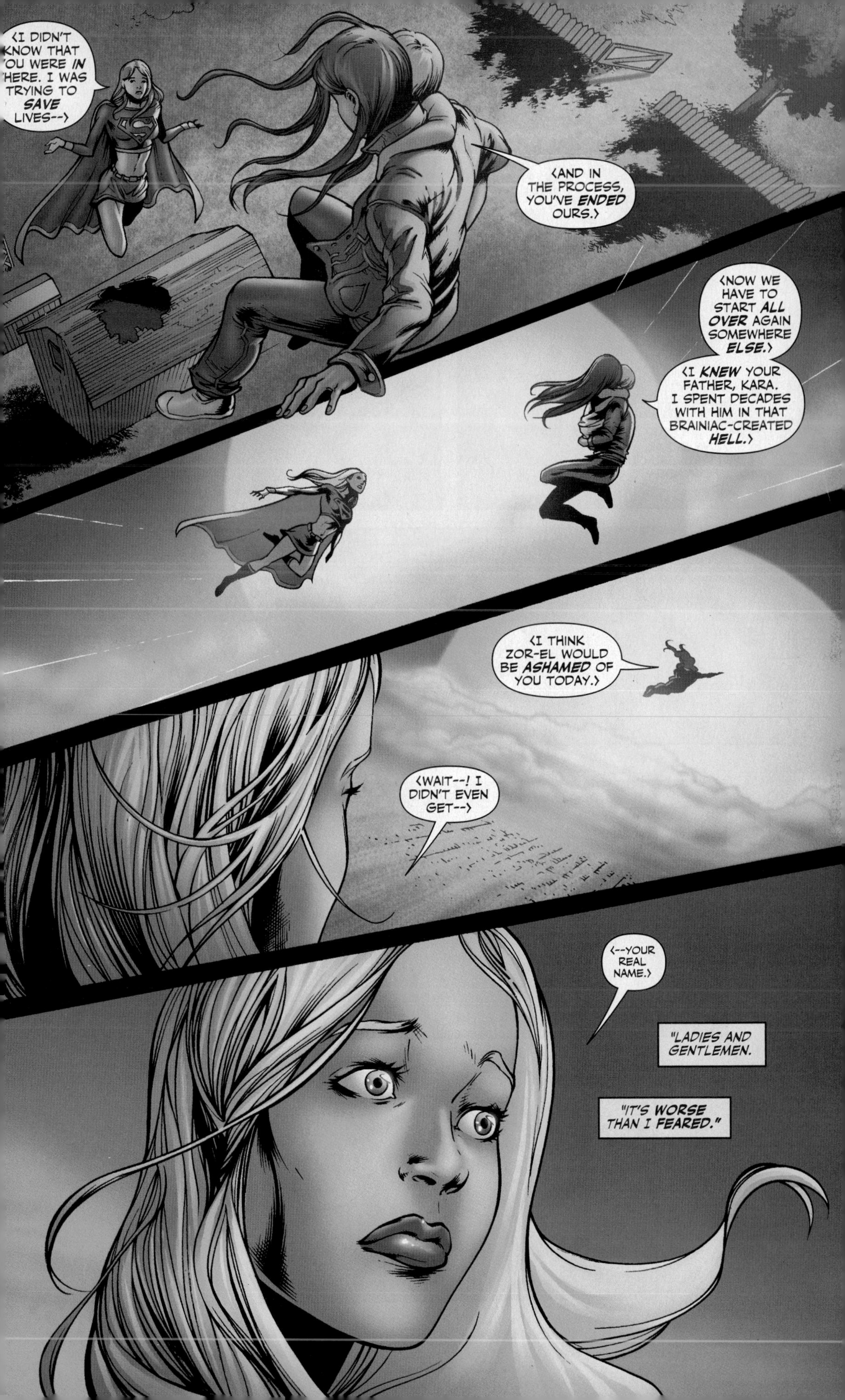

<I DIDN'T KNOW THAT YOU WERE *IN* HERE. I WAS TRYING TO *SAVE* LIVES-->
<AND IN THE PROCESS, YOU'VE *ENDED* OURS.>
<NOW WE HAVE TO START *ALL OVER* AGAIN SOMEWHERE *ELSE.*>
<I *KNEW* YOUR FATHER, KARA. I SPENT DECADES WITH HIM IN THAT BRAINIAC-CREATED *HELL.*>
<I THINK ZOR-EL WOULD BE *ASHAMED* OF YOU TODAY.>
<WAIT--! I DIDN'T EVEN GET-->
<--YOUR REAL NAME.>
"LADIES AND GENTLEMEN.
"IT'S *WORSE* THAN I *FEARED.*"

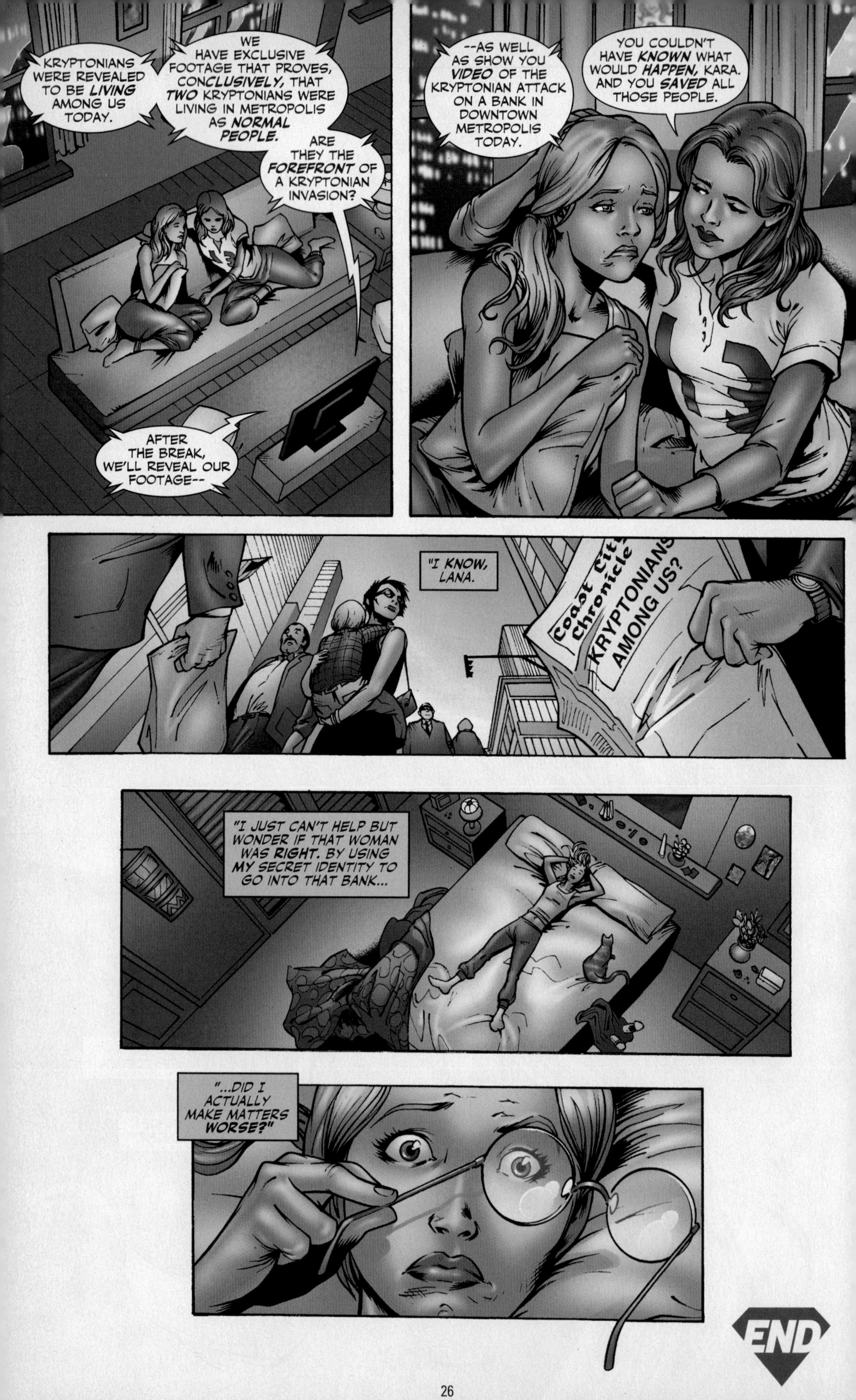
KRYPTONIANS WERE REVEALED TO BE LIVING AMONG US TODAY.
WE HAVE EXCLUSIVE FOOTAGE THAT PROVES, CONCLUSIVELY, THAT TWO KRYPTONIANS WERE LIVING IN METROPOLIS AS NORMAL PEOPLE.
ARE THEY THE FOREFRONT OF A KRYPTONIAN INVASION?
AFTER THE BREAK, WE'LL REVEAL OUR FOOTAGE--
--AS WELL AS SHOW YOU VIDEO OF THE KRYPTONIAN ATTACK ON A BANK IN DOWNTOWN METROPOLIS TODAY.
YOU COULDN'T HAVE KNOWN WHAT WOULD HAPPEN, KARA. AND YOU SAVED ALL THOSE PEOPLE.
"I KNOW, LANA.
Coast City Chronicle
KRYPTONIANS AMONG US?
"I JUST CAN'T HELP BUT WONDER IF THAT WOMAN WAS RIGHT. BY USING MY SECRET IDENTITY TO GO INTO THAT BANK...
"...DID I ACTUALLY MAKE MATTERS WORSE?"
END

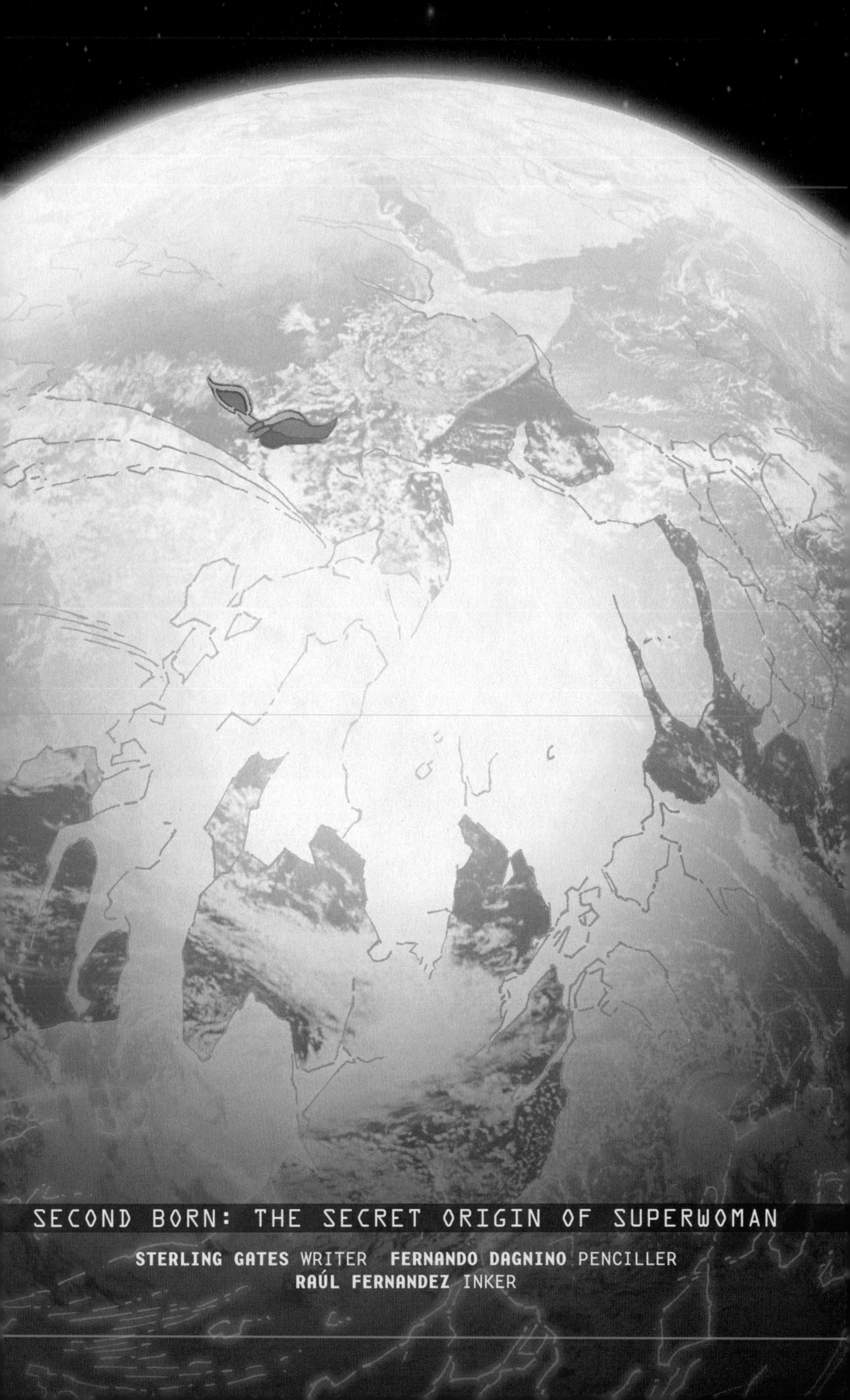
SECOND BORN: THE SECRET ORIGIN OF SUPERWOMAN
STERLING GATES WRITER FERNANDO DAGNINO PENCILLER
RAÚL FERNANDEZ INKER

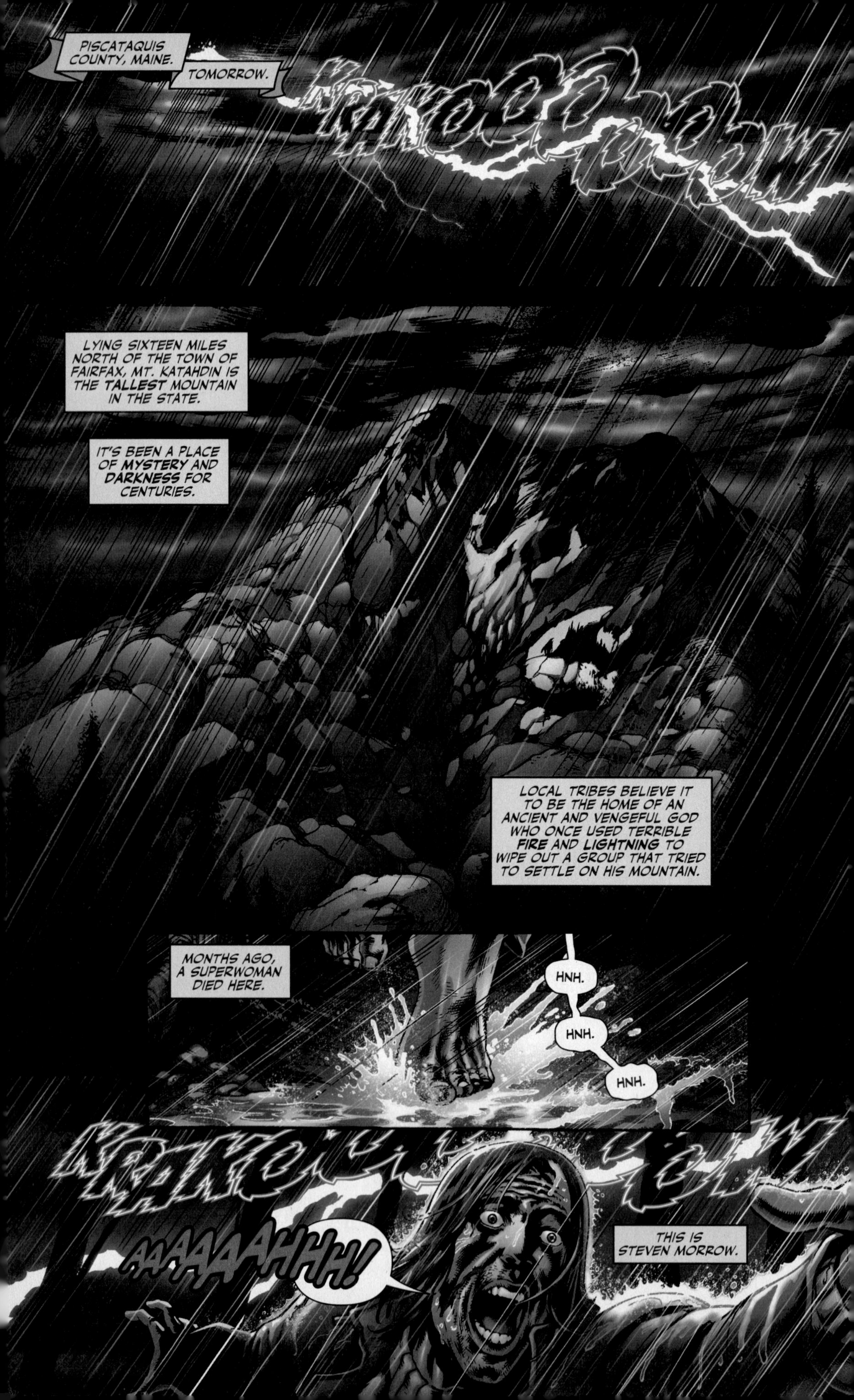
PISCATAQUIS COUNTY, MAINE.
TOMORROW.
LYING SIXTEEN MILES NORTH OF THE TOWN OF FAIRFAX, MT. KATAHDIN IS THE TALLEST MOUNTAIN IN THE STATE.
IT'S BEEN A PLACE OF MYSTERY AND DARKNESS FOR CENTURIES.
LOCAL TRIBES BELIEVE IT TO BE THE HOME OF AN ANCIENT AND VENGEFUL GOD WHO ONCE USED TERRIBLE FIRE AND LIGHTNING TO WIPE OUT A GROUP THAT TRIED TO SETTLE ON HIS MOUNTAIN.
MONTHS AGO, A SUPERWOMAN DIED HERE.
HNH.
HNH.
HNH.
AAAAAAHHH!
THIS IS STEVEN MORROW.

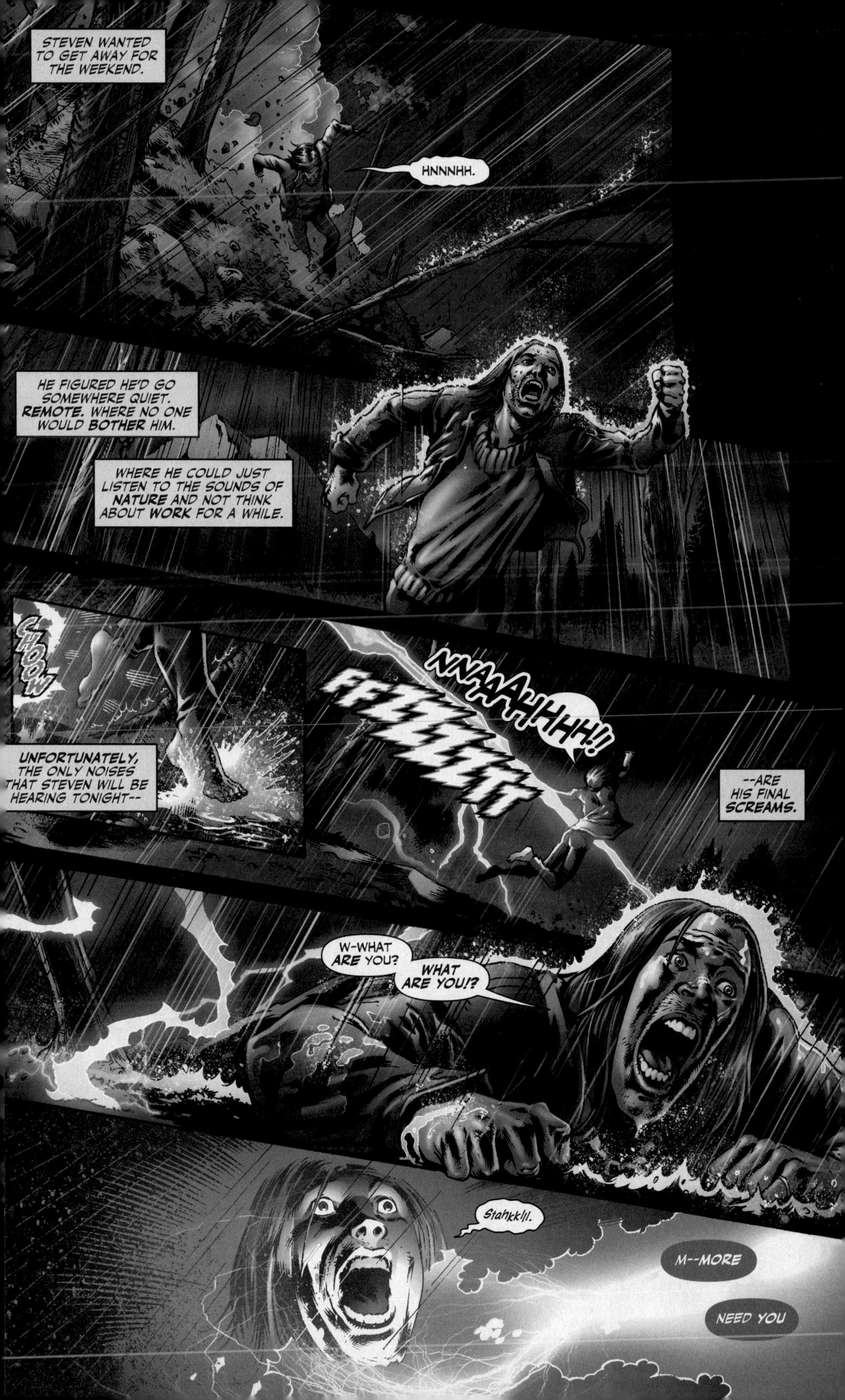
STEVEN WANTED TO GET AWAY FOR THE WEEKEND.
HNNNHH.
HE FIGURED HE'D GO SOMEWHERE QUIET. REMOTE. WHERE NO ONE WOULD BOTHER HIM.
WHERE HE COULD JUST LISTEN TO THE SOUNDS OF NATURE AND NOT THINK ABOUT WORK FOR A WHILE.
CHOOW
UNFORTUNATELY, THE ONLY NOISES THAT STEVEN WILL BE HEARING TONIGHT--
FFZZZZTT
NNAAAHHHH!!
--ARE HIS FINAL SCREAMS.
W-WHAT ARE YOU?
WHAT ARE YOU!?
Stahkklll.
M--MORE
NEED YOU

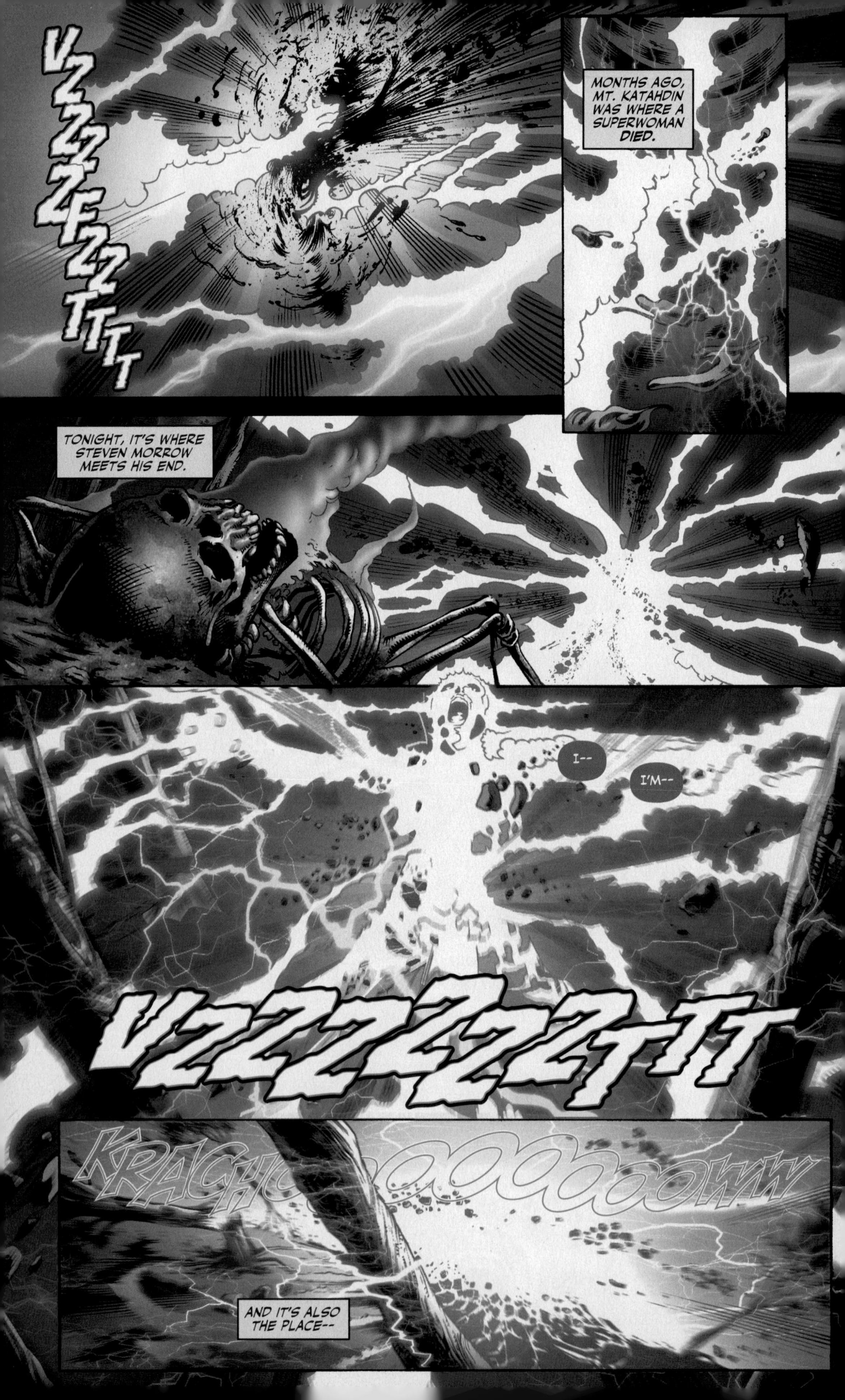
VZZZZFZZTTTT
MONTHS AGO, MT. KATAHDIN WAS WHERE A SUPERWOMAN DIED.
TONIGHT, IT'S WHERE STEVEN MORROW MEETS HIS END.
I--
I'M--
VZZZZZZT-TT
KRACHOOOOOOOOOWW
AND IT'S ALSO THE PLACE--

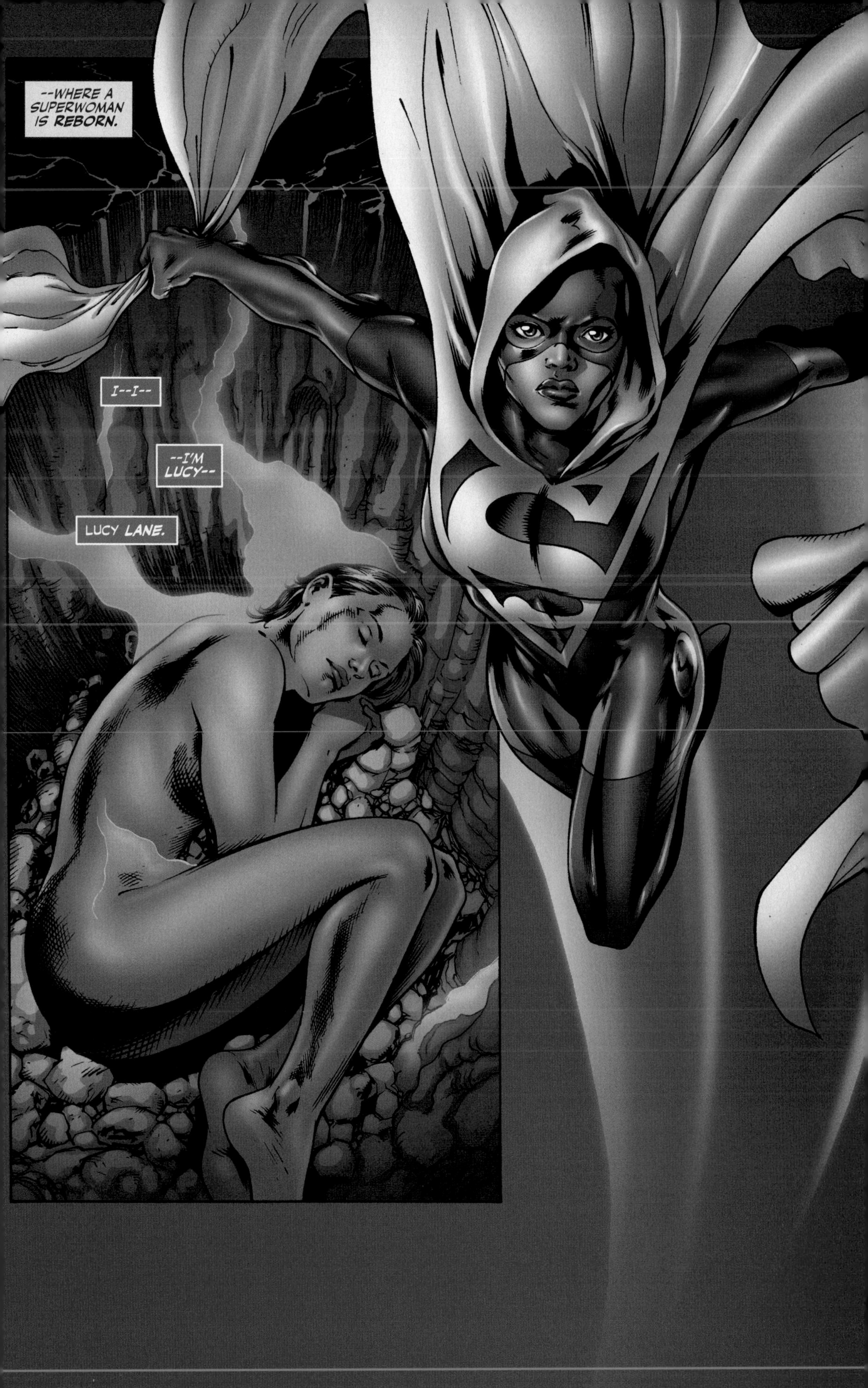
--WHERE A SUPERWOMAN IS REBORN.
I--I--
--I'M LUCY--
LUCY LANE.

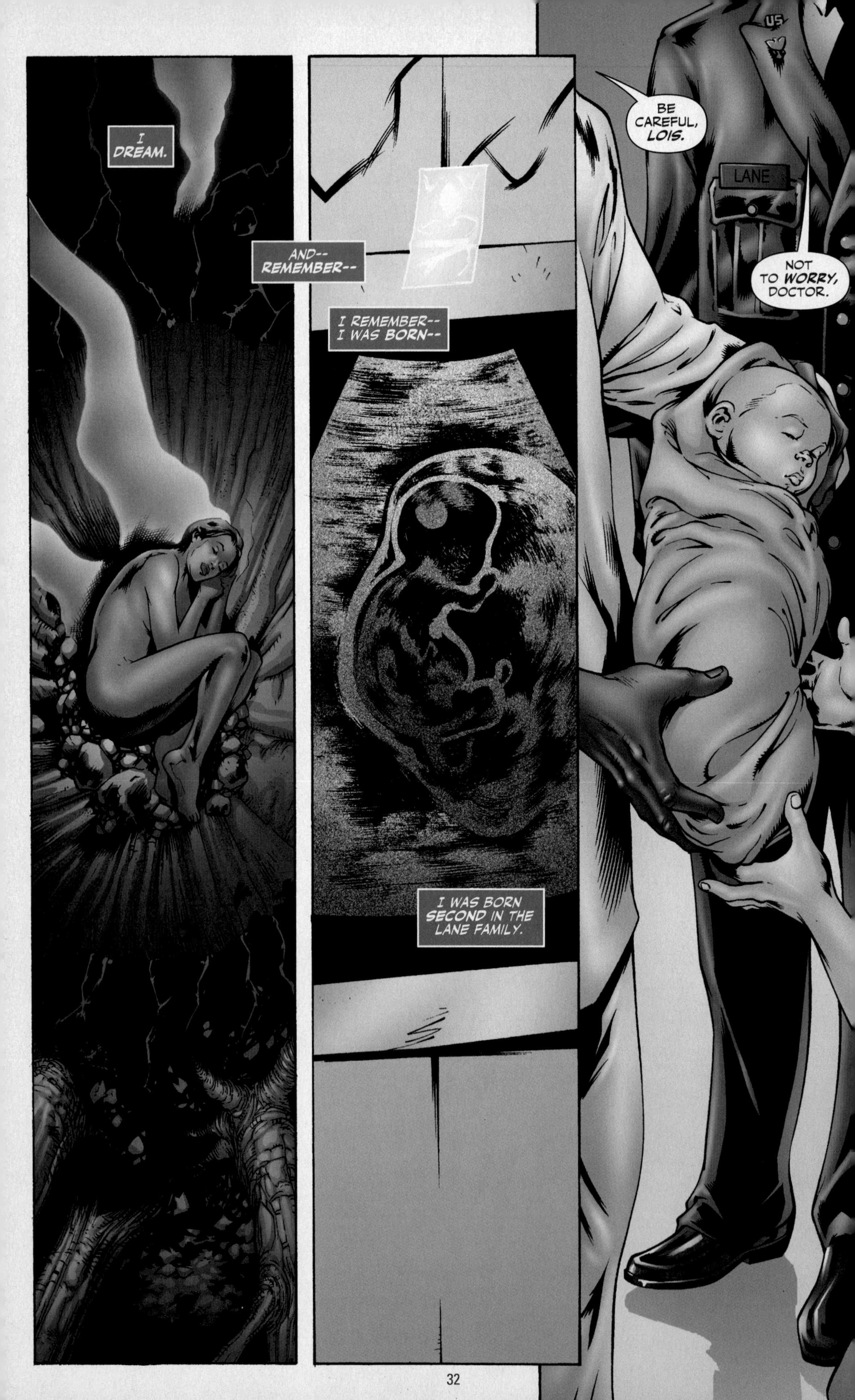
I DREAM.
AND-- REMEMBER--
I REMEMBER-- I WAS BORN--
I WAS BORN SECOND IN THE LANE FAMILY.
BE CAREFUL, LOIS.
NOT TO WORRY, DOCTOR.
LANE
US

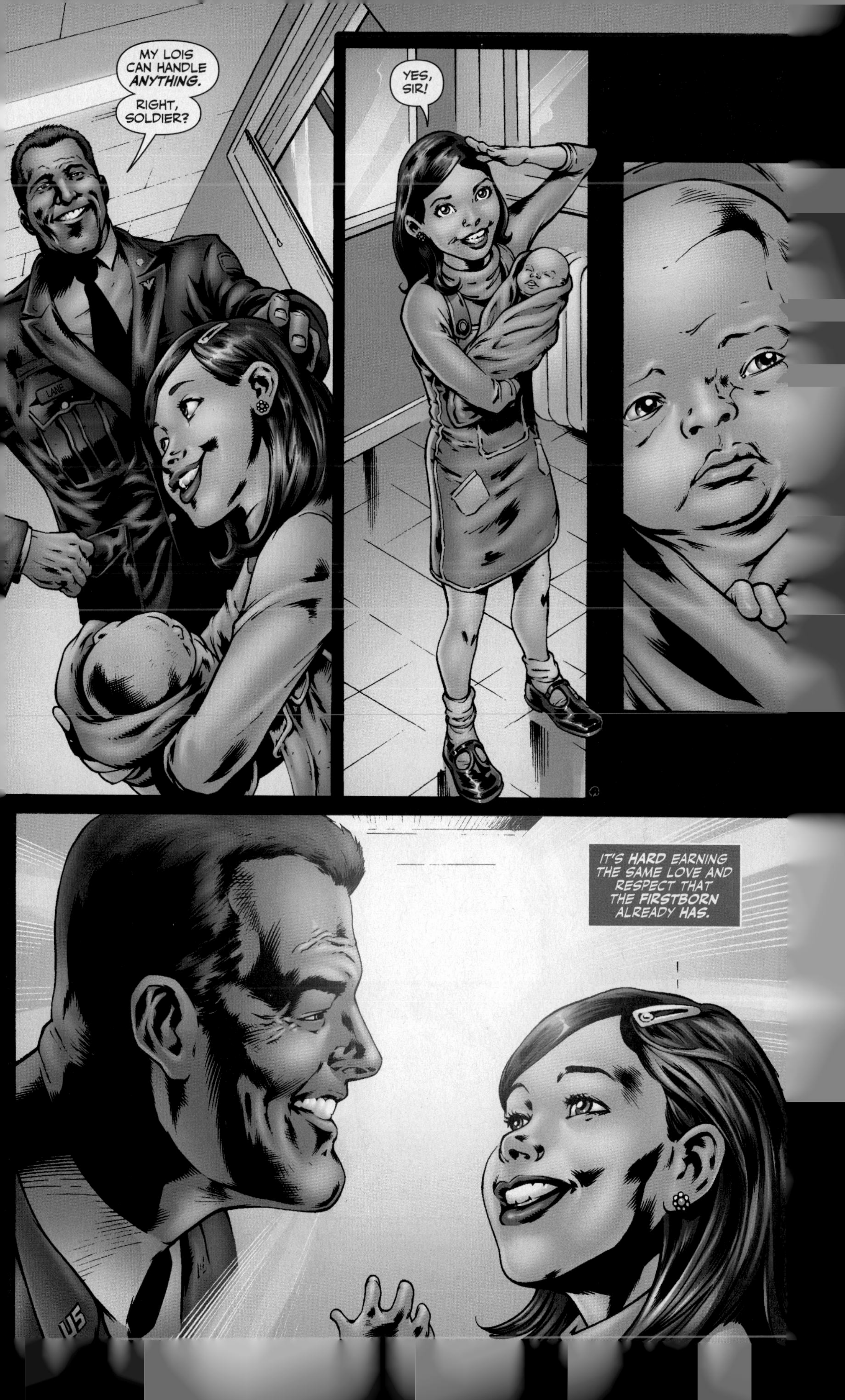
MY LOIS CAN HANDLE ANYTHING.
RIGHT, SOLDIER?
YES, SIR!
IT'S HARD EARNING THE SAME LOVE AND RESPECT THAT THE FIRSTBORN ALREADY HAS.
LANE
US

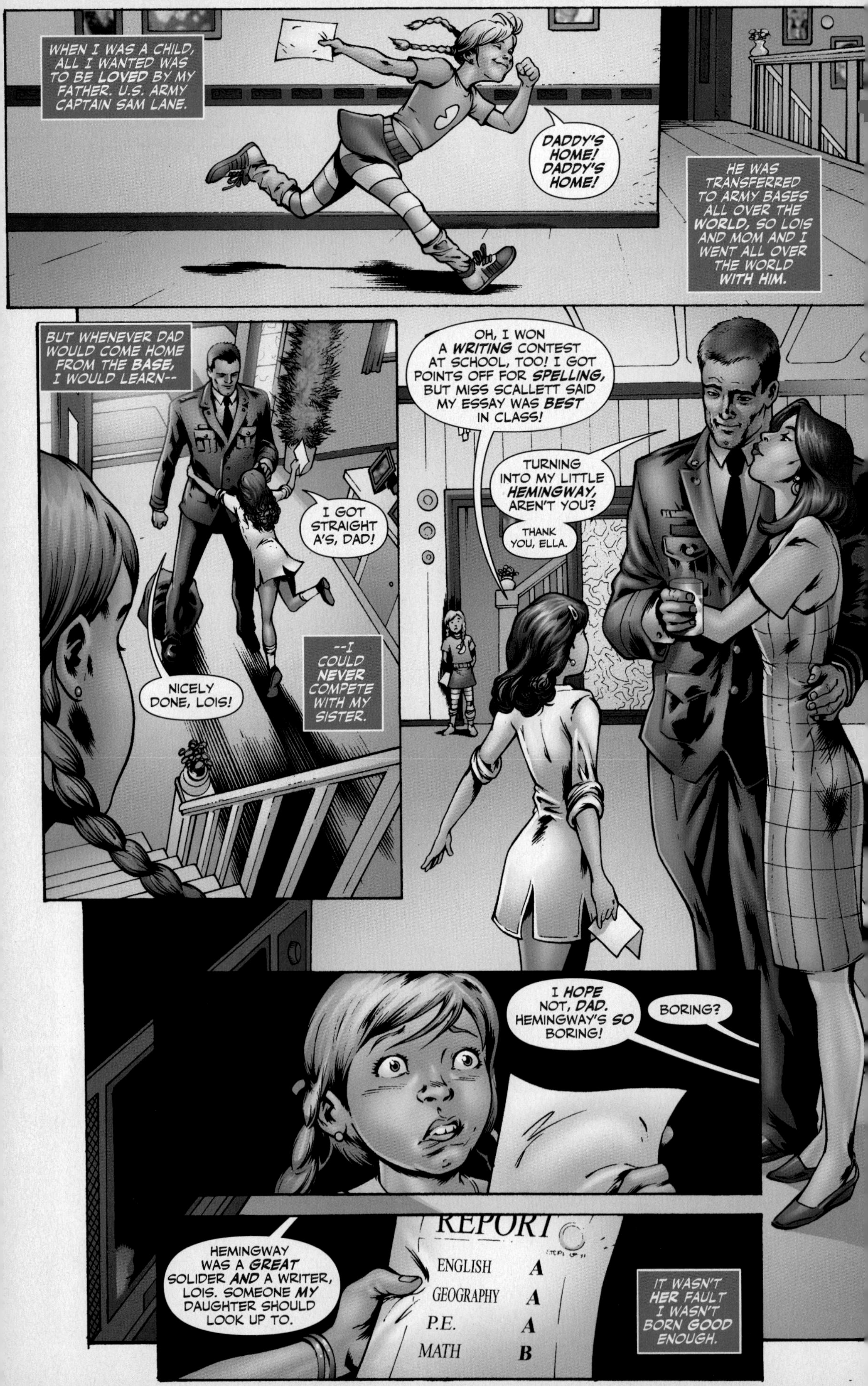

WHEN I WAS A CHILD, ALL I WANTED WAS TO BE LOVED BY MY FATHER. U.S. ARMY CAPTAIN SAM LANE.
DADDY'S HOME! DADDY'S HOME!
HE WAS TRANSFERRED TO ARMY BASES ALL OVER THE WORLD, SO LOIS AND MOM AND I WENT ALL OVER THE WORLD WITH HIM.
BUT WHENEVER DAD WOULD COME HOME FROM THE BASE, I WOULD LEARN--
I GOT STRAIGHT A'S, DAD!
NICELY DONE, LOIS!
--I COULD NEVER COMPETE WITH MY SISTER.
OH, I WON A WRITING CONTEST AT SCHOOL, TOO! I GOT POINTS OFF FOR SPELLING, BUT MISS SCALLETT SAID MY ESSAY WAS BEST IN CLASS!
TURNING INTO MY LITTLE HEMINGWAY, AREN'T YOU?
THANK YOU, ELLA.
I HOPE NOT, DAD. HEMINGWAY'S SO BORING!
BORING?
HEMINGWAY WAS A GREAT SOLIDER AND A WRITER, LOIS. SOMEONE MY DAUGHTER SHOULD LOOK UP TO.
REPORT
ENGLISH A
GEOGRAPHY A
P.E. A
MATH B
IT WASN'T HER FAULT I WASN'T BORN GOOD ENOUGH.

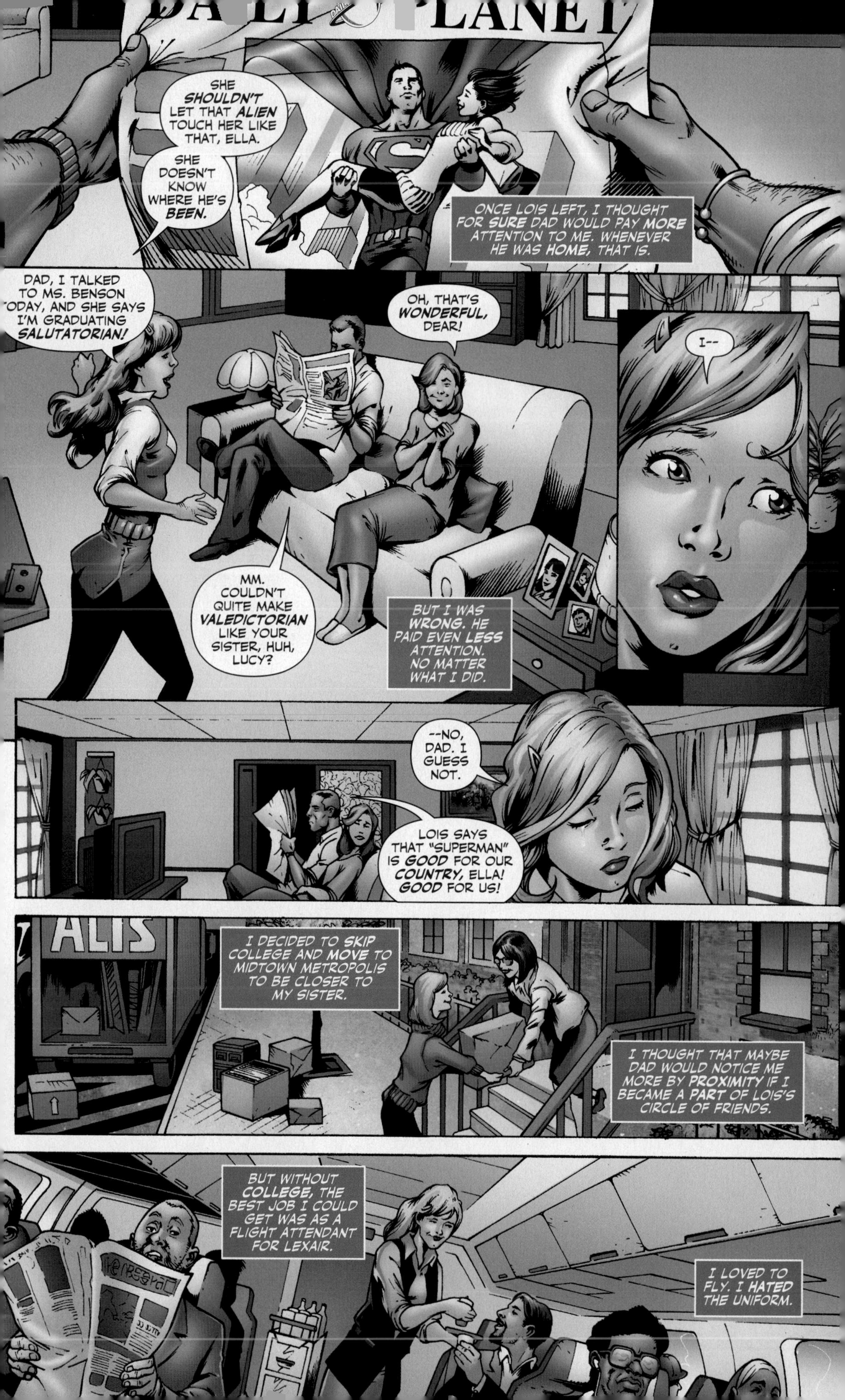
DAILY PLANET
SHE SHOULDN'T LET THAT ALIEN TOUCH HER LIKE THAT, ELLA.
SHE DOESN'T KNOW WHERE HE'S BEEN.
ONCE LOIS LEFT, I THOUGHT FOR SURE DAD WOULD PAY MORE ATTENTION TO ME. WHENEVER HE WAS HOME, THAT IS.
DAD, I TALKED TO MS. BENSON TODAY, AND SHE SAYS I'M GRADUATING SALUTATORIAN!
OH, THAT'S WONDERFUL, DEAR!
MM. COULDN'T QUITE MAKE VALEDICTORIAN LIKE YOUR SISTER, HUH, LUCY?
BUT I WAS WRONG. HE PAID EVEN LESS ATTENTION. NO MATTER WHAT I DID.
I--
--NO, DAD. I GUESS NOT.
LOIS SAYS THAT "SUPERMAN" IS GOOD FOR OUR COUNTRY, ELLA! GOOD FOR US!
ALIS
I DECIDED TO SKIP COLLEGE AND MOVE TO MIDTOWN METROPOLIS TO BE CLOSER TO MY SISTER.
I THOUGHT THAT MAYBE DAD WOULD NOTICE ME MORE BY PROXIMITY IF I BECAME A PART OF LOIS'S CIRCLE OF FRIENDS.
BUT WITHOUT COLLEGE, THE BEST JOB I COULD GET WAS AS A FLIGHT ATTENDANT FOR LEXAIR.
I LOVED TO FLY. I HATED THE UNIFORM.

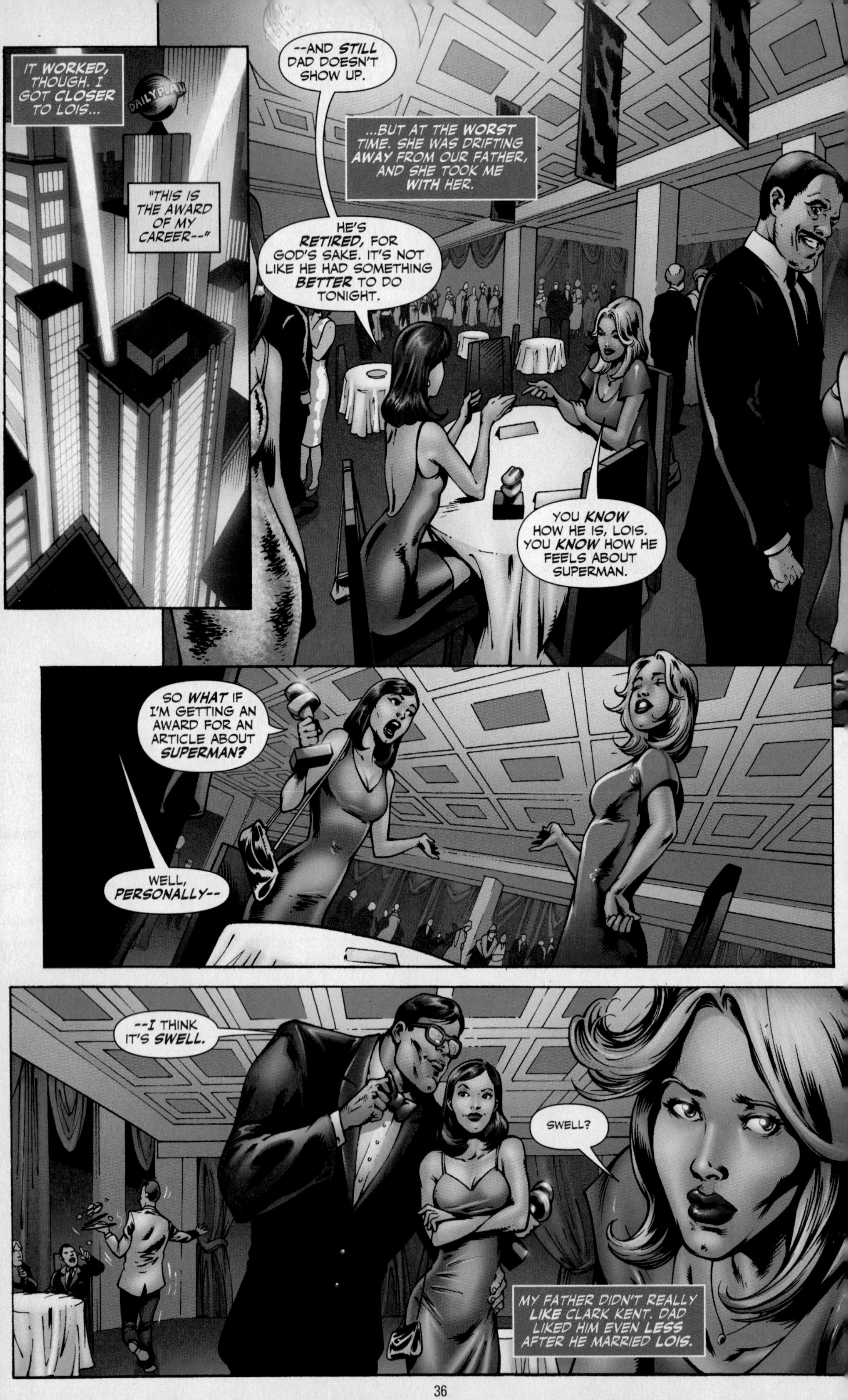
IT WORKED, THOUGH. I GOT CLOSER TO LOIS...
DAILY PLANET
"THIS IS THE AWARD OF MY CAREER--"
--AND STILL DAD DOESN'T SHOW UP.
...BUT AT THE WORST TIME. SHE WAS DRIFTING AWAY FROM OUR FATHER, AND SHE TOOK ME WITH HER.
HE'S RETIRED, FOR GOD'S SAKE. IT'S NOT LIKE HE HAD SOMETHING BETTER TO DO TONIGHT.
YOU KNOW HOW HE IS, LOIS. YOU KNOW HOW HE FEELS ABOUT SUPERMAN.
SO WHAT IF I'M GETTING AN AWARD FOR AN ARTICLE ABOUT SUPERMAN?
WELL, PERSONALLY--
--I THINK IT'S SWELL.
SWELL?
MY FATHER DIDN'T REALLY LIKE CLARK KENT. DAD LIKED HIM EVEN LESS AFTER HE MARRIED LOIS.

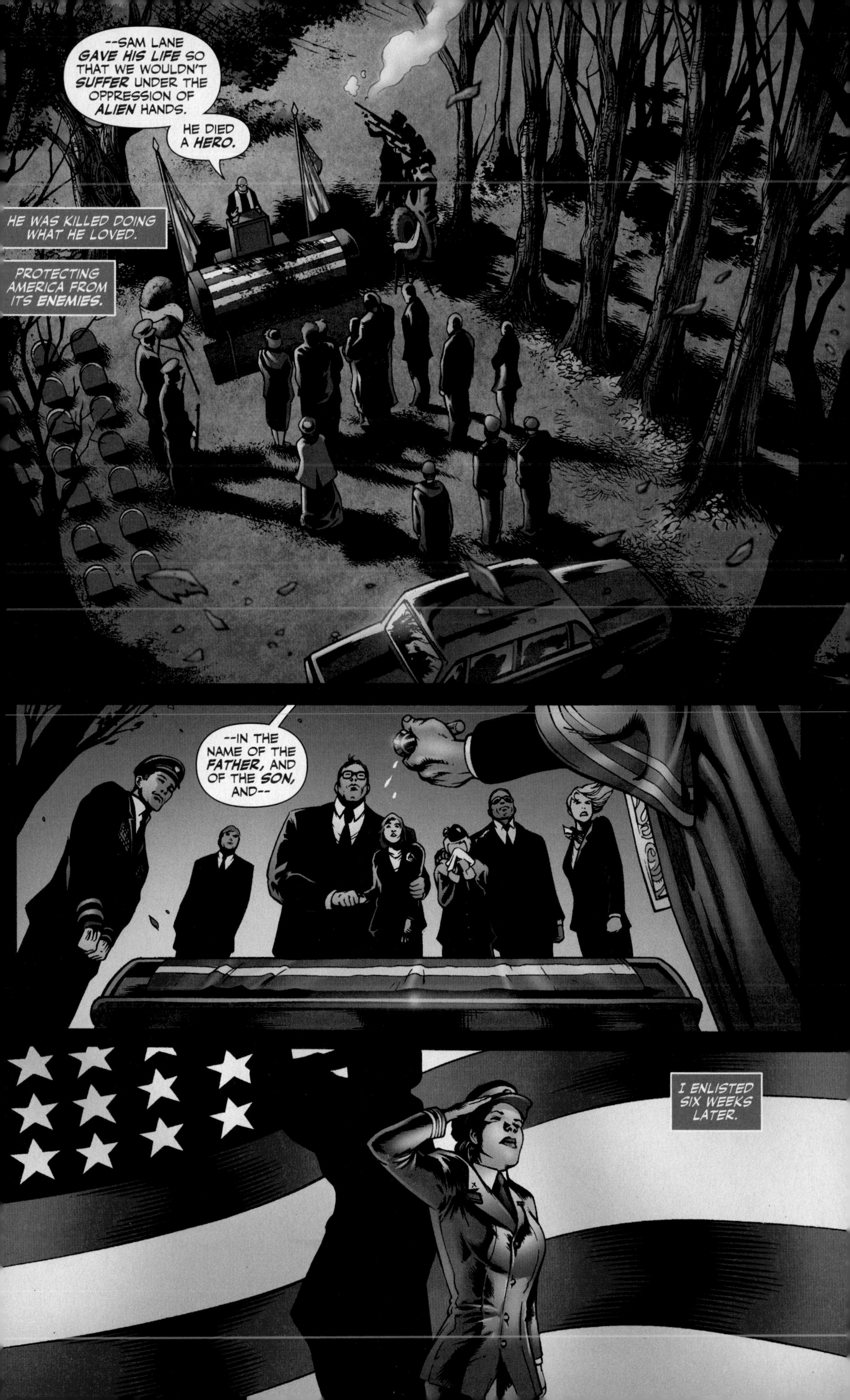
--SAM LANE GAVE HIS LIFE SO THAT WE WOULDN'T SUFFER UNDER THE OPPRESSION OF ALIEN HANDS.
HE DIED A HERO.
HE WAS KILLED DOING WHAT HE LOVED.
PROTECTING AMERICA FROM ITS ENEMIES.
--IN THE NAME OF THE FATHER, AND OF THE SON, AND--
I ENLISTED SIX WEEKS LATER.

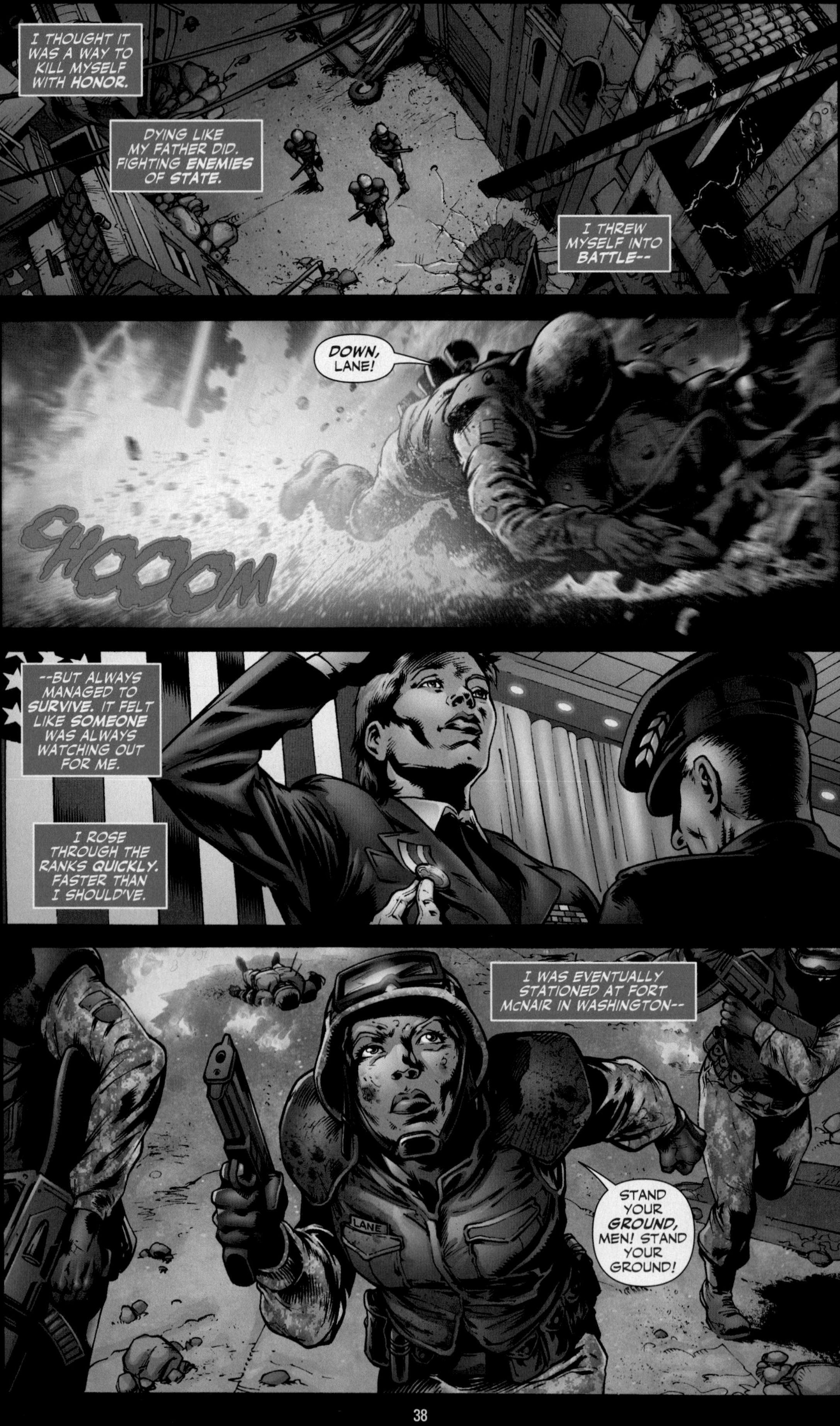
I THOUGHT IT WAS A WAY TO KILL MYSELF WITH HONOR.
DYING LIKE MY FATHER DID. FIGHTING ENEMIES OF STATE.
I THREW MYSELF INTO BATTLE--
DOWN, LANE!
CHOOOM
--BUT ALWAYS MANAGED TO SURVIVE. IT FELT LIKE SOMEONE WAS ALWAYS WATCHING OUT FOR ME.
I ROSE THROUGH THE RANKS QUICKLY. FASTER THAN I SHOULD'VE.
I WAS EVENTUALLY STATIONED AT FORT McNAIR IN WASHINGTON--
LANE
STAND YOUR GROUND, MEN! STAND YOUR GROUND!

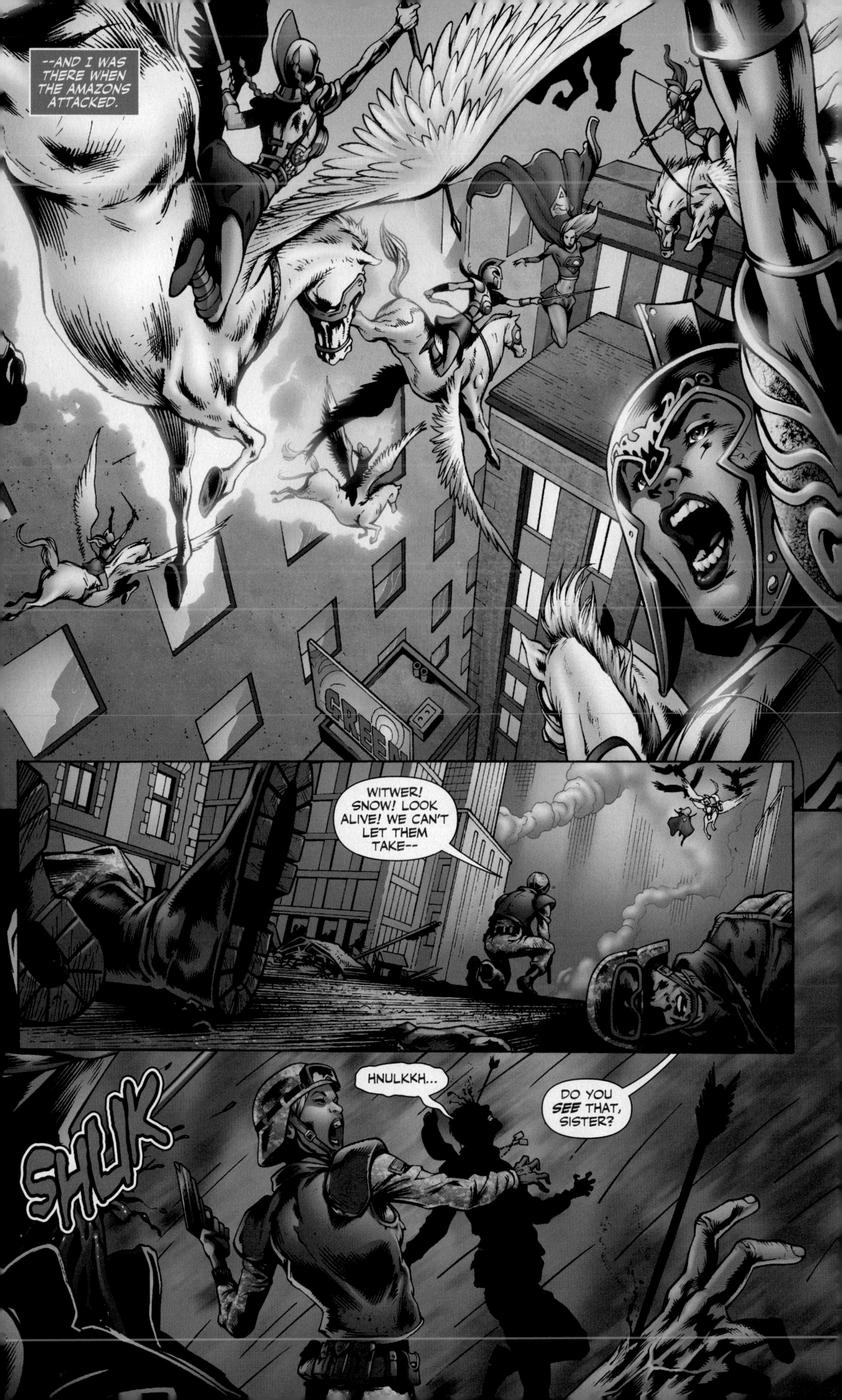
--AND I WAS THERE WHEN THE AMAZONS ATTACKED.
GREEN
WITWER! SNOW! LOOK ALIVE! WE CAN'T LET THEM TAKE--
SHLK
HNULKKH...
DO YOU SEE THAT, SISTER?

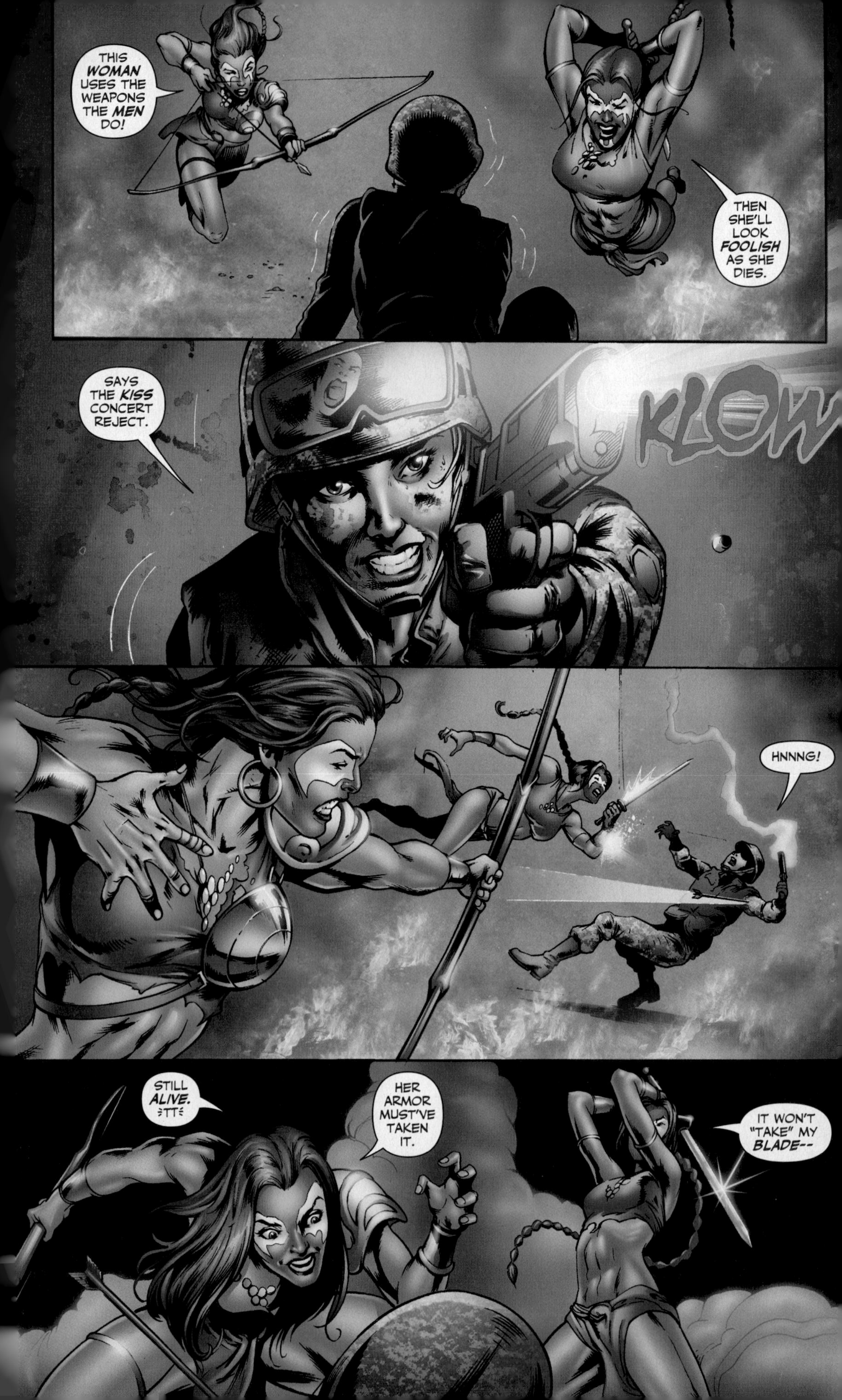
THIS WOMAN USES THE WEAPONS THE MEN DO!
THEN SHE'LL LOOK FOOLISH AS SHE DIES.
SAYS THE KISS CONCERT REJECT.
KLOW
HNNNG!
STILL ALIVE. TT
HER ARMOR MUST'VE TAKEN IT.
IT WON'T "TAKE" MY BLADE--

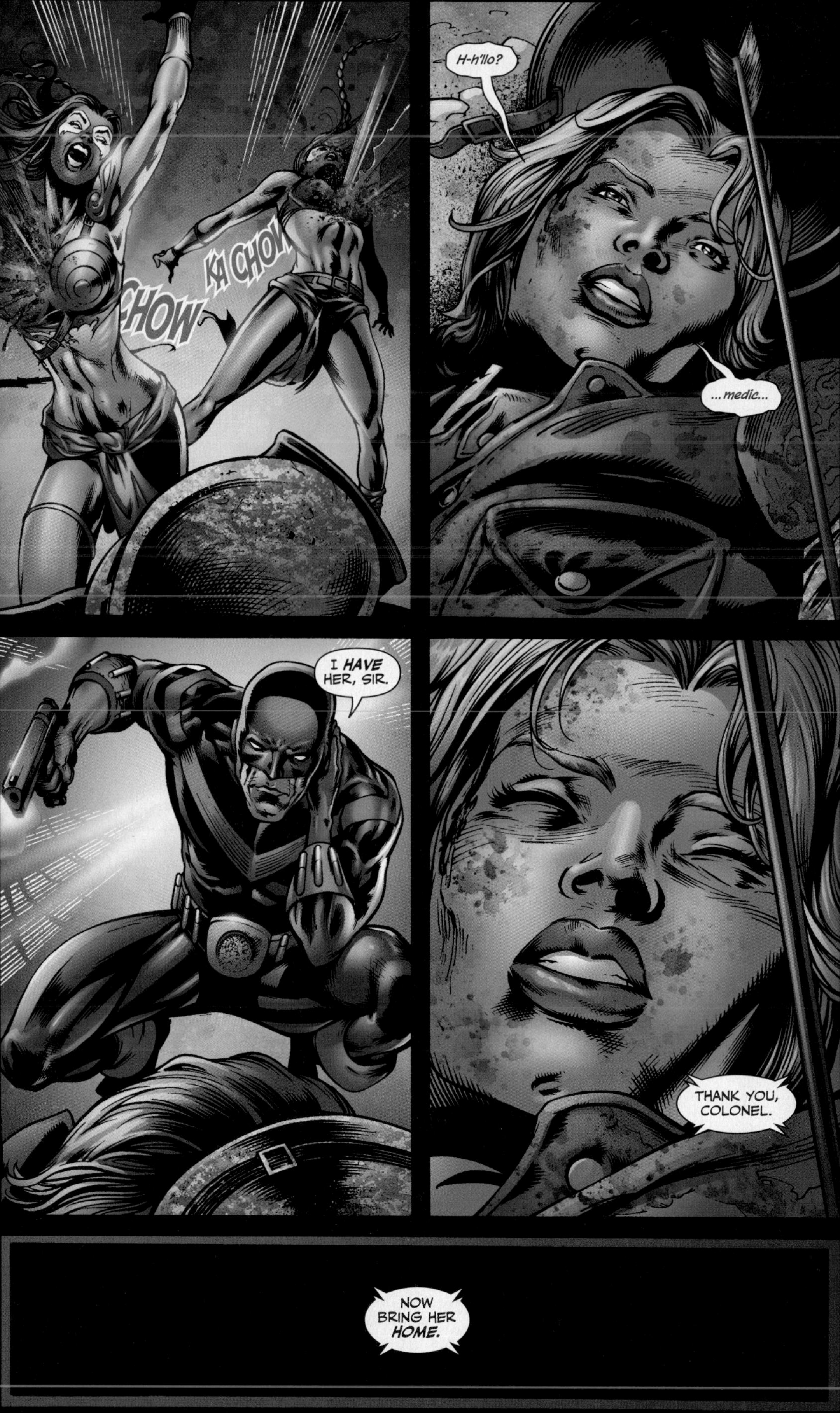
CHOW
KA CHOW
H-h'llo?
...medic...
I HAVE HER, SIR.
THANK YOU, COLONEL.
NOW BRING HER HOME.

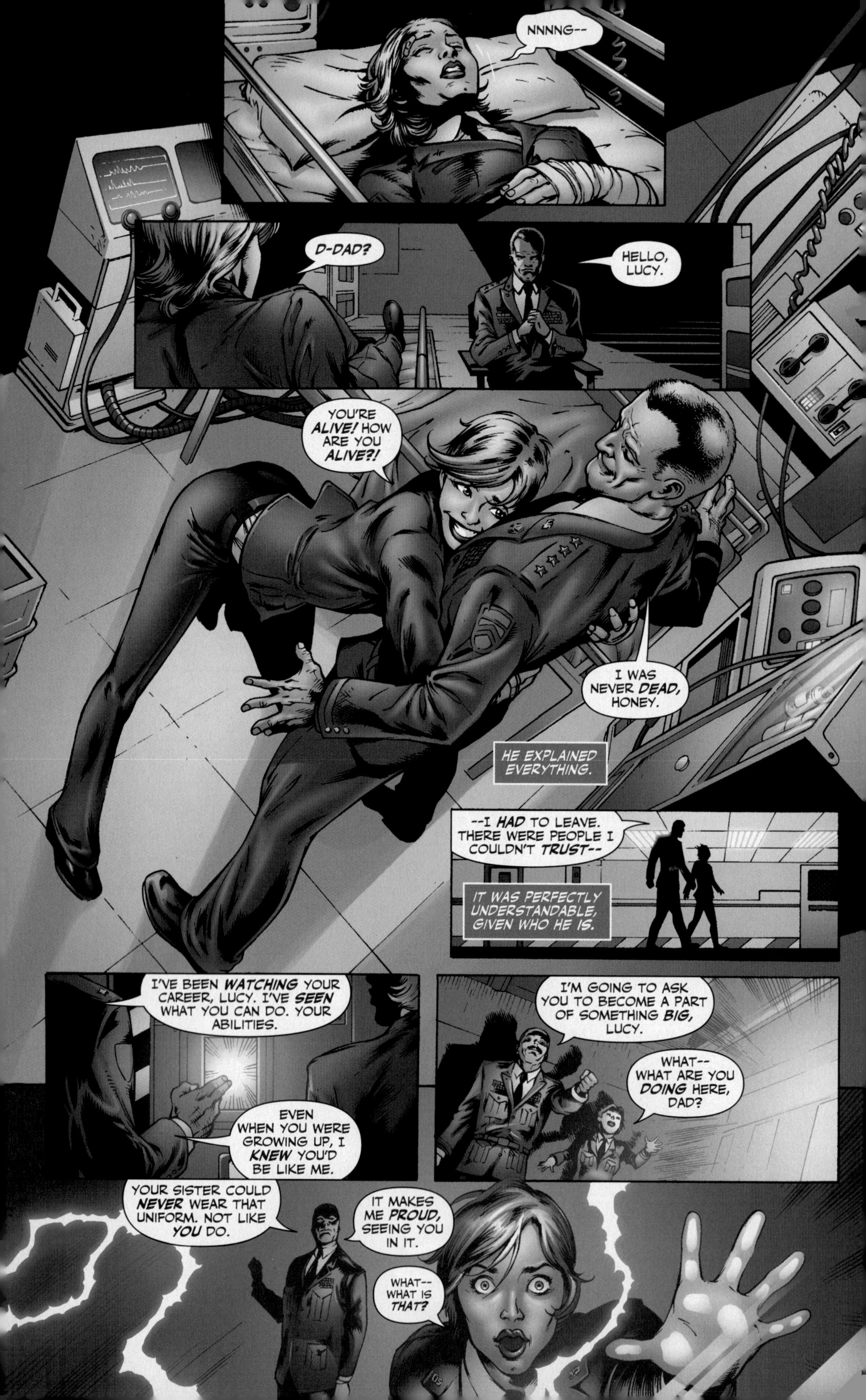
NNNNG--
D-DAD?
HELLO, LUCY.
YOU'RE ALIVE! HOW ARE YOU ALIVE?!
I WAS NEVER DEAD, HONEY.
HE EXPLAINED EVERYTHING.
--I HAD TO LEAVE. THERE WERE PEOPLE I COULDN'T TRUST--
IT WAS PERFECTLY UNDERSTANDABLE, GIVEN WHO HE IS.
I'VE BEEN WATCHING YOUR CAREER, LUCY. I'VE SEEN WHAT YOU CAN DO. YOUR ABILITIES.
EVEN WHEN YOU WERE GROWING UP, I KNEW YOU'D BE LIKE ME.
I'M GOING TO ASK YOU TO BECOME A PART OF SOMETHING BIG, LUCY.
WHAT-- WHAT ARE YOU DOING HERE, DAD?
YOUR SISTER COULD NEVER WEAR THAT UNIFORM. NOT LIKE YOU DO.
IT MAKES ME PROUD, SEEING YOU IN IT.
WHAT-- WHAT IS THAT?

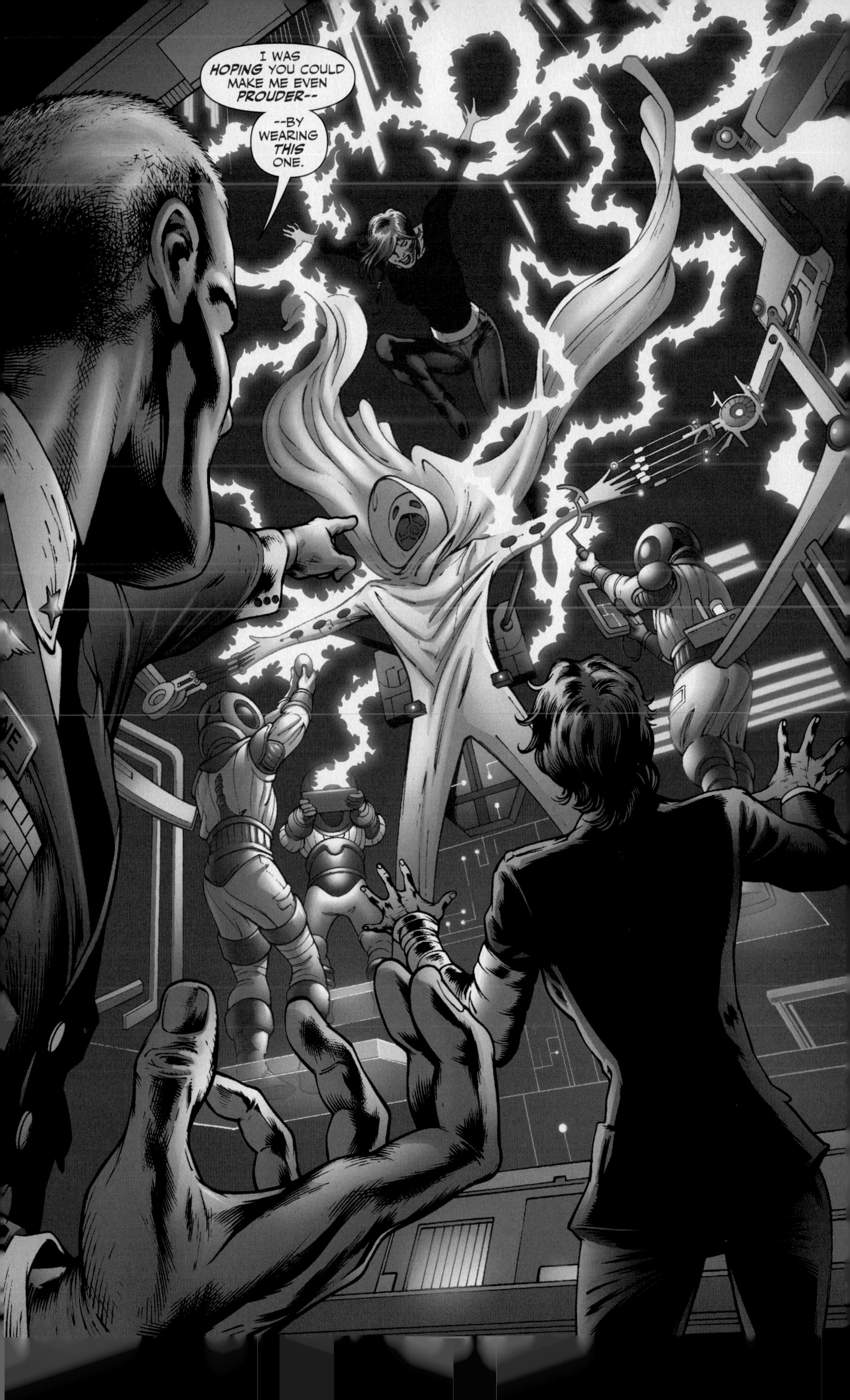
I WAS HOPING YOU COULD MAKE ME EVEN PROUDER--
--BY WEARING THIS ONE.

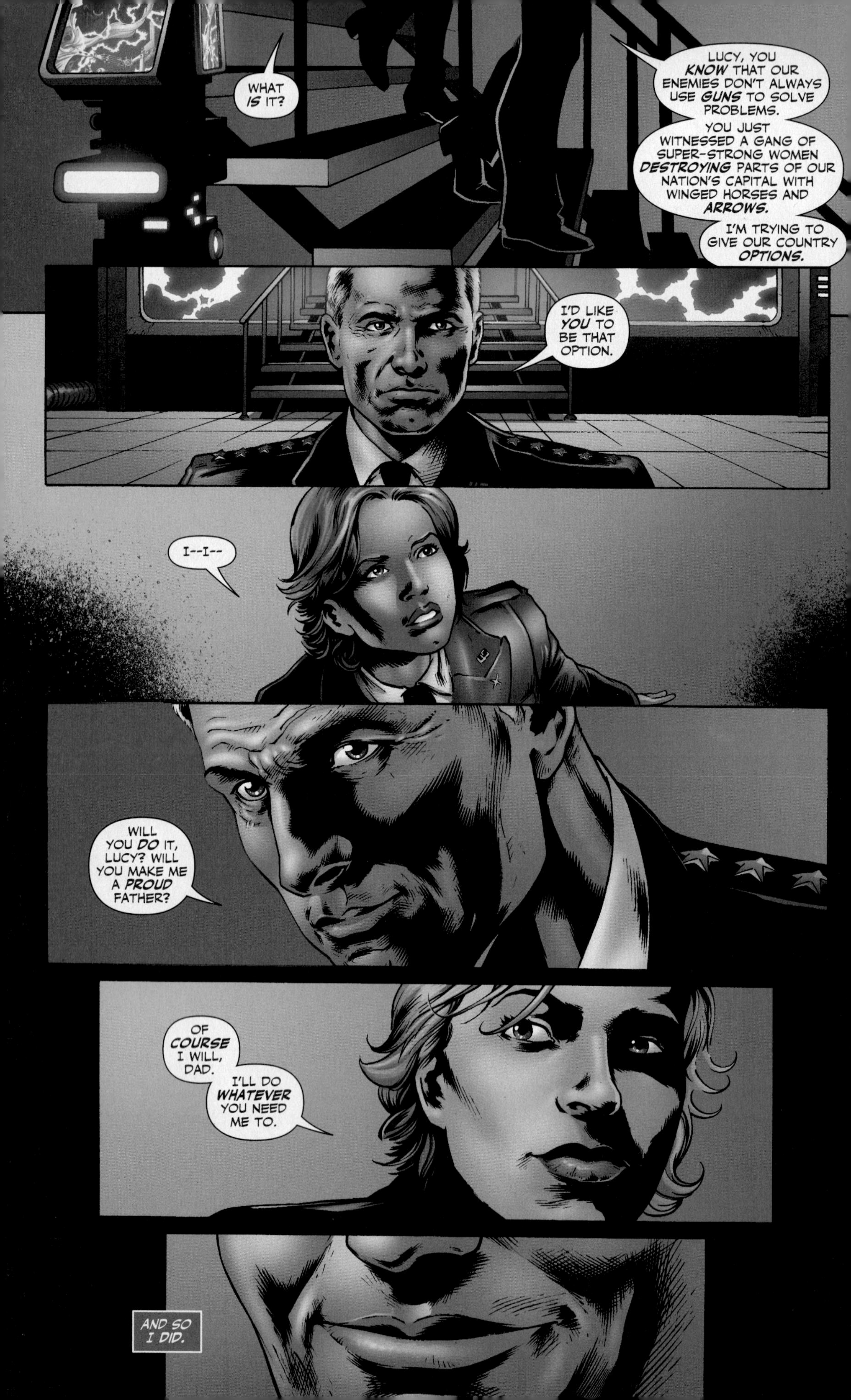
WHAT IS IT?
LUCY, YOU KNOW THAT OUR ENEMIES DON'T ALWAYS USE GUNS TO SOLVE PROBLEMS.
YOU JUST WITNESSED A GANG OF SUPER-STRONG WOMEN DESTROYING PARTS OF OUR NATION'S CAPITAL WITH WINGED HORSES AND ARROWS.
I'M TRYING TO GIVE OUR COUNTRY OPTIONS.
I'D LIKE YOU TO BE THAT OPTION.
I--I--
WILL YOU DO IT, LUCY? WILL YOU MAKE ME A PROUD FATHER?
OF COURSE I WILL, DAD.
I'LL DO WHATEVER YOU NEED ME TO.
AND SO I DID.

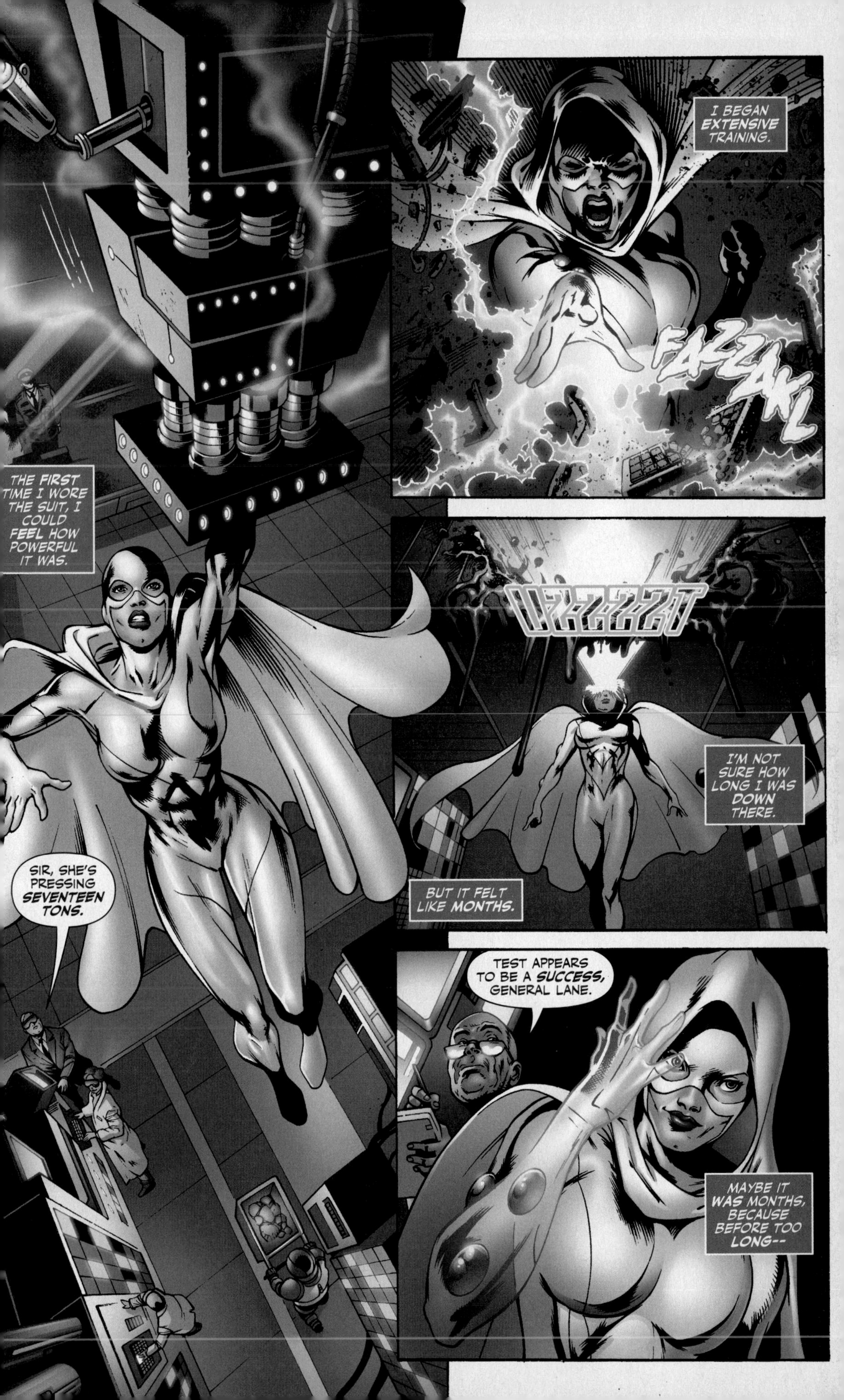

THE FIRST TIME I WORE THE SUIT, I COULD FEEL HOW POWERFUL IT WAS.
SIR, SHE'S PRESSING SEVENTEEN TONS.
I BEGAN EXTENSIVE TRAINING.
FAZZAKL
UZZZZZT
I'M NOT SURE HOW LONG I WAS DOWN THERE.
BUT IT FELT LIKE MONTHS.
TEST APPEARS TO BE A SUCCESS, GENERAL LANE.
MAYBE IT WAS MONTHS, BECAUSE BEFORE TOO LONG--

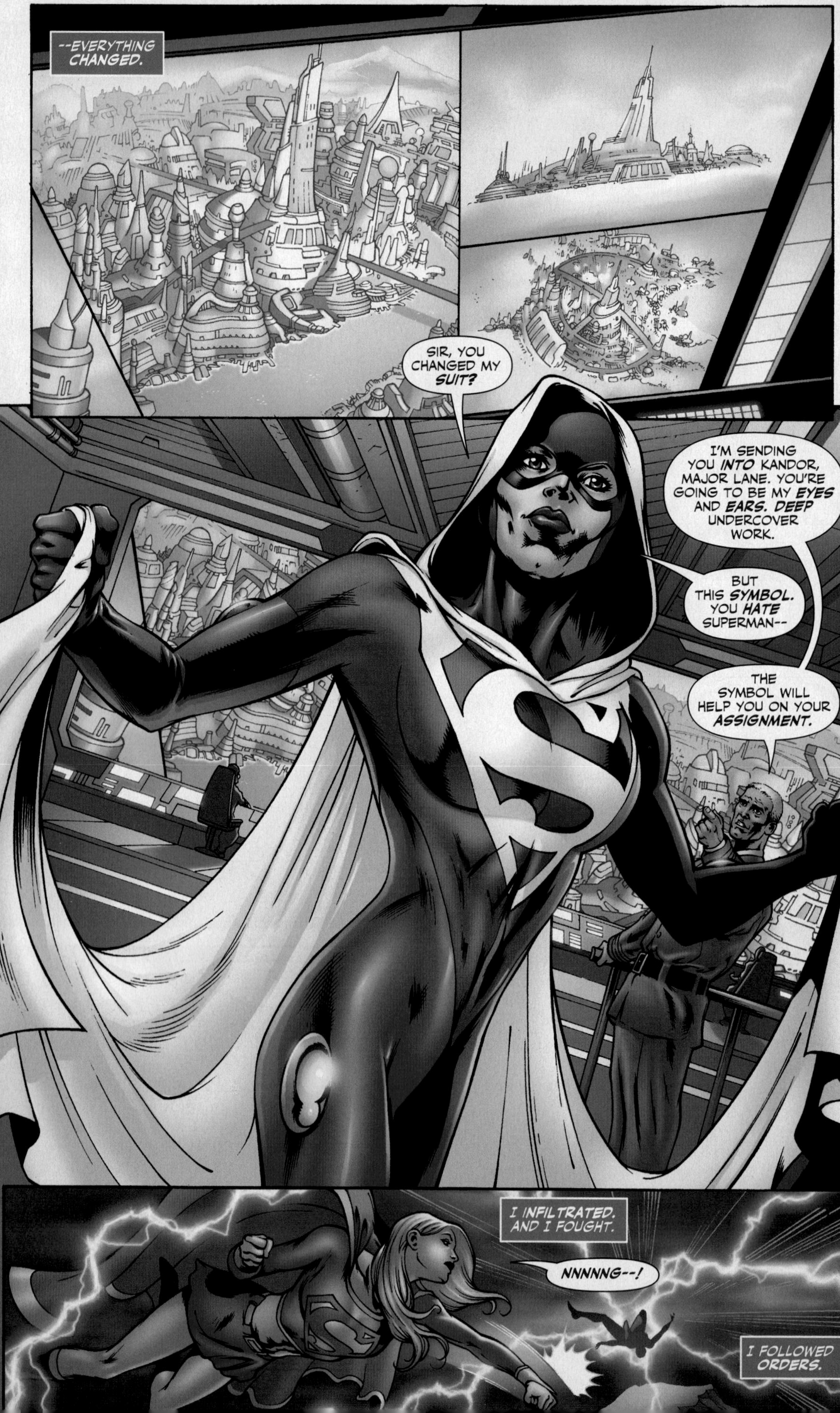
--EVERYTHING CHANGED.
SIR, YOU CHANGED MY SUIT?
I'M SENDING YOU INTO KANDOR, MAJOR LANE. YOU'RE GOING TO BE MY EYES AND EARS. DEEP UNDERCOVER WORK.
BUT THIS SYMBOL. YOU HATE SUPERMAN--
THE SYMBOL WILL HELP YOU ON YOUR ASSIGNMENT.
I INFILTRATED. AND I FOUGHT.
NNNNNG--!
I FOLLOWED ORDERS.

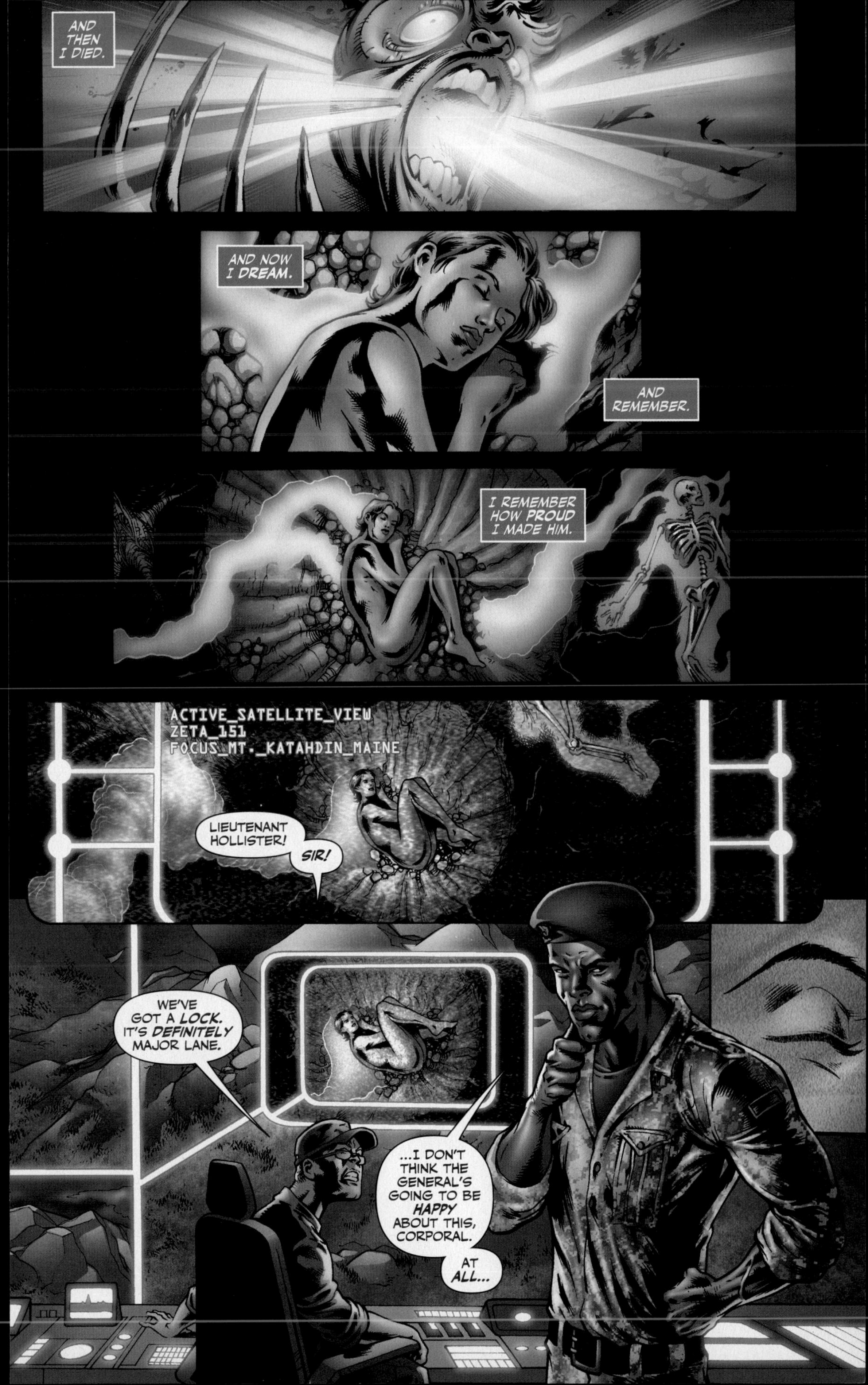
AND THEN I DIED.
AND NOW I DREAM.
AND REMEMBER.
I REMEMBER HOW PROUD I MADE HIM.
ACTIVE_SATELLITE_VIEW
ZETA_151
FOCUS_MT._KATAHDIN_MAINE
LIEUTENANT HOLLISTER!
SIR!
WE'VE GOT A LOCK. IT'S DEFINITELY MAJOR LANE.
...I DON'T THINK THE GENERAL'S GOING TO BE HAPPY ABOUT THIS, CORPORAL.
AT ALL...

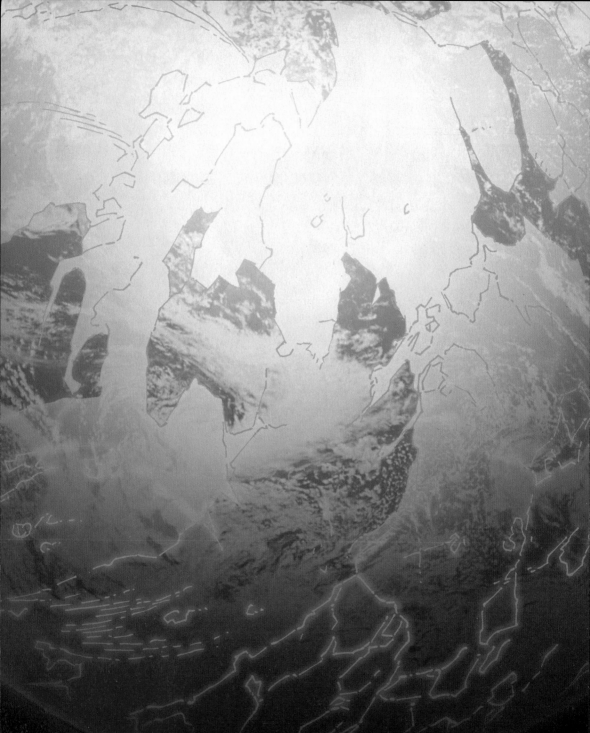

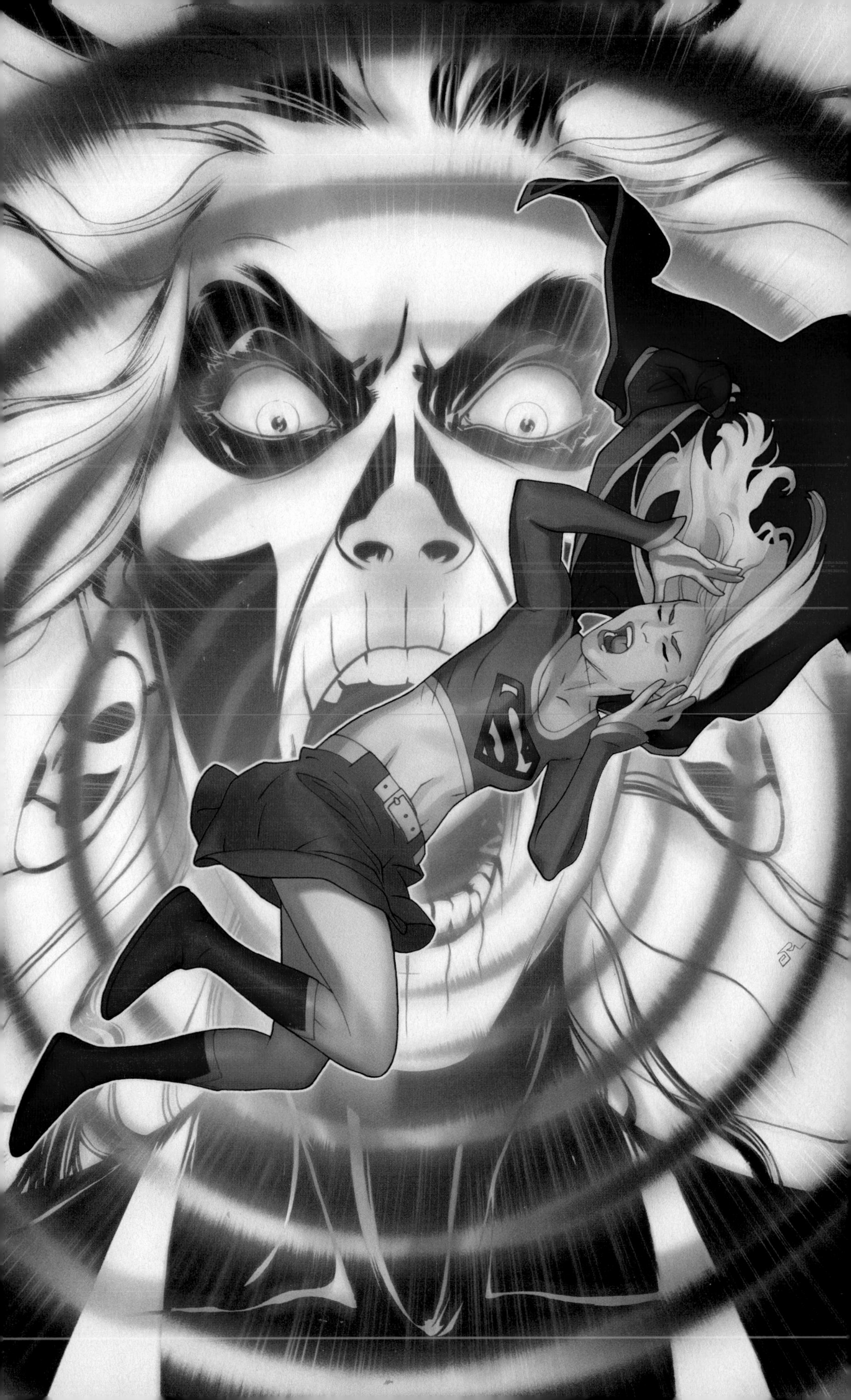

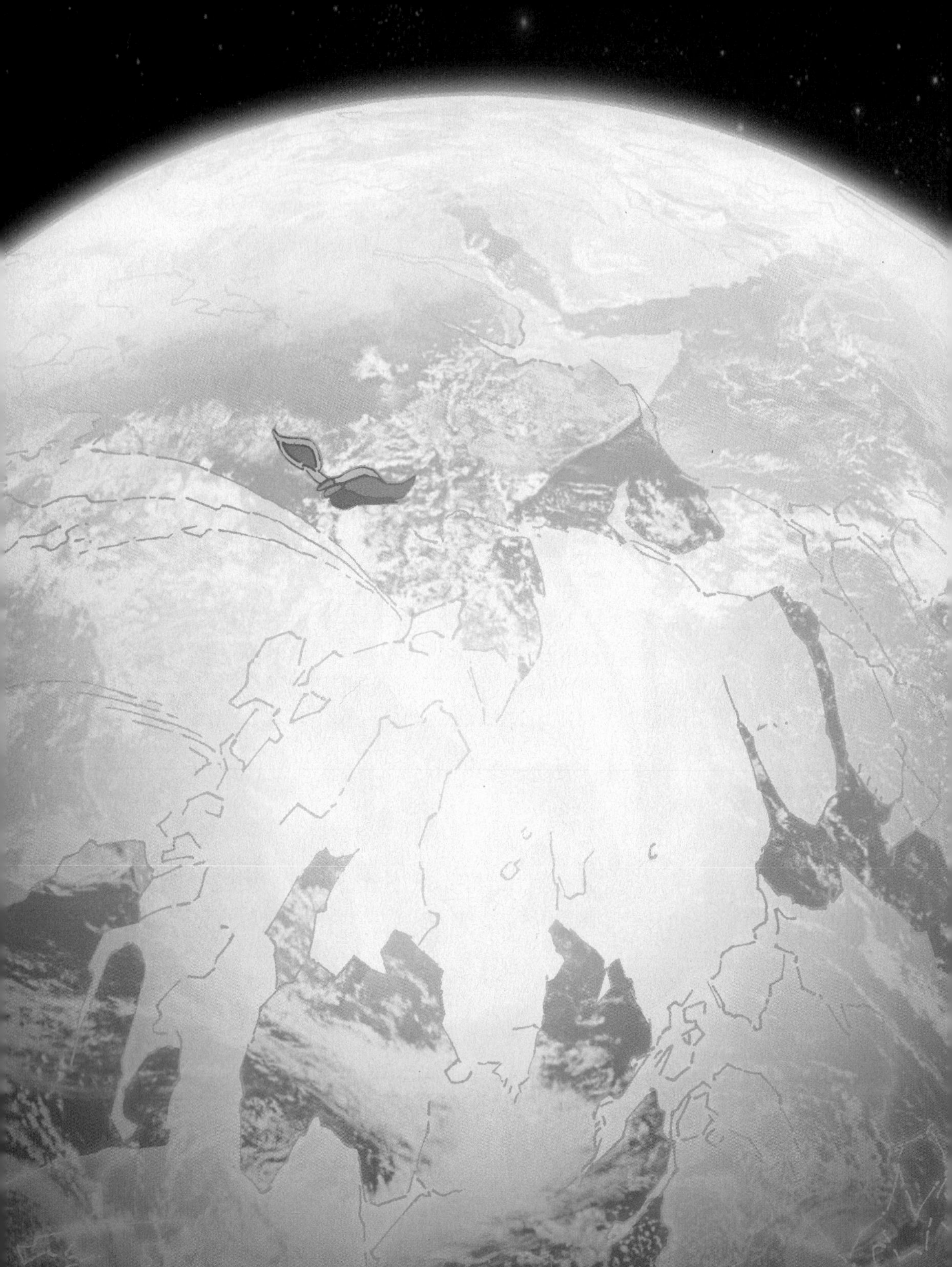

SONG OF THE SILVER BANSHEE

STERLING GATES WRITER **FERNANDO DAGNINO** PENCILLER
RAÚL FERNANDEZ INKER

COVER BY **JOSHUA MIDDLETON**

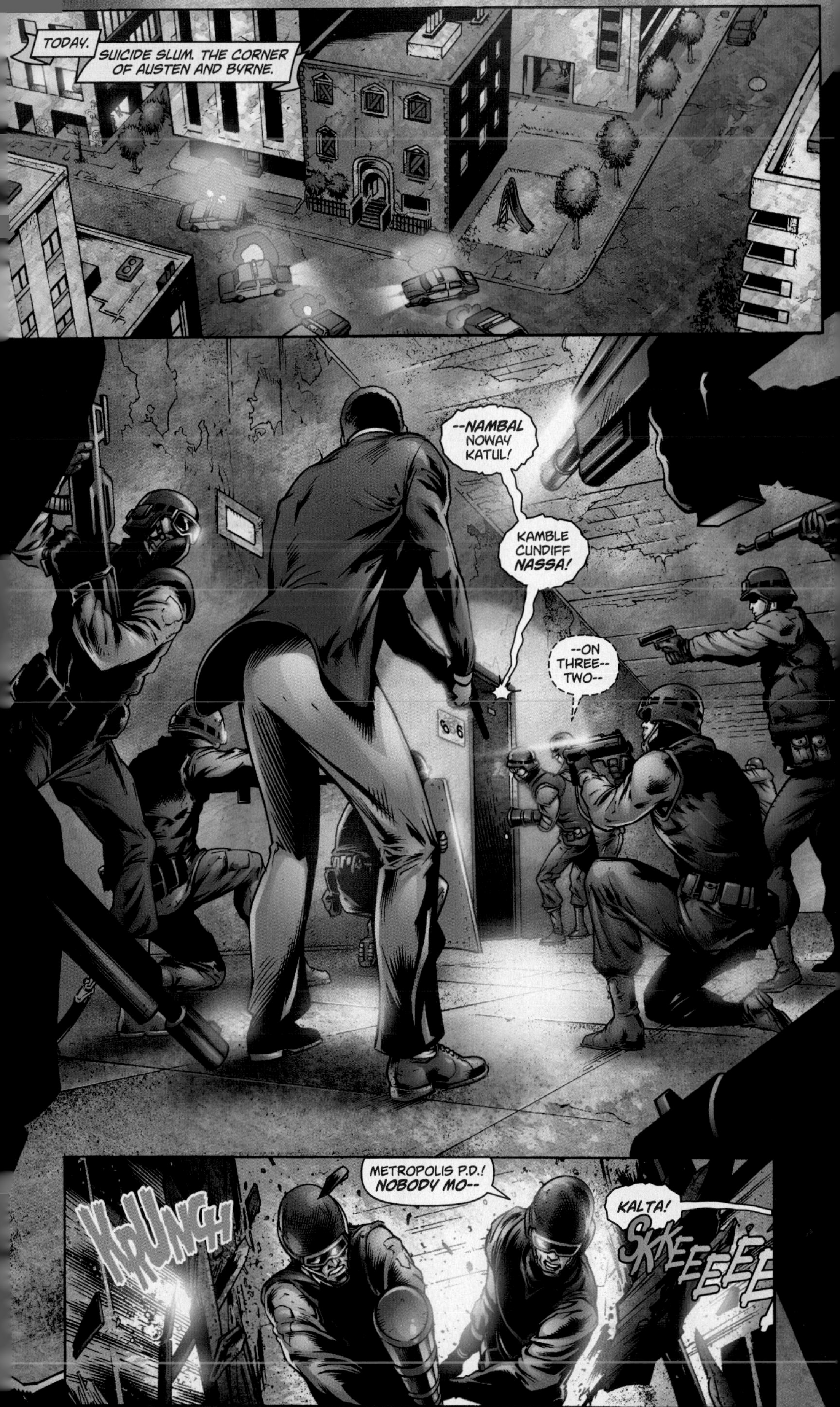
TODAY.
SUICIDE SLUM. THE CORNER OF AUSTEN AND BYRNE.
--NAMBAL NOWAY KATUL!
KAMBLE CUNDIFF NASSA!
--ON THREE-- TWO--
KRUNCH
METROPOLIS P.D.! NOBODY MO--
KALTA!
SKKEEEEE

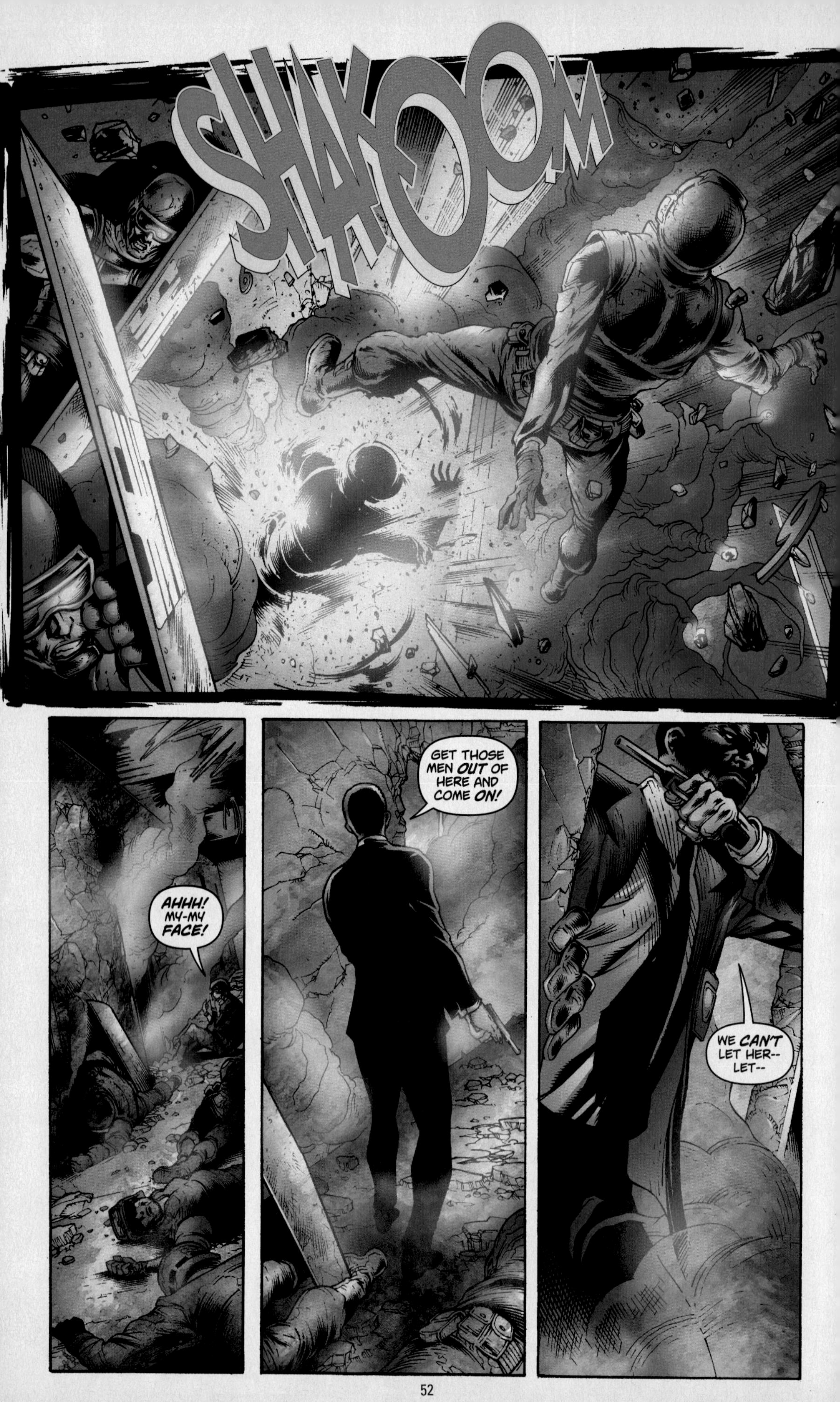
SHAKOOM
AHHH! MY-MY FACE!
GET THOSE MEN OUT OF HERE AND COME ON!
WE CAN'T LET HER-- LET--

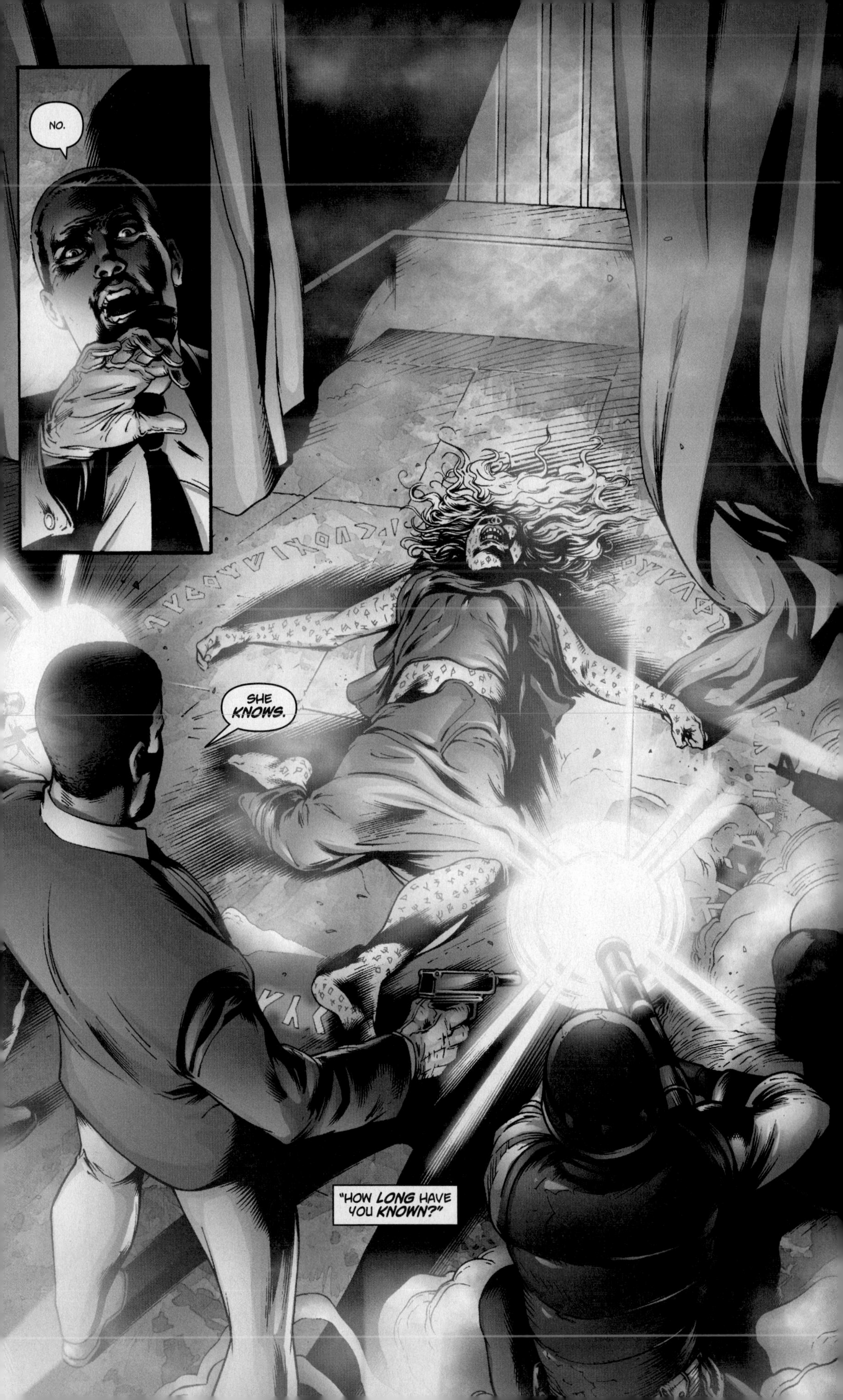
NO.
SHE KNOWS.
"HOW LONG HAVE YOU KNOWN?"

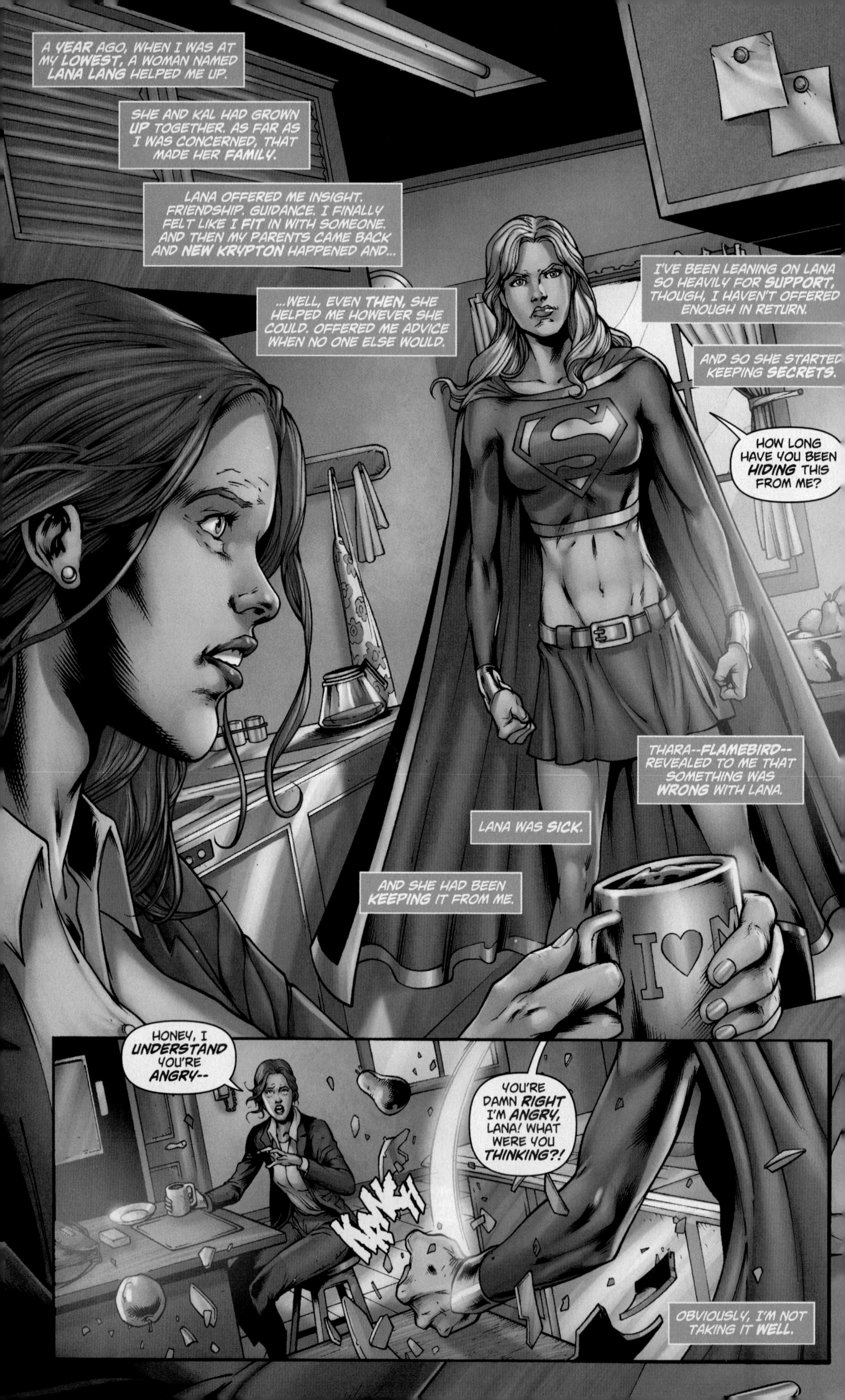
A YEAR AGO, WHEN I WAS AT MY LOWEST, A WOMAN NAMED LANA LANG HELPED ME UP.
SHE AND KAL HAD GROWN UP TOGETHER. AS FAR AS I WAS CONCERNED, THAT MADE HER FAMILY.
LANA OFFERED ME INSIGHT. FRIENDSHIP. GUIDANCE. I FINALLY FELT LIKE I FIT IN WITH SOMEONE. AND THEN MY PARENTS CAME BACK AND NEW KRYPTON HAPPENED AND...
...WELL, EVEN THEN, SHE HELPED ME HOWEVER SHE COULD. OFFERED ME ADVICE WHEN NO ONE ELSE WOULD.
I'VE BEEN LEANING ON LANA SO HEAVILY FOR SUPPORT, THOUGH, I HAVEN'T OFFERED ENOUGH IN RETURN.
AND SO SHE STARTED KEEPING SECRETS.
HOW LONG HAVE YOU BEEN HIDING THIS FROM ME?
THARA--FLAMEBIRD--REVEALED TO ME THAT SOMETHING WAS WRONG WITH LANA.
LANA WAS SICK.
AND SHE HAD BEEN KEEPING IT FROM ME.
HONEY, I UNDERSTAND YOU'RE ANGRY--
YOU'RE DAMN RIGHT I'M ANGRY, LANA! WHAT WERE YOU THINKING?!
KRASH
OBVIOUSLY, I'M NOT TAKING IT WELL.

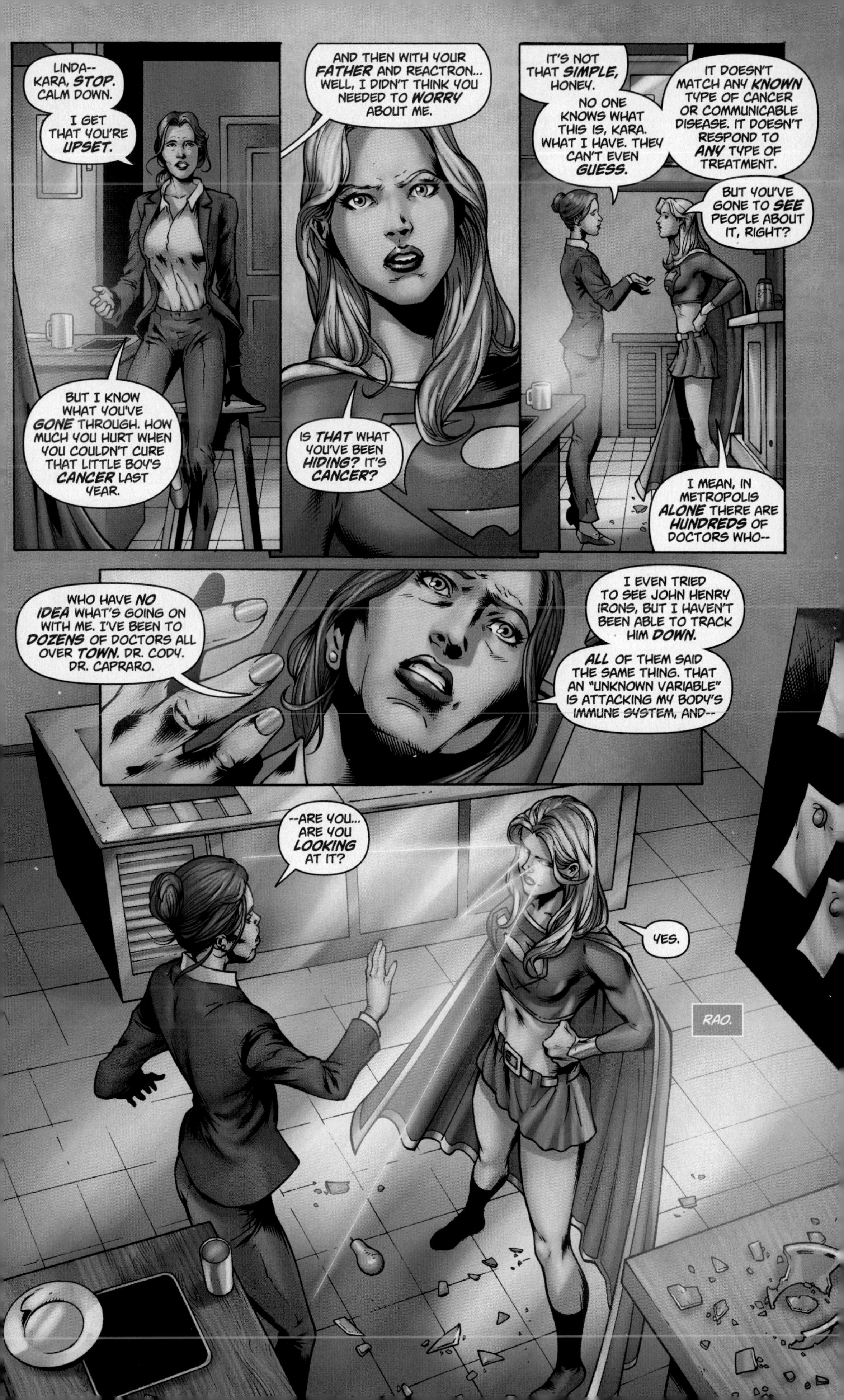

LINDA-- KARA, STOP. CALM DOWN.
I GET THAT YOU'RE UPSET.
BUT I KNOW WHAT YOU'VE GONE THROUGH. HOW MUCH YOU HURT WHEN YOU COULDN'T CURE THAT LITTLE BOY'S CANCER LAST YEAR.
AND THEN WITH YOUR FATHER AND REACTRON... WELL, I DIDN'T THINK YOU NEEDED TO WORRY ABOUT ME.
IS THAT WHAT YOU'VE BEEN HIDING? IT'S CANCER?
IT'S NOT THAT SIMPLE, HONEY.
NO ONE KNOWS WHAT THIS IS, KARA. WHAT I HAVE. THEY CAN'T EVEN GUESS.
IT DOESN'T MATCH ANY KNOWN TYPE OF CANCER OR COMMUNICABLE DISEASE. IT DOESN'T RESPOND TO ANY TYPE OF TREATMENT.
BUT YOU'VE GONE TO SEE PEOPLE ABOUT IT, RIGHT?
I MEAN, IN METROPOLIS ALONE THERE ARE HUNDREDS OF DOCTORS WHO--
WHO HAVE NO IDEA WHAT'S GOING ON WITH ME. I'VE BEEN TO DOZENS OF DOCTORS ALL OVER TOWN. DR. CODY. DR. CAPRARO.
I EVEN TRIED TO SEE JOHN HENRY IRONS, BUT I HAVEN'T BEEN ABLE TO TRACK HIM DOWN.
ALL OF THEM SAID THE SAME THING. THAT AN "UNKNOWN VARIABLE" IS ATTACKING MY BODY'S IMMUNE SYSTEM, AND--
--ARE YOU... ARE YOU LOOKING AT IT?
YES.
RAO.

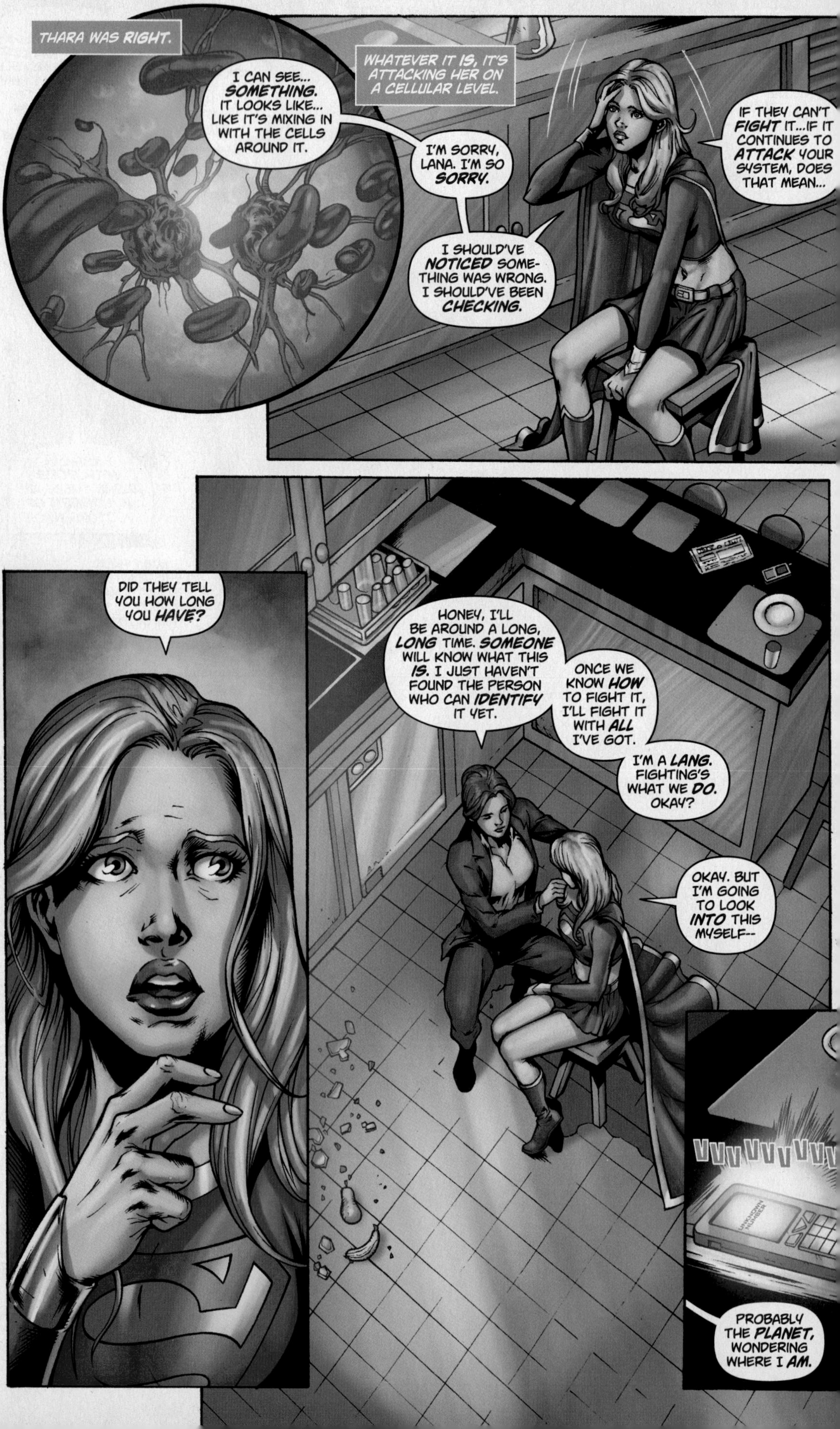
THARA WAS RIGHT.
I CAN SEE... SOMETHING. IT LOOKS LIKE... LIKE IT'S MIXING IN WITH THE CELLS AROUND IT.
WHATEVER IT IS, IT'S ATTACKING HER ON A CELLULAR LEVEL.
I'M SORRY, LANA. I'M SO SORRY.
I SHOULD'VE NOTICED SOMETHING WAS WRONG. I SHOULD'VE BEEN CHECKING.
IF THEY CAN'T FIGHT IT...IF IT CONTINUES TO ATTACK YOUR SYSTEM, DOES THAT MEAN...
DID THEY TELL YOU HOW LONG YOU HAVE?
HONEY, I'LL BE AROUND A LONG, LONG TIME. SOMEONE WILL KNOW WHAT THIS IS. I JUST HAVEN'T FOUND THE PERSON WHO CAN IDENTIFY IT YET.
ONCE WE KNOW HOW TO FIGHT IT, I'LL FIGHT IT WITH ALL I'VE GOT.
I'M A LANG. FIGHTING'S WHAT WE DO. OKAY?
OKAY. BUT I'M GOING TO LOOK INTO THIS MYSELF--
VVVVVVVVVV
PROBABLY THE PLANET, WONDERING WHERE I AM.

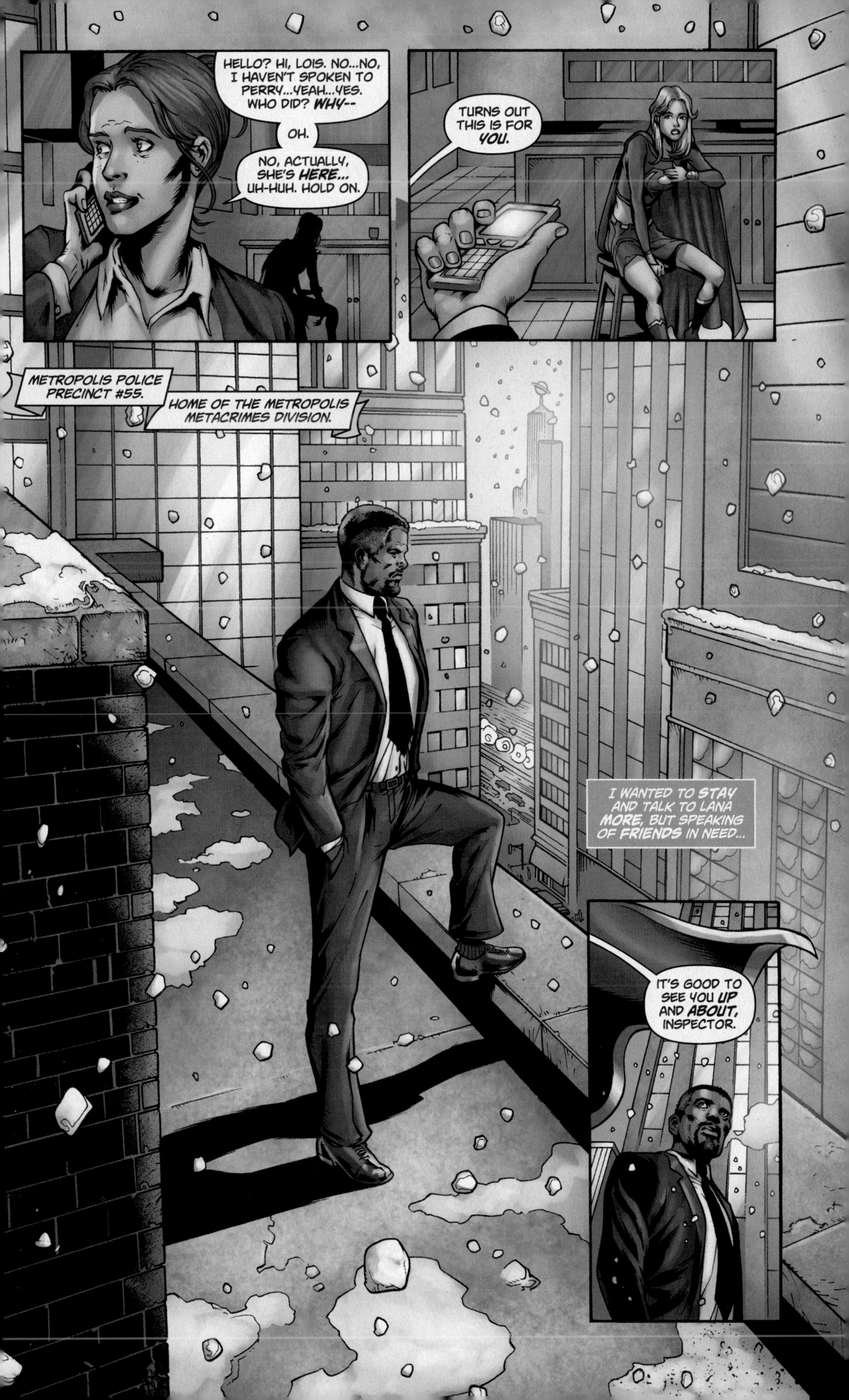
HELLO? HI, LOIS. NO...NO, I HAVEN'T SPOKEN TO PERRY...YEAH...YES. WHO DID? WHY--
OH.
NO, ACTUALLY, SHE'S HERE... UH-HUH. HOLD ON.
TURNS OUT THIS IS FOR YOU.
METROPOLIS POLICE PRECINCT #55.
HOME OF THE METROPOLIS METACRIMES DIVISION.
I WANTED TO STAY AND TALK TO LANA MORE, BUT SPEAKING OF FRIENDS IN NEED...
IT'S GOOD TO SEE YOU UP AND ABOUT, INSPECTOR.

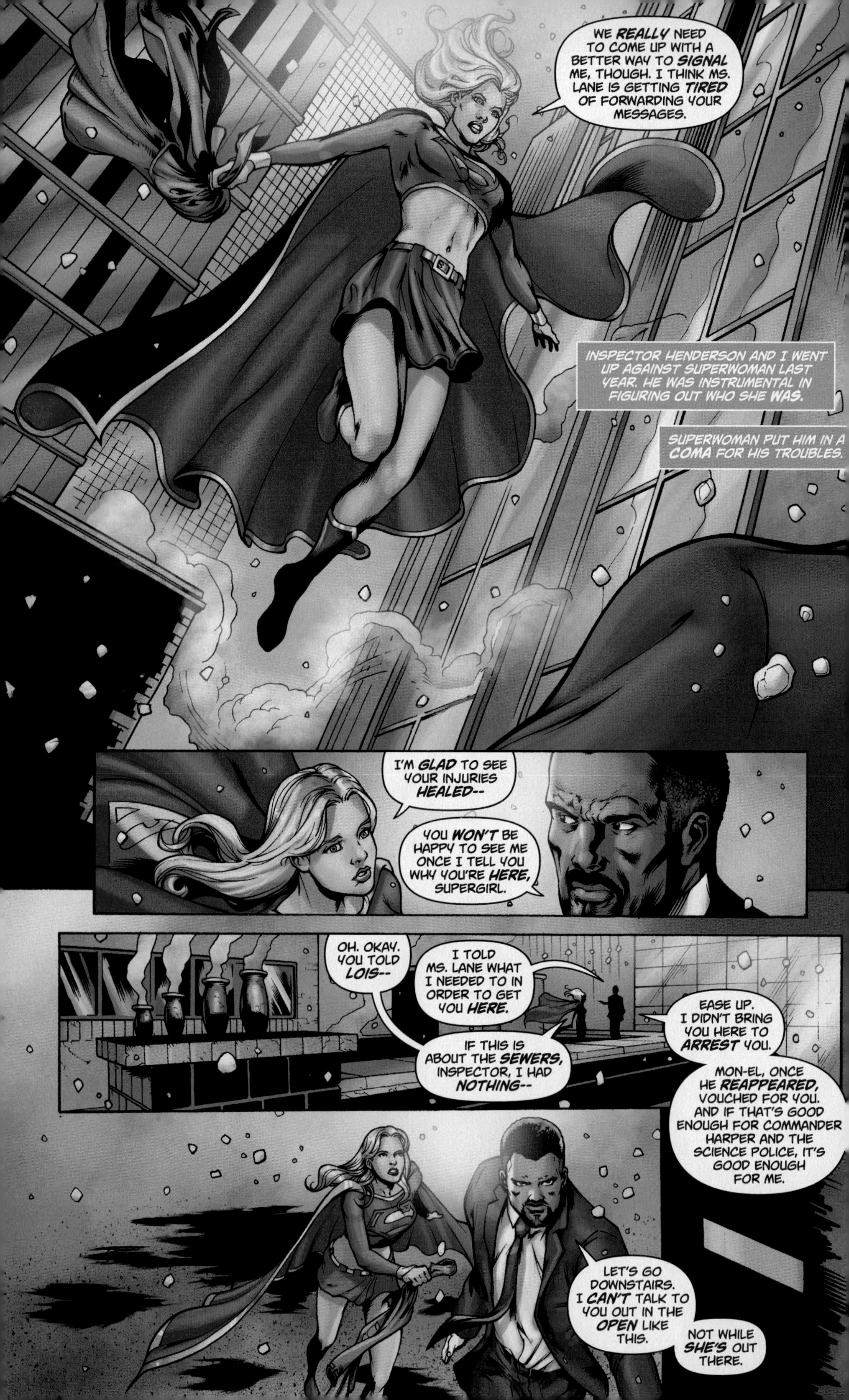

WE REALLY NEED TO COME UP WITH A BETTER WAY TO SIGNAL ME, THOUGH. I THINK MS. LANE IS GETTING TIRED OF FORWARDING YOUR MESSAGES.
INSPECTOR HENDERSON AND I WENT UP AGAINST SUPERWOMAN LAST YEAR. HE WAS INSTRUMENTAL IN FIGURING OUT WHO SHE WAS.
SUPERWOMAN PUT HIM IN A COMA FOR HIS TROUBLES.
I'M GLAD TO SEE YOUR INJURIES HEALED--
YOU WON'T BE HAPPY TO SEE ME ONCE I TELL YOU WHY YOU'RE HERE, SUPERGIRL.
OH. OKAY. YOU TOLD LOIS--
I TOLD MS. LANE WHAT I NEEDED TO IN ORDER TO GET YOU HERE.
IF THIS IS ABOUT THE SEWERS, INSPECTOR, I HAD NOTHING--
EASE UP. I DIDN'T BRING YOU HERE TO ARREST YOU.
MON-EL, ONCE HE REAPPEARED, VOUCHED FOR YOU. AND IF THAT'S GOOD ENOUGH FOR COMMANDER HARPER AND THE SCIENCE POLICE, IT'S GOOD ENOUGH FOR ME.
LET'S GO DOWNSTAIRS. I CAN'T TALK TO YOU OUT IN THE OPEN LIKE THIS.
NOT WHILE SHE'S OUT THERE.

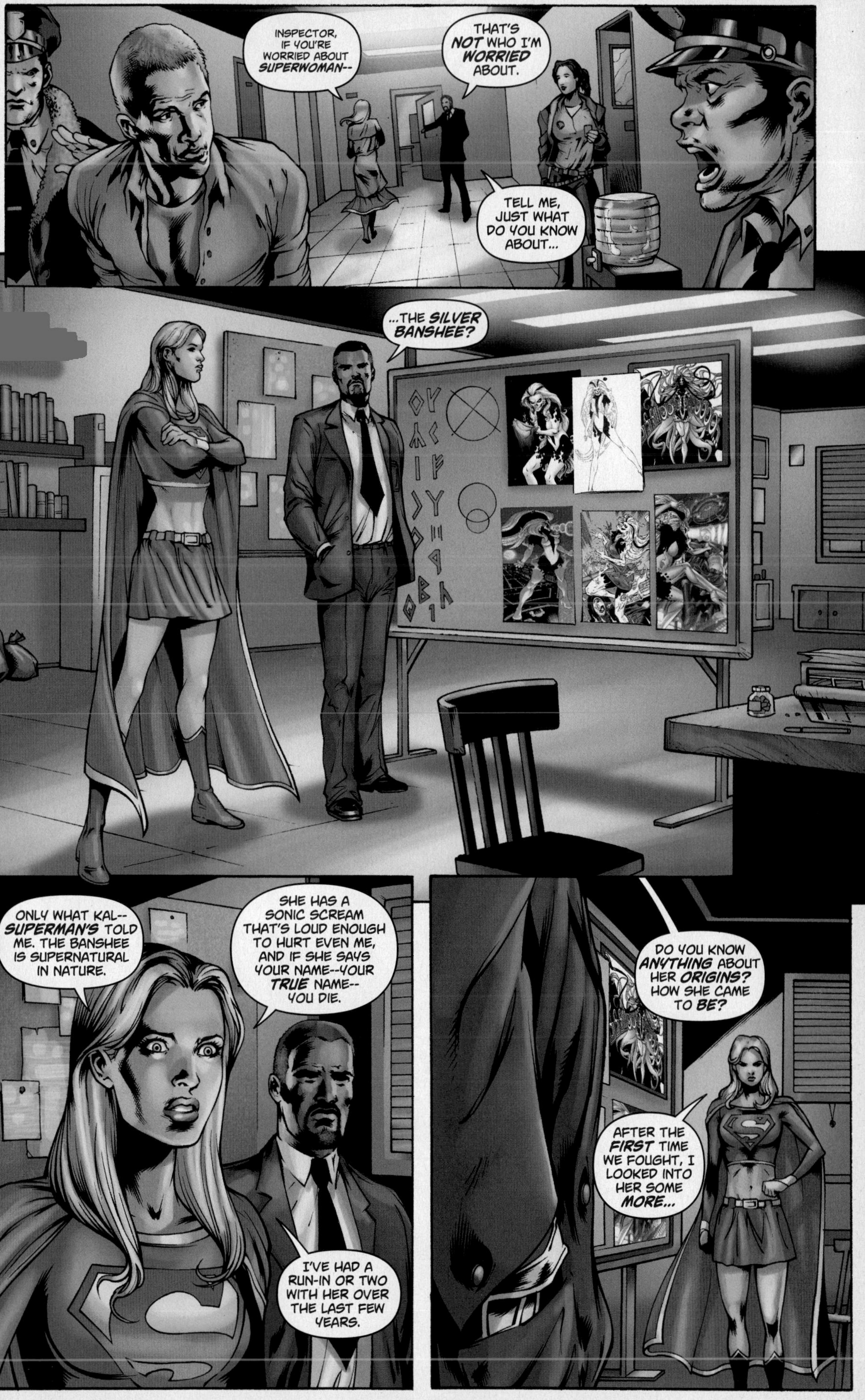
INSPECTOR, IF YOU'RE WORRIED ABOUT SUPERWOMAN--
THAT'S NOT WHO I'M WORRIED ABOUT.
TELL ME, JUST WHAT DO YOU KNOW ABOUT...
...THE SILVER BANSHEE?
ONLY WHAT KAL-- SUPERMAN'S TOLD ME. THE BANSHEE IS SUPERNATURAL IN NATURE.
SHE HAS A SONIC SCREAM THAT'S LOUD ENOUGH TO HURT EVEN ME, AND IF SHE SAYS YOUR NAME--YOUR TRUE NAME-- YOU DIE.
I'VE HAD A RUN-IN OR TWO WITH HER OVER THE LAST FEW YEARS.
DO YOU KNOW ANYTHING ABOUT HER ORIGINS? HOW SHE CAME TO BE?
AFTER THE FIRST TIME WE FOUGHT, I LOOKED INTO HER SOME MORE...

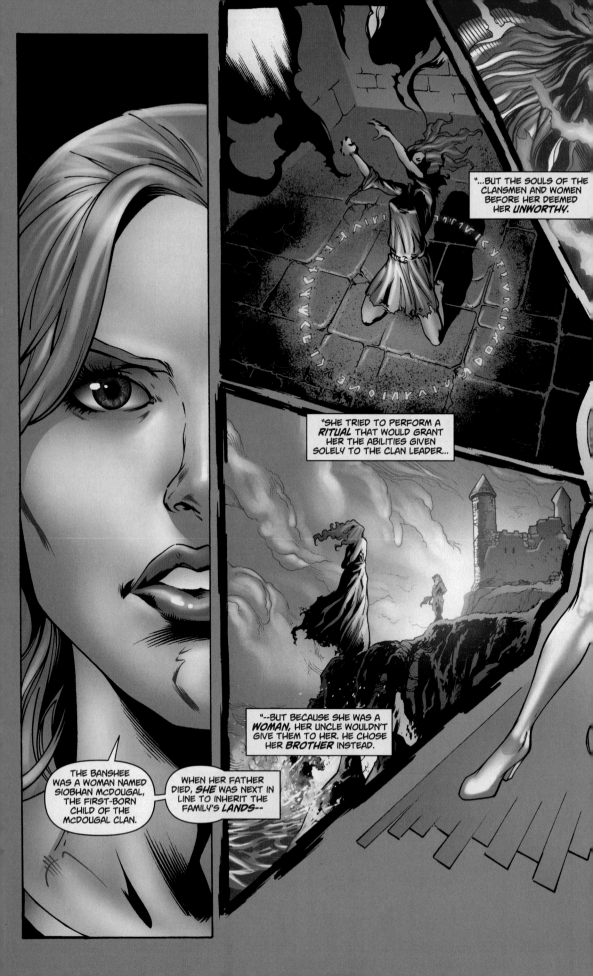

"...BUT THE SOULS OF THE CLANSMEN AND WOMEN BEFORE HER DEEMED HER *UNWORTHY*.

"SHE TRIED TO PERFORM A *RITUAL* THAT WOULD GRANT HER THE ABILITIES GIVEN SOLELY TO THE CLAN LEADER...

"--BUT BECAUSE SHE WAS A *WOMAN*, HER UNCLE WOULDN'T GIVE THEM TO HER. HE CHOSE HER *BROTHER* INSTEAD.

THE BANSHEE WAS A WOMAN NAMED SIOBHAN MCDOUGAL, THE FIRST-BORN CHILD OF THE MCDOUGAL CLAN.

WHEN HER FATHER DIED, *SHE* WAS NEXT IN LINE TO INHERIT THE FAMILY'S *LANDS*--

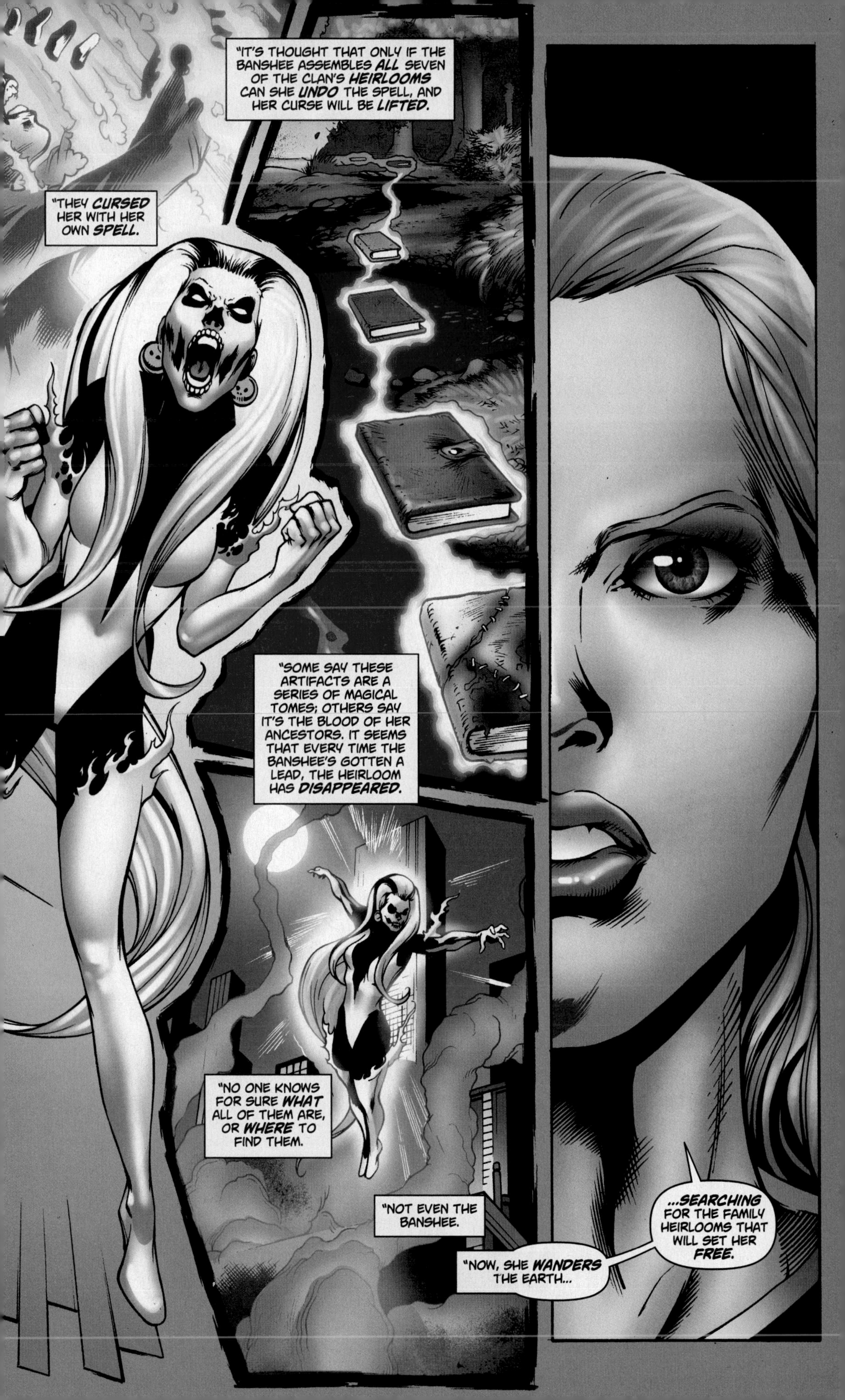
"THEY CURSED HER WITH HER OWN SPELL.
"IT'S THOUGHT THAT ONLY IF THE BANSHEE ASSEMBLES ALL SEVEN OF THE CLAN'S HEIRLOOMS CAN SHE UNDO THE SPELL, AND HER CURSE WILL BE LIFTED.
"SOME SAY THESE ARTIFACTS ARE A SERIES OF MAGICAL TOMES; OTHERS SAY IT'S THE BLOOD OF HER ANCESTORS. IT SEEMS THAT EVERY TIME THE BANSHEE'S GOTTEN A LEAD, THE HEIRLOOM HAS DISAPPEARED.
"NO ONE KNOWS FOR SURE WHAT ALL OF THEM ARE, OR WHERE TO FIND THEM.
"NOT EVEN THE BANSHEE.
"NOW, SHE WANDERS THE EARTH...
...SEARCHING FOR THE FAMILY HEIRLOOMS THAT WILL SET HER FREE.

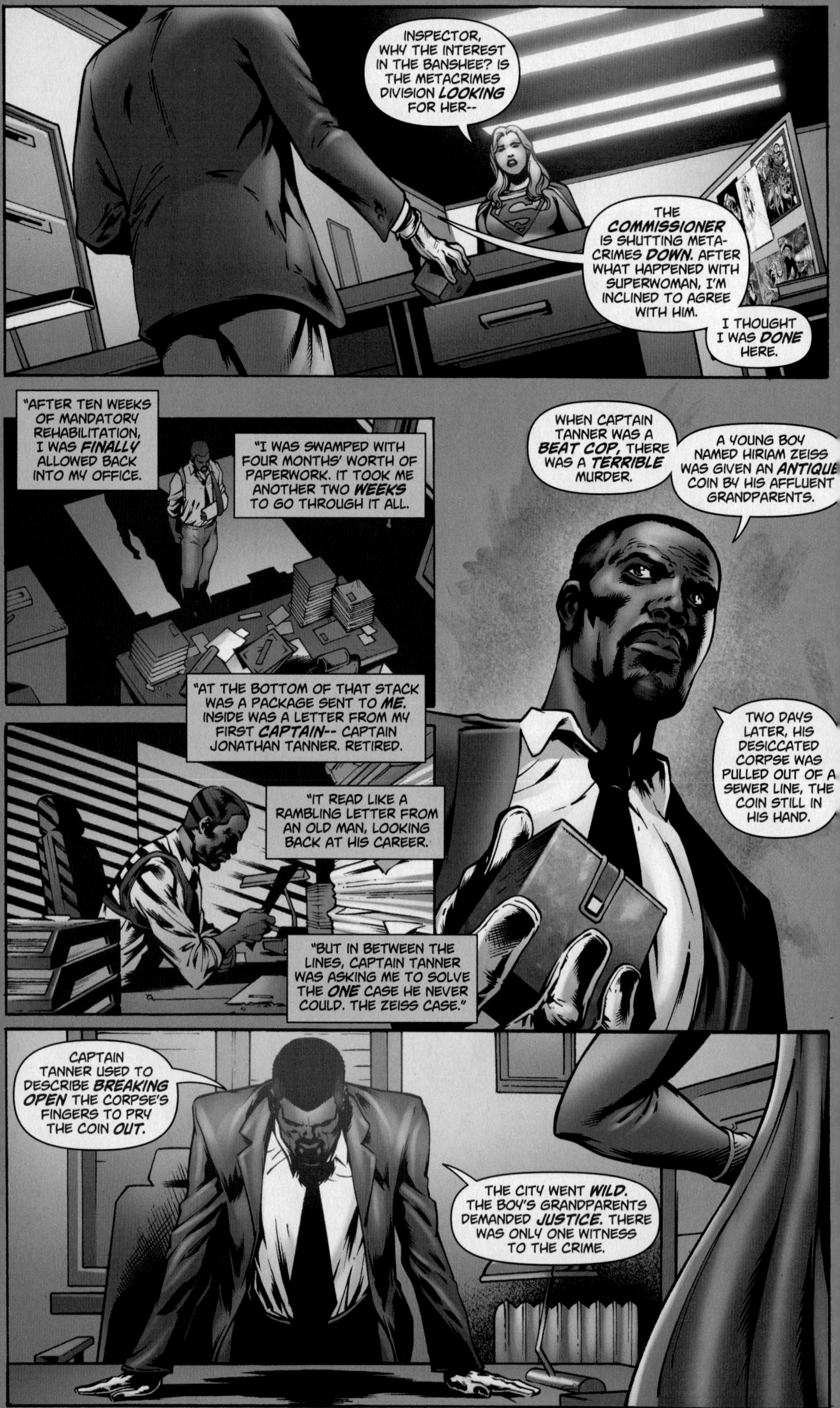
INSPECTOR, WHY THE INTEREST IN THE BANSHEE? IS THE METACRIMES DIVISION LOOKING FOR HER--
THE COMMISSIONER IS SHUTTING METACRIMES DOWN. AFTER WHAT HAPPENED WITH SUPERWOMAN, I'M INCLINED TO AGREE WITH HIM.
I THOUGHT I WAS DONE HERE.
"AFTER TEN WEEKS OF MANDATORY REHABILITATION, I WAS FINALLY ALLOWED BACK INTO MY OFFICE.
"I WAS SWAMPED WITH FOUR MONTHS' WORTH OF PAPERWORK. IT TOOK ME ANOTHER TWO WEEKS TO GO THROUGH IT ALL.
"AT THE BOTTOM OF THAT STACK WAS A PACKAGE SENT TO ME. INSIDE WAS A LETTER FROM MY FIRST CAPTAIN-- CAPTAIN JONATHAN TANNER. RETIRED.
"IT READ LIKE A RAMBLING LETTER FROM AN OLD MAN, LOOKING BACK AT HIS CAREER.
"BUT IN BETWEEN THE LINES, CAPTAIN TANNER WAS ASKING ME TO SOLVE THE ONE CASE HE NEVER COULD. THE ZEISS CASE."
WHEN CAPTAIN TANNER WAS A BEAT COP, THERE WAS A TERRIBLE MURDER.
A YOUNG BOY NAMED HIRIAM ZEISS WAS GIVEN AN ANTIQUE COIN BY HIS AFFLUENT GRANDPARENTS.
TWO DAYS LATER, HIS DESICCATED CORPSE WAS PULLED OUT OF A SEWER LINE, THE COIN STILL IN HIS HAND.
CAPTAIN TANNER USED TO DESCRIBE BREAKING OPEN THE CORPSE'S FINGERS TO PRY THE COIN OUT.
THE CITY WENT WILD. THE BOY'S GRANDPARENTS DEMANDED JUSTICE. THERE WAS ONLY ONE WITNESS TO THE CRIME.

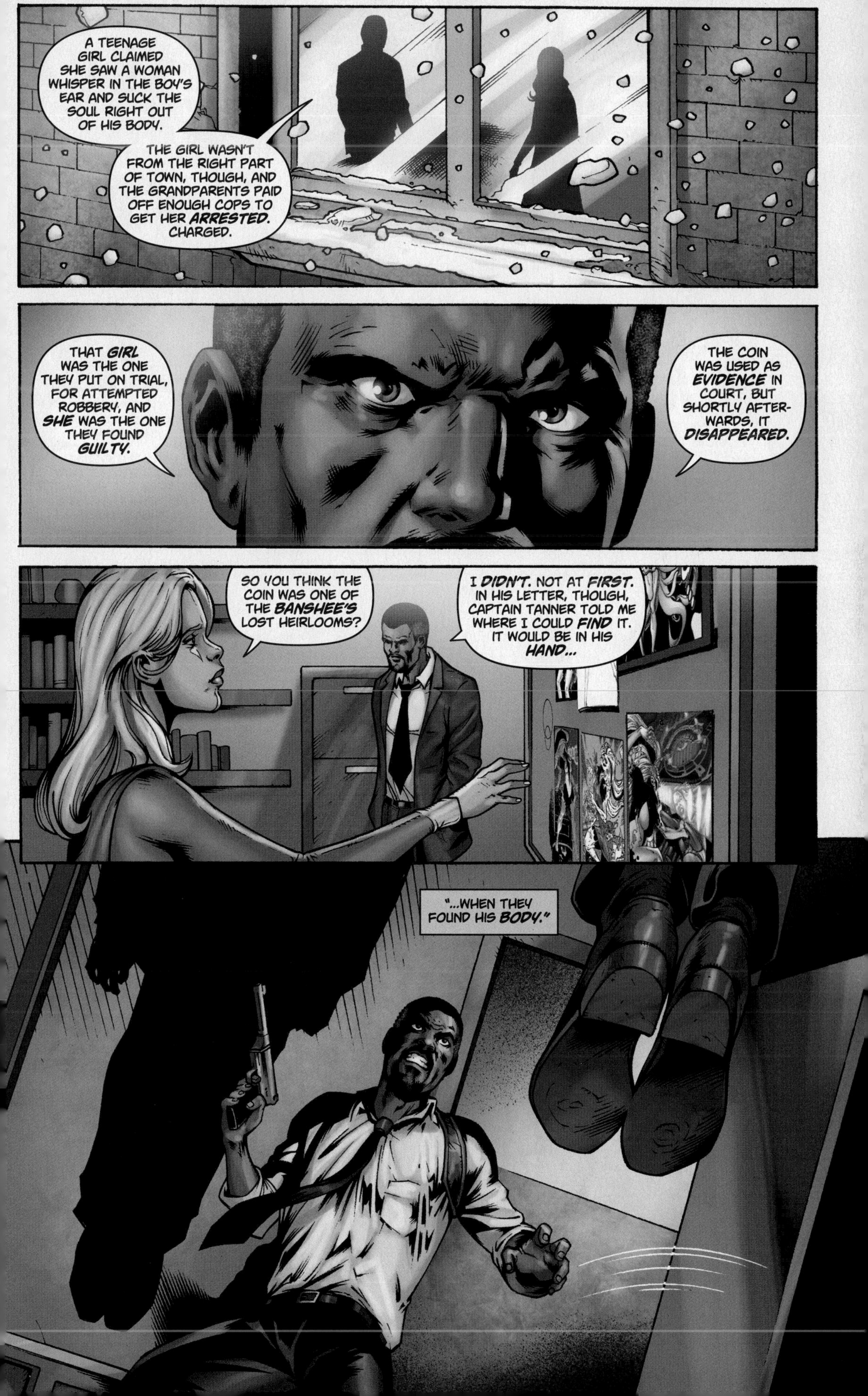
A TEENAGE GIRL CLAIMED SHE SAW A WOMAN WHISPER IN THE BOY'S EAR AND SUCK THE SOUL RIGHT OUT OF HIS BODY.
THE GIRL WASN'T FROM THE RIGHT PART OF TOWN, THOUGH, AND THE GRANDPARENTS PAID OFF ENOUGH COPS TO GET HER ARRESTED. CHARGED.
THAT GIRL WAS THE ONE THEY PUT ON TRIAL, FOR ATTEMPTED ROBBERY, AND SHE WAS THE ONE THEY FOUND GUILTY.
THE COIN WAS USED AS EVIDENCE IN COURT, BUT SHORTLY AFTER-WARDS, IT DISAPPEARED.
SO YOU THINK THE COIN WAS ONE OF THE BANSHEE'S LOST HEIRLOOMS?
I DIDN'T. NOT AT FIRST. IN HIS LETTER, THOUGH, CAPTAIN TANNER TOLD ME WHERE I COULD FIND IT. IT WOULD BE IN HIS HAND...
"...WHEN THEY FOUND HIS BODY."

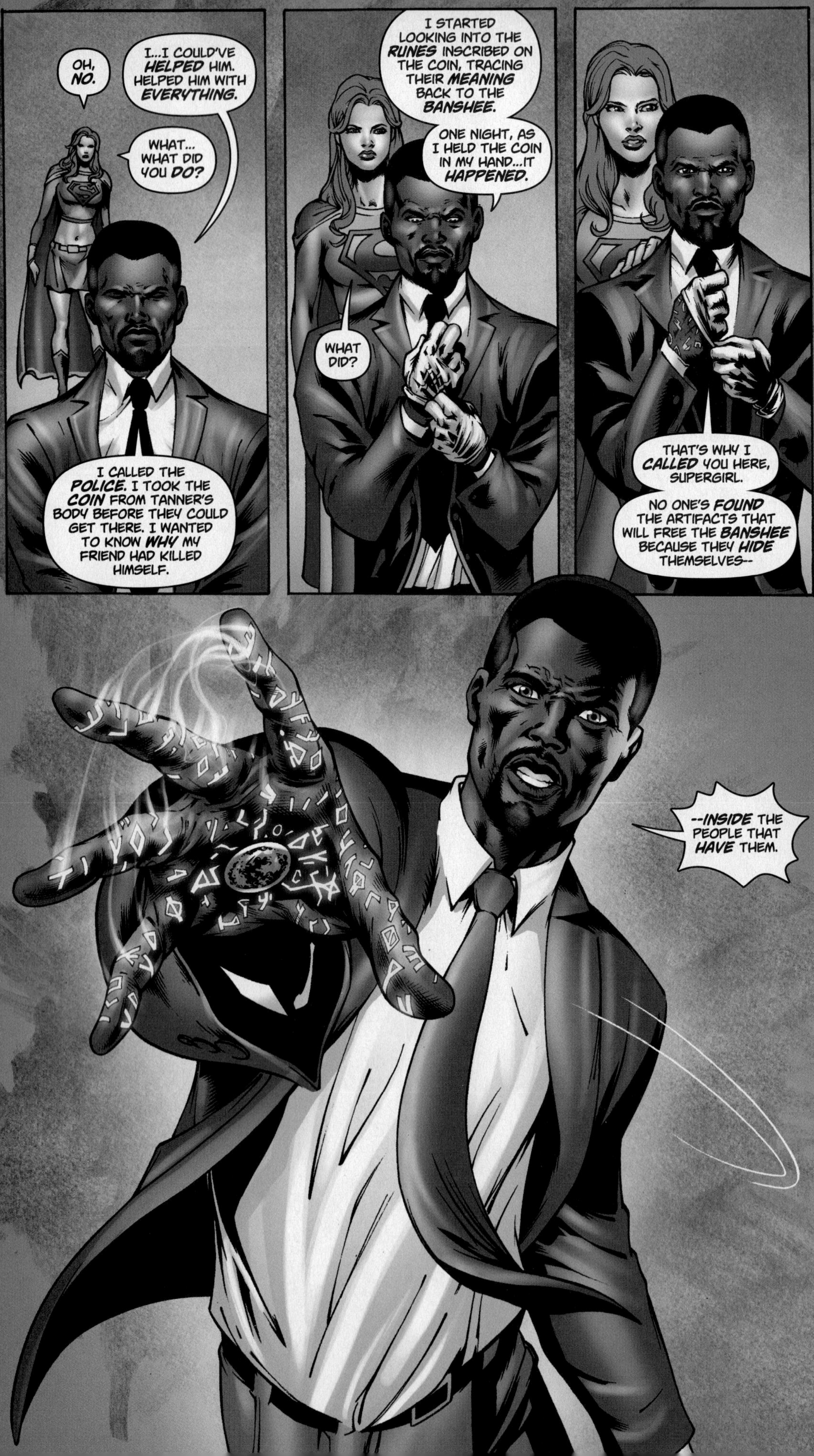
OH, NO.
I...I COULD'VE HELPED HIM. HELPED HIM WITH EVERYTHING.
WHAT... WHAT DID YOU DO?
I CALLED THE POLICE. I TOOK THE COIN FROM TANNER'S BODY BEFORE THEY COULD GET THERE. I WANTED TO KNOW WHY MY FRIEND HAD KILLED HIMSELF.
I STARTED LOOKING INTO THE RUNES INSCRIBED ON THE COIN, TRACING THEIR MEANING BACK TO THE BANSHEE.
ONE NIGHT, AS I HELD THE COIN IN MY HAND...IT HAPPENED.
WHAT DID?
THAT'S WHY I CALLED YOU HERE, SUPERGIRL.
NO ONE'S FOUND THE ARTIFACTS THAT WILL FREE THE BANSHEE BECAUSE THEY HIDE THEMSELVES--
--INSIDE THE PEOPLE THAT HAVE THEM.

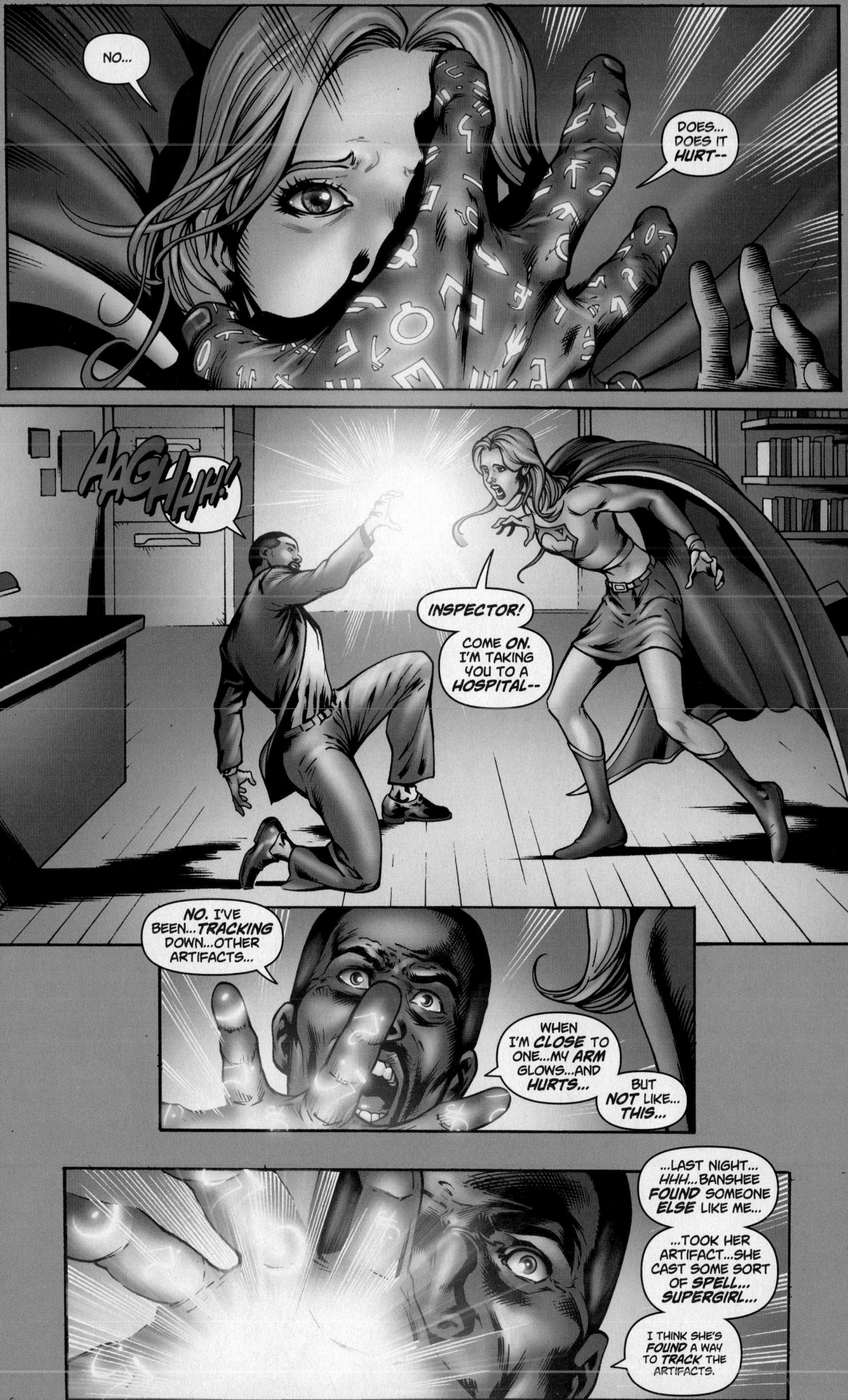
NO...
DOES... DOES IT HURT--
AAGHHH!
INSPECTOR!
COME ON. I'M TAKING YOU TO A HOSPITAL--
NO. I'VE BEEN...TRACKING DOWN...OTHER ARTIFACTS...
WHEN I'M CLOSE TO ONE...MY ARM GLOWS...AND HURTS...
BUT NOT LIKE... THIS...
...LAST NIGHT... HHH...BANSHEE FOUND SOMEONE ELSE LIKE ME...
...TOOK HER ARTIFACT...SHE CAST SOME SORT OF SPELL... SUPERGIRL...
I THINK SHE'S FOUND A WAY TO TRACK THE ARTIFACTS.

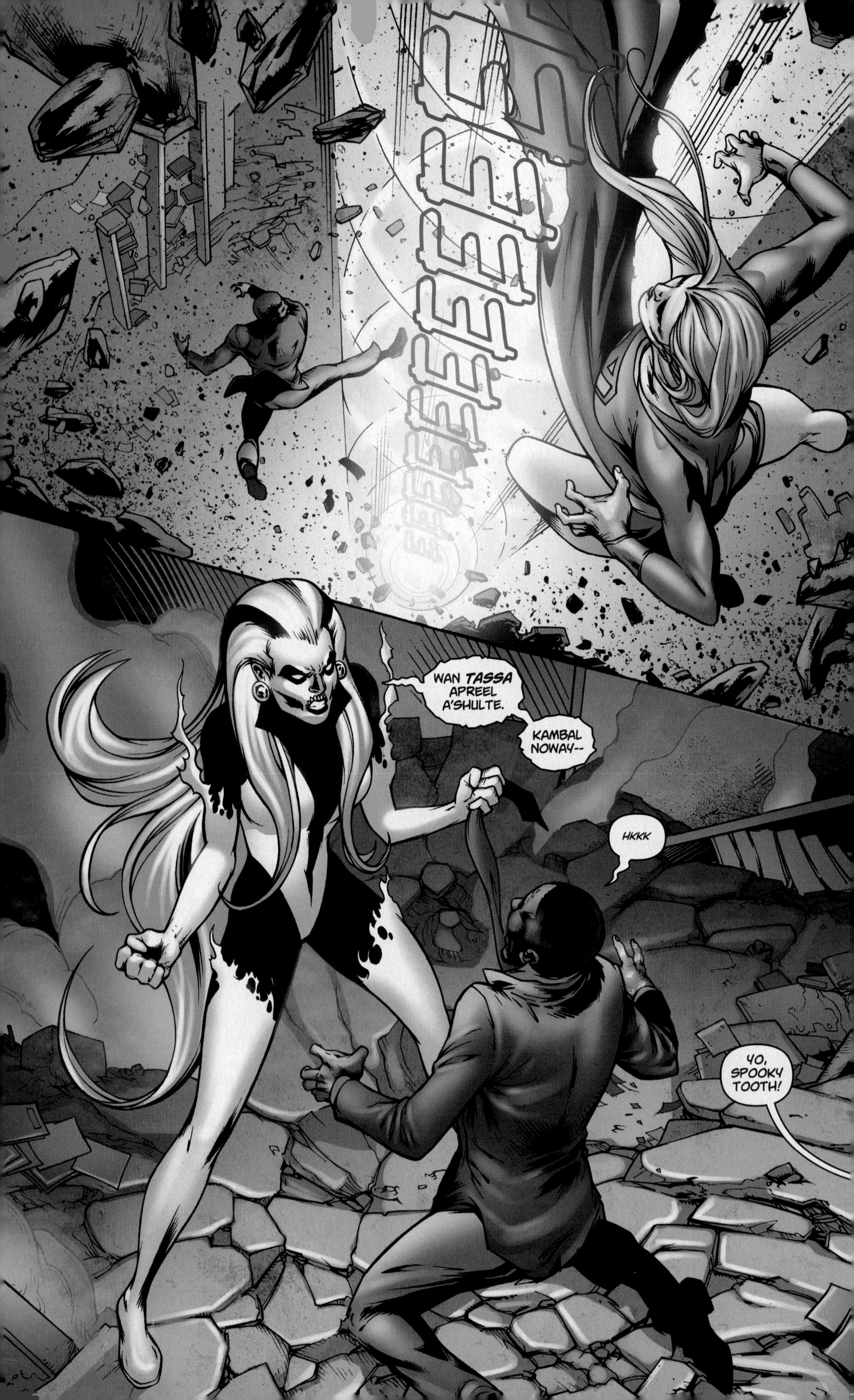
SSSHEEEEEEEEEEEEE
WAN TASSA APREEL A'SHULTE.
KAMBAL NOWAY--
HKKK
YO, SPOOKY TOOTH!

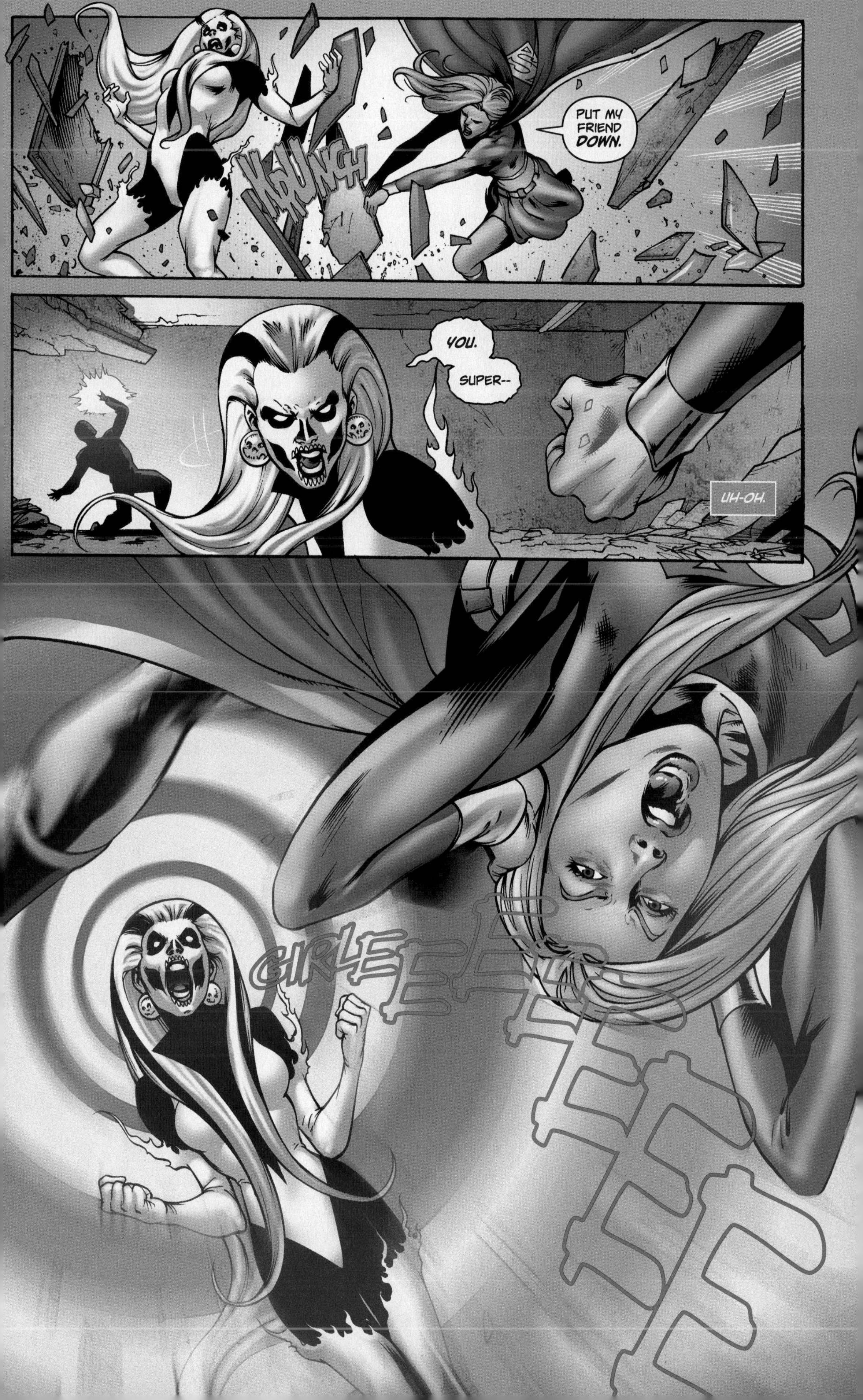
KRUNCH
PUT MY FRIEND DOWN.
YOU.
SUPER--
UH-OH.
GIRLEEEEEEE

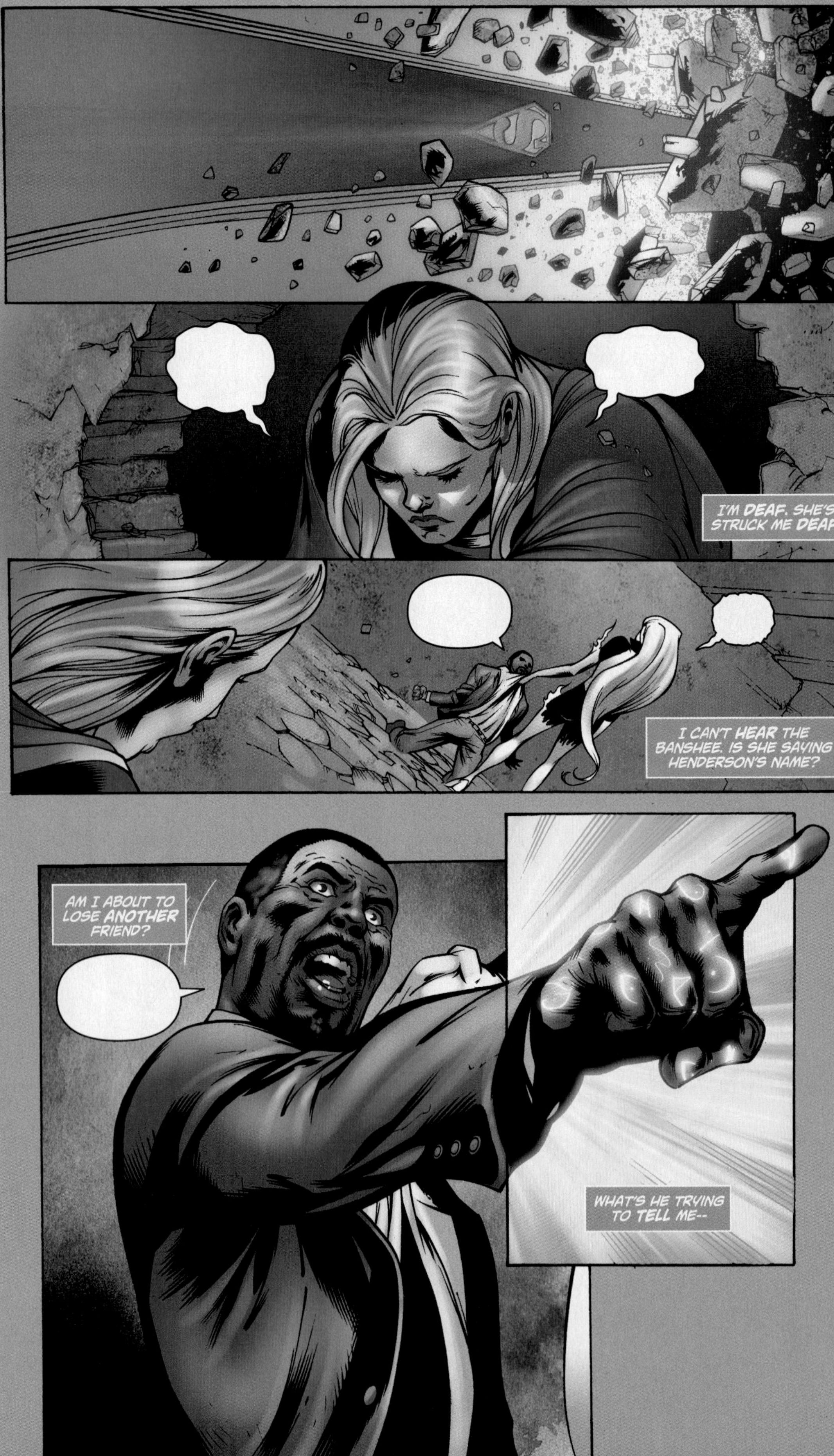
I'M DEAF. SHE'S STRUCK ME DEAF.
I CAN'T HEAR THE BANSHEE. IS SHE SAYING HENDERSON'S NAME?
AM I ABOUT TO LOSE ANOTHER FRIEND?
WHAT'S HE TRYING TO TELL ME--

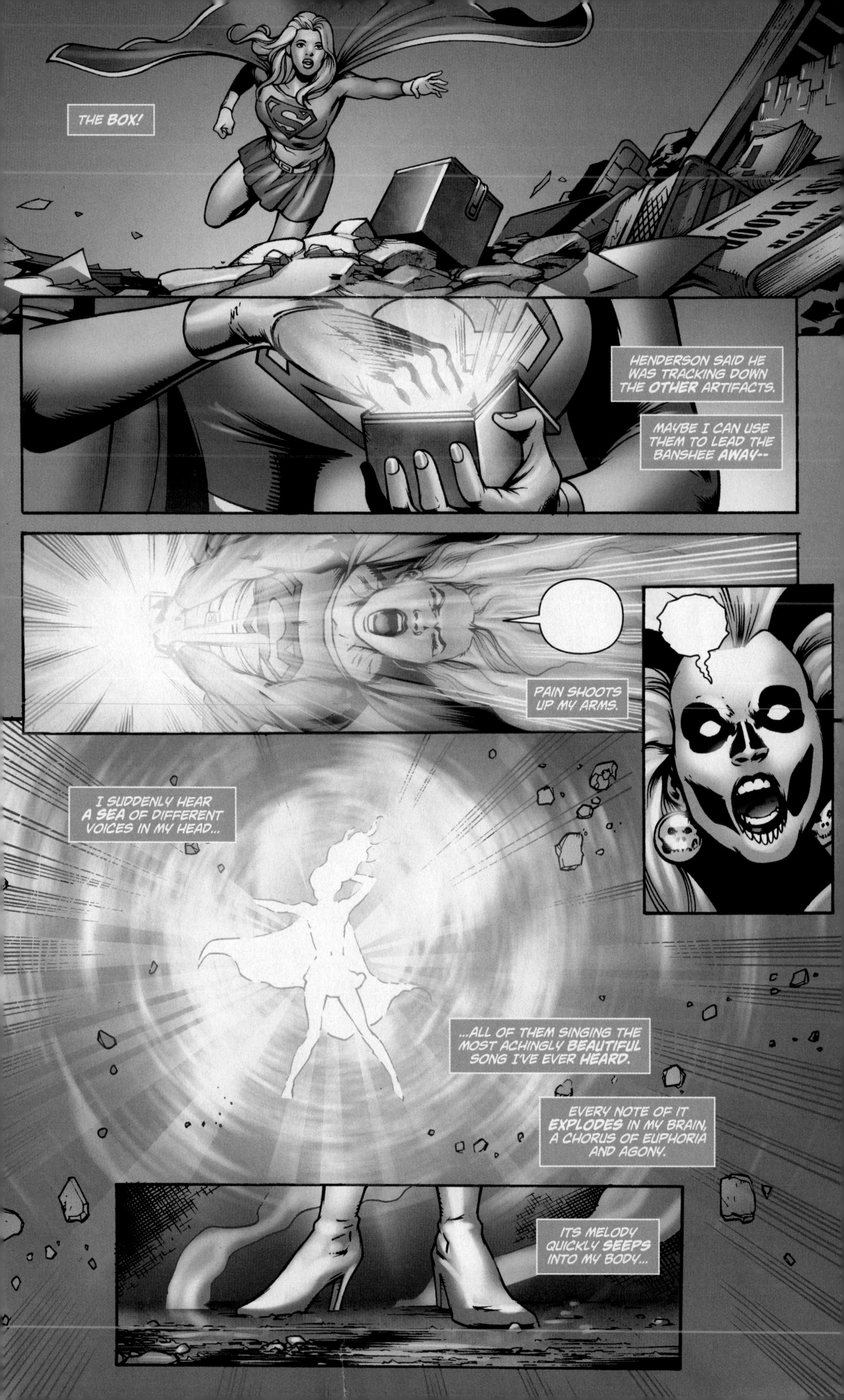
THE BOX!
HENDERSON SAID HE WAS TRACKING DOWN THE OTHER ARTIFACTS.
MAYBE I CAN USE THEM TO LEAD THE BANSHEE AWAY--
PAIN SHOOTS UP MY ARMS.
I SUDDENLY HEAR A SEA OF DIFFERENT VOICES IN MY HEAD...
...ALL OF THEM SINGING THE MOST ACHINGLY BEAUTIFUL SONG I'VE EVER HEARD.
EVERY NOTE OF IT EXPLODES IN MY BRAIN, A CHORUS OF EUPHORIA AND AGONY.
ITS MELODY QUICKLY SEEPS INTO MY BODY...

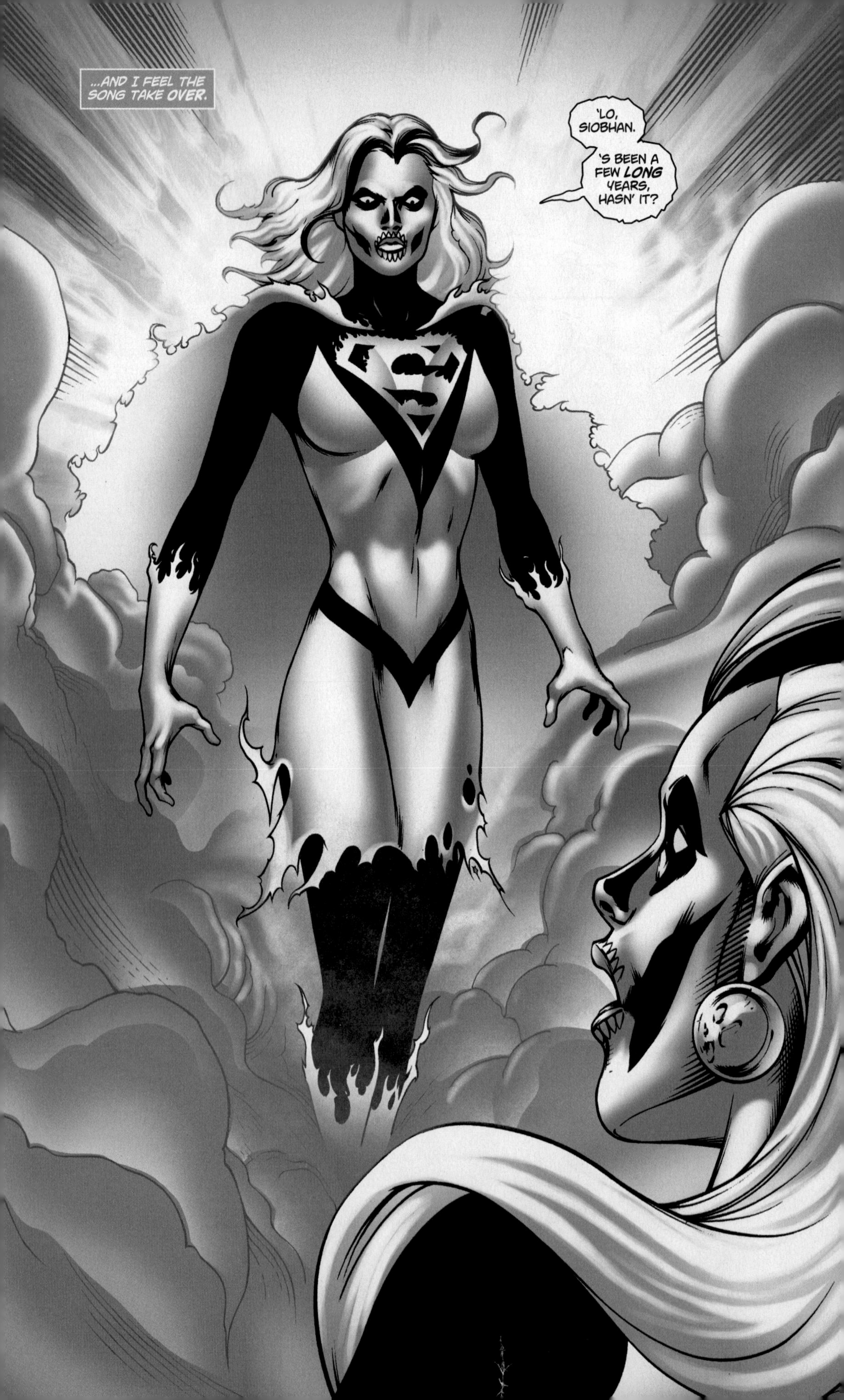
...AND I FEEL THE SONG TAKE OVER.
'LO, SIOBHAN.
'S BEEN A FEW LONG YEARS, HASN' IT?

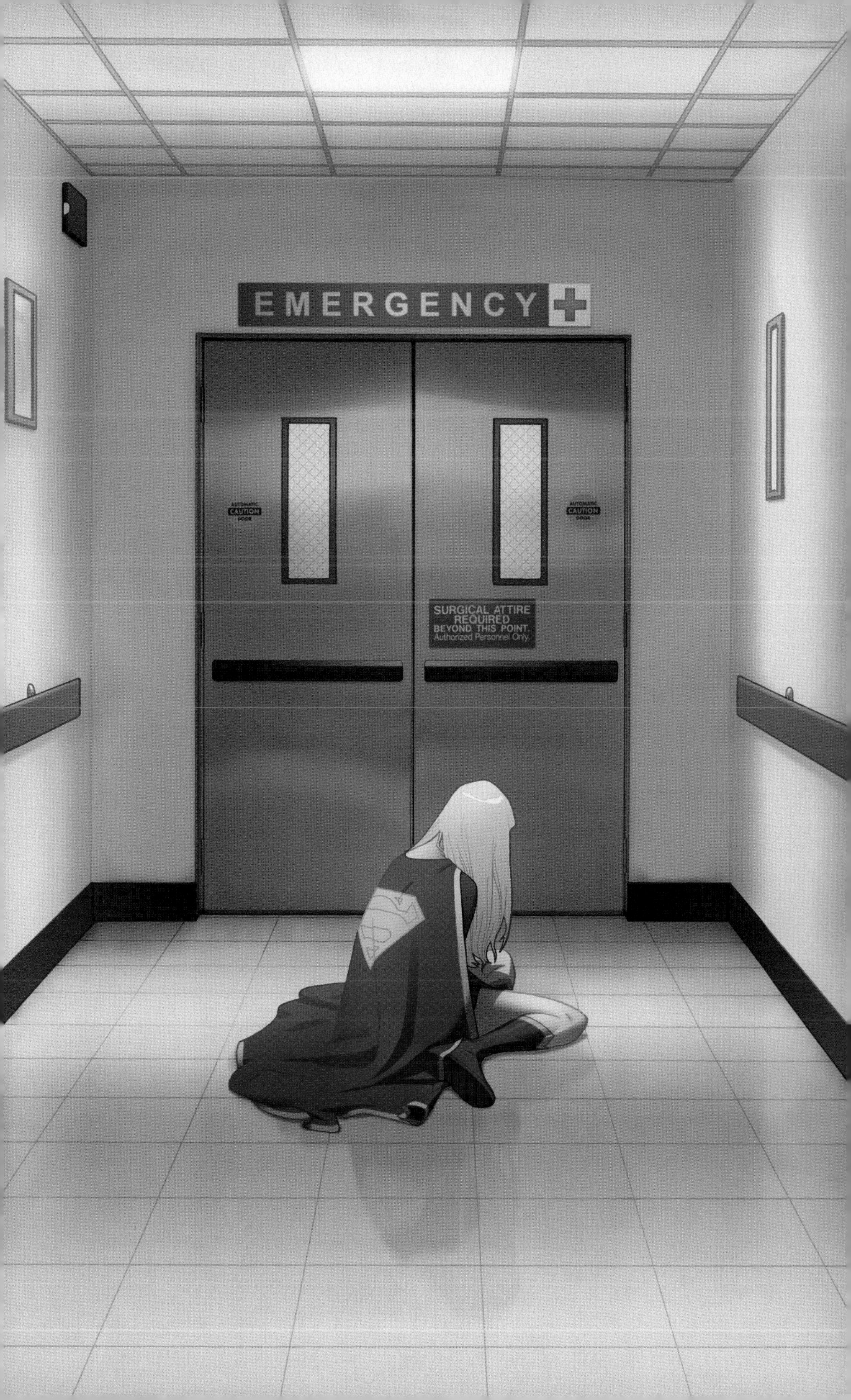
EMERGENCY
AUTOMATIC CAUTION DOOR
AUTOMATIC CAUTION DOOR
SURGICAL ATTIRE REQUIRED BEYOND THIS POINT. Authorized Personnel Only.

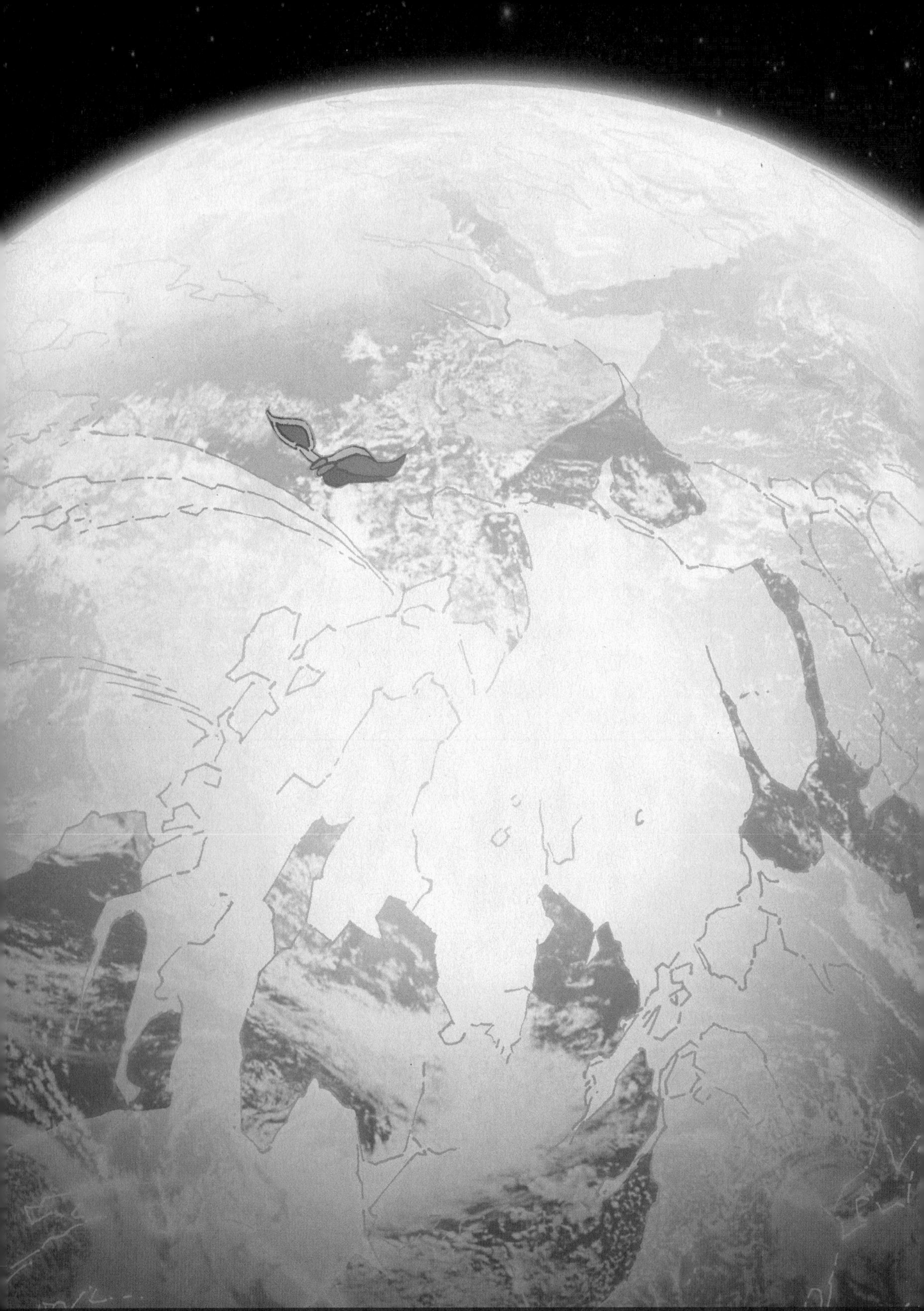

DEATH & THE FAMILY

STERLING GATES WRITER
MATT CAMP ARTIST

COVER BY **JOSHUA MIDDLETON**

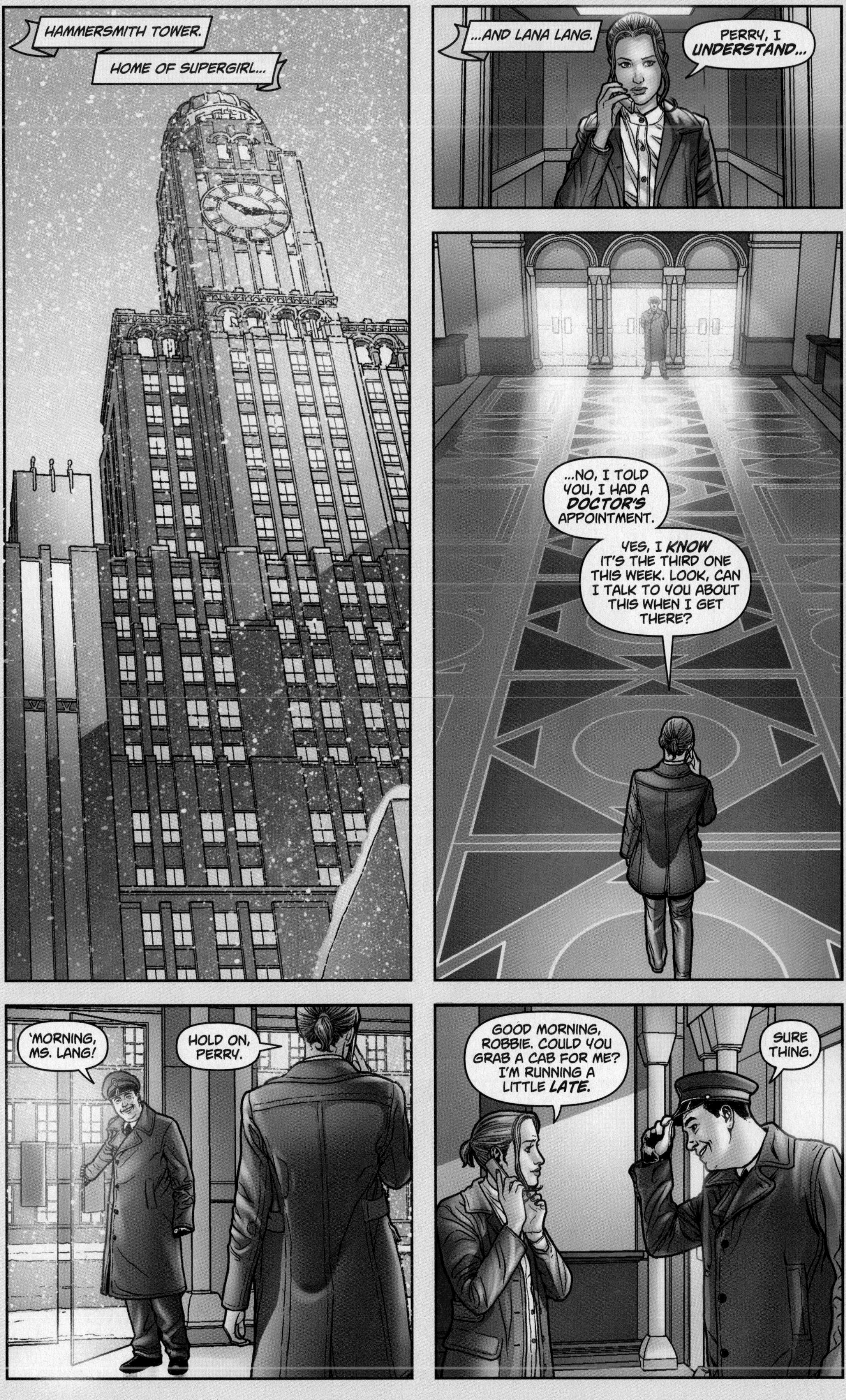
HAMMERSMITH TOWER.
HOME OF SUPERGIRL...
...AND LANA LANG.
PERRY, I UNDERSTAND...
...NO, I TOLD YOU, I HAD A DOCTOR'S APPOINTMENT.
YES, I KNOW IT'S THE THIRD ONE THIS WEEK. LOOK, CAN I TALK TO YOU ABOUT THIS WHEN I GET THERE?
'MORNING, MS. LANG!
HOLD ON, PERRY.
GOOD MORNING, ROBBIE. COULD YOU GRAB A CAB FOR ME? I'M RUNNING A LITTLE LATE.
SURE THING.

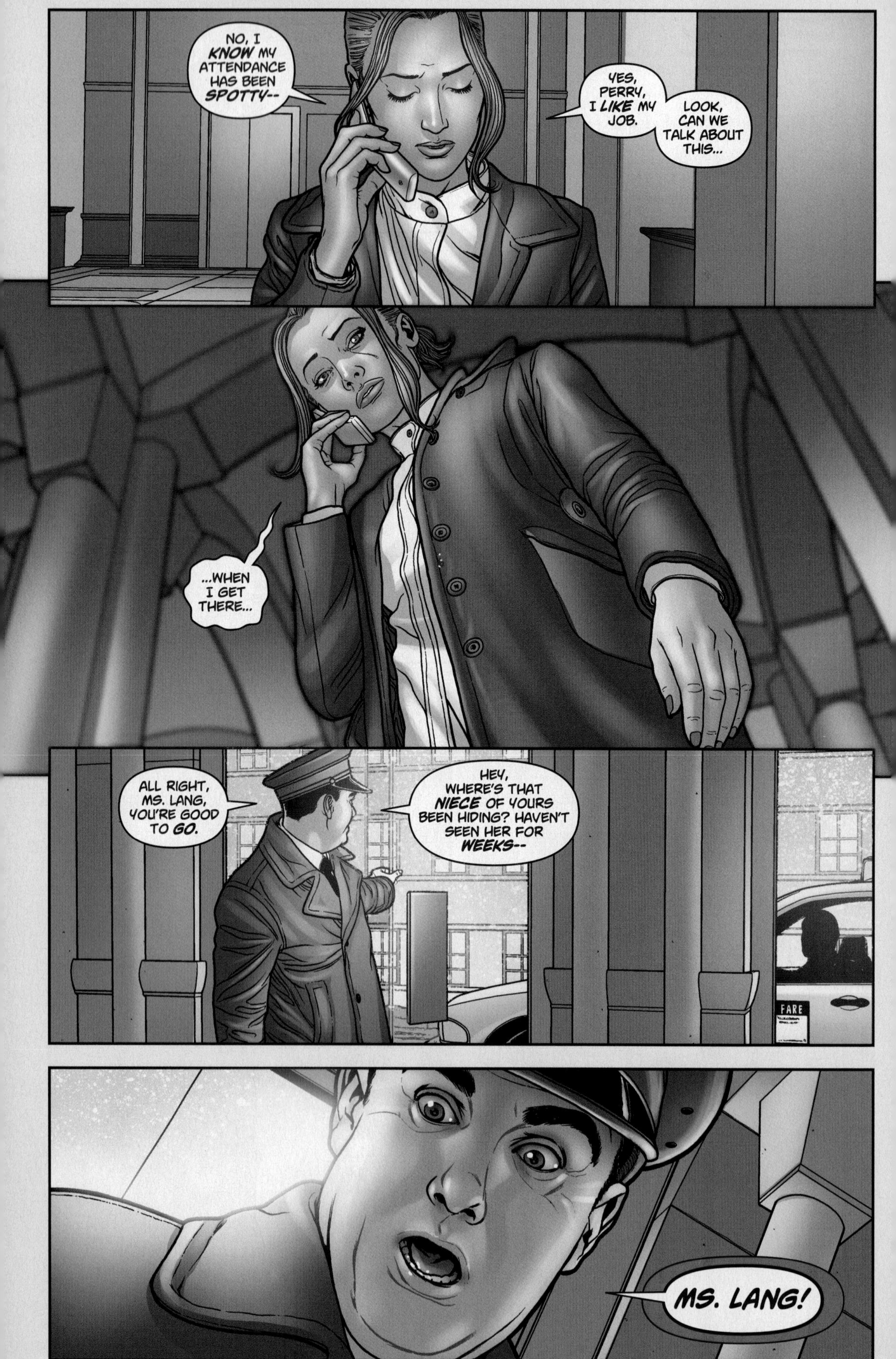
NO, I KNOW MY ATTENDANCE HAS BEEN SPOTTY--
YES, PERRY, I LIKE MY JOB.
LOOK, CAN WE TALK ABOUT THIS...
...WHEN I GET THERE...
ALL RIGHT, MS. LANG, YOU'RE GOOD TO GO.
HEY, WHERE'S THAT NIECE OF YOURS BEEN HIDING? HAVEN'T SEEN HER FOR WEEKS--
FARE
MS. LANG!

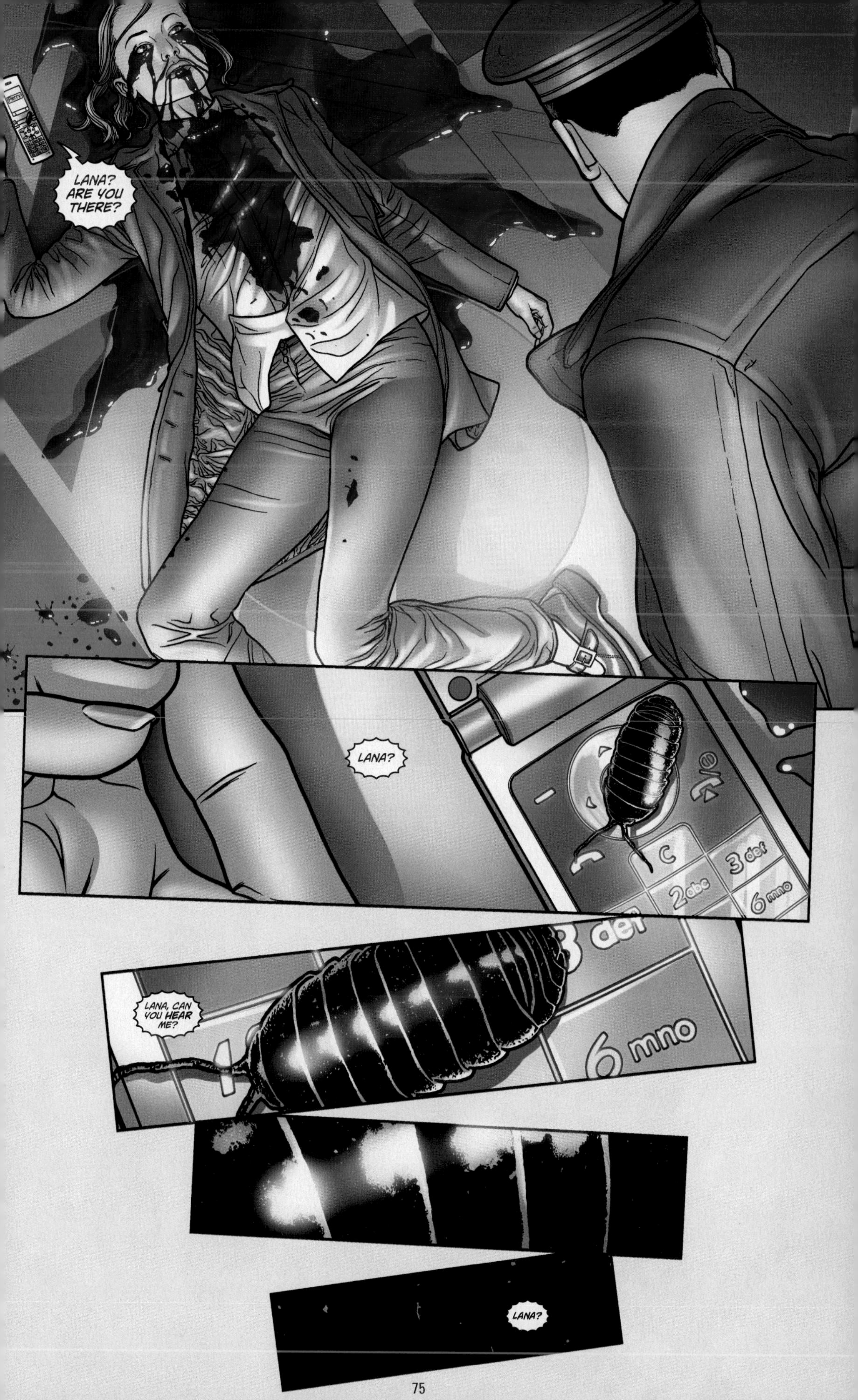
LANA? ARE YOU THERE?
LANA?
LANA, CAN YOU HEAR ME?
LANA?

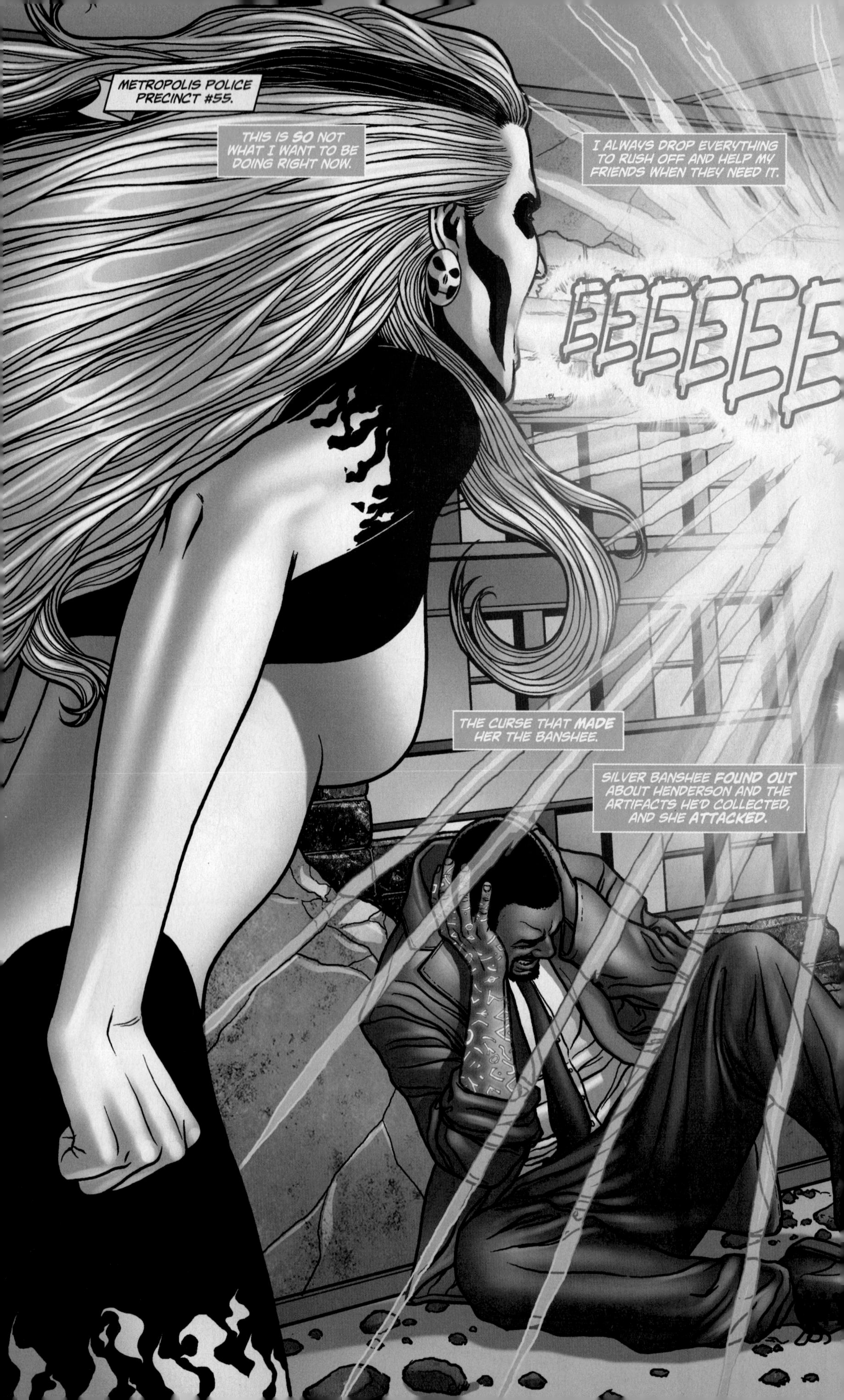
METROPOLIS POLICE PRECINCT #55.
THIS IS SO NOT WHAT I WANT TO BE DOING RIGHT NOW.
I ALWAYS DROP EVERYTHING TO RUSH OFF AND HELP MY FRIENDS WHEN THEY NEED IT.
EEEEEEE
THE CURSE THAT MADE HER THE BANSHEE.
SILVER BANSHEE FOUND OUT ABOUT HENDERSON AND THE ARTIFACTS HE'D COLLECTED, AND SHE ATTACKED.

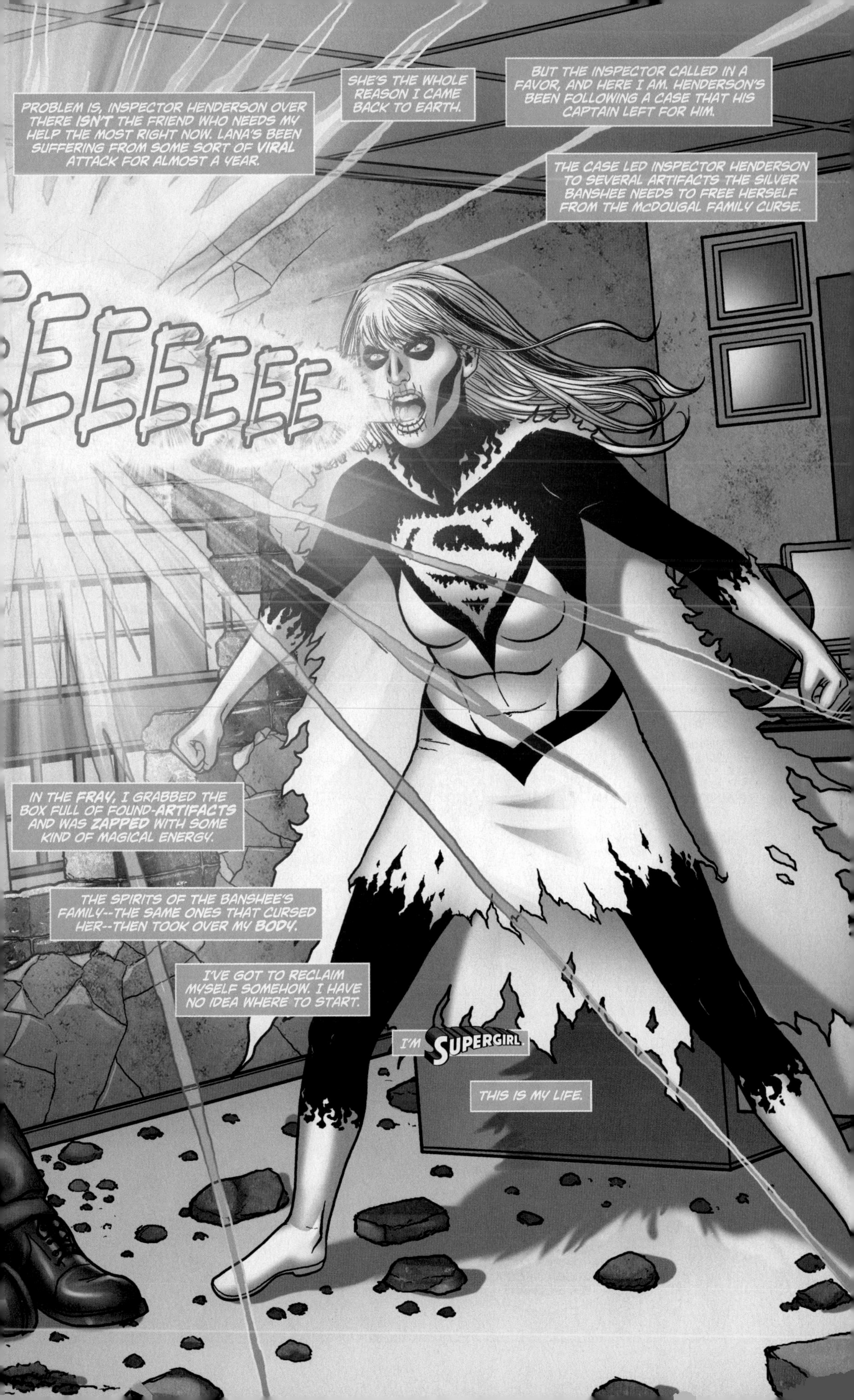
PROBLEM IS, INSPECTOR HENDERSON OVER THERE ISN'T THE FRIEND WHO NEEDS MY HELP THE MOST RIGHT NOW. LANA'S BEEN SUFFERING FROM SOME SORT OF VIRAL ATTACK FOR ALMOST A YEAR.
SHE'S THE WHOLE REASON I CAME BACK TO EARTH.
BUT THE INSPECTOR CALLED IN A FAVOR, AND HERE I AM. HENDERSON'S BEEN FOLLOWING A CASE THAT HIS CAPTAIN LEFT FOR HIM.
THE CASE LED INSPECTOR HENDERSON TO SEVERAL ARTIFACTS THE SILVER BANSHEE NEEDS TO FREE HERSELF FROM THE McDOUGAL FAMILY CURSE.
EEEEEEE
IN THE FRAY, I GRABBED THE BOX FULL OF FOUND-ARTIFACTS AND WAS ZAPPED WITH SOME KIND OF MAGICAL ENERGY.
THE SPIRITS OF THE BANSHEE'S FAMILY--THE SAME ONES THAT CURSED HER--THEN TOOK OVER MY BODY.
I'VE GOT TO RECLAIM MYSELF SOMEHOW. I HAVE NO IDEA WHERE TO START.
I'M SUPERGIRL.
THIS IS MY LIFE.

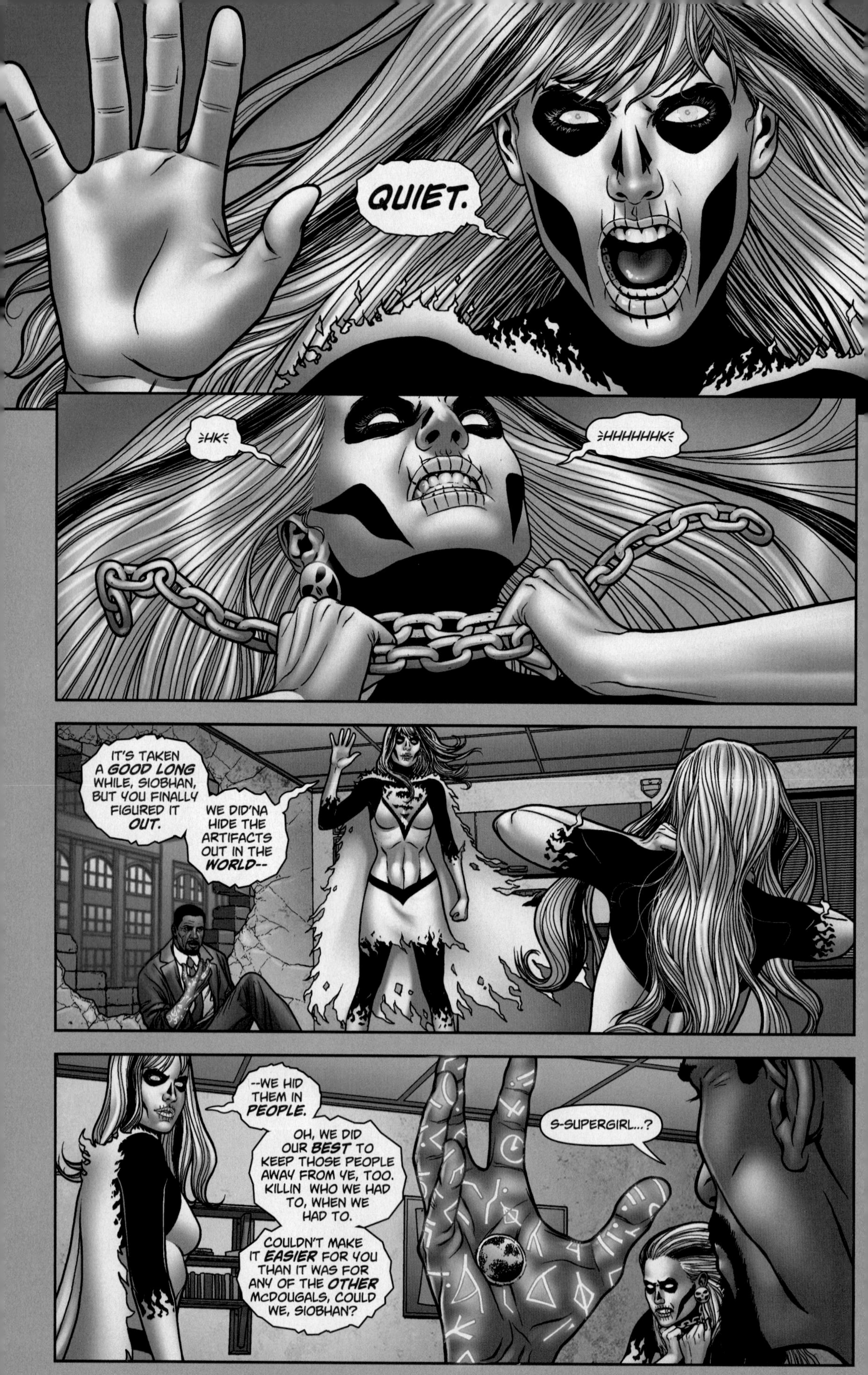
QUIET.
HK
HHHHHHK
IT'S TAKEN A GOOD LONG WHILE, SIOBHAN, BUT YOU FINALLY FIGURED IT OUT.
WE DID'NA HIDE THE ARTIFACTS OUT IN THE WORLD--
--WE HID THEM IN PEOPLE.
OH, WE DID OUR BEST TO KEEP THOSE PEOPLE AWAY FROM YE, TOO. KILLIN WHO WE HAD TO, WHEN WE HAD TO.
COULDN'T MAKE IT EASIER FOR YOU THAN IT WAS FOR ANY OF THE OTHER McDOUGALS, COULD WE, SIOBHAN?
S-SUPERGIRL...?

AND THEN THERE'S THE *ONE* YOU *WERE* ABLE TO *FIND*.

THE *ONLY* ONE YOU'VE *FOUND* IN NEARLY A *HUNDRED* YEARS.

THE ONE YOU USED TO *TRACK* THE OTHERS.

THE ONE *INSIDE* YOU.

LET'S SEE IT.

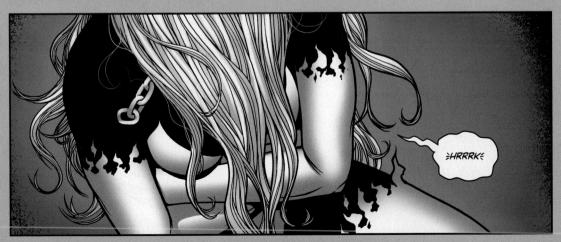

⌐HRRRK⌐

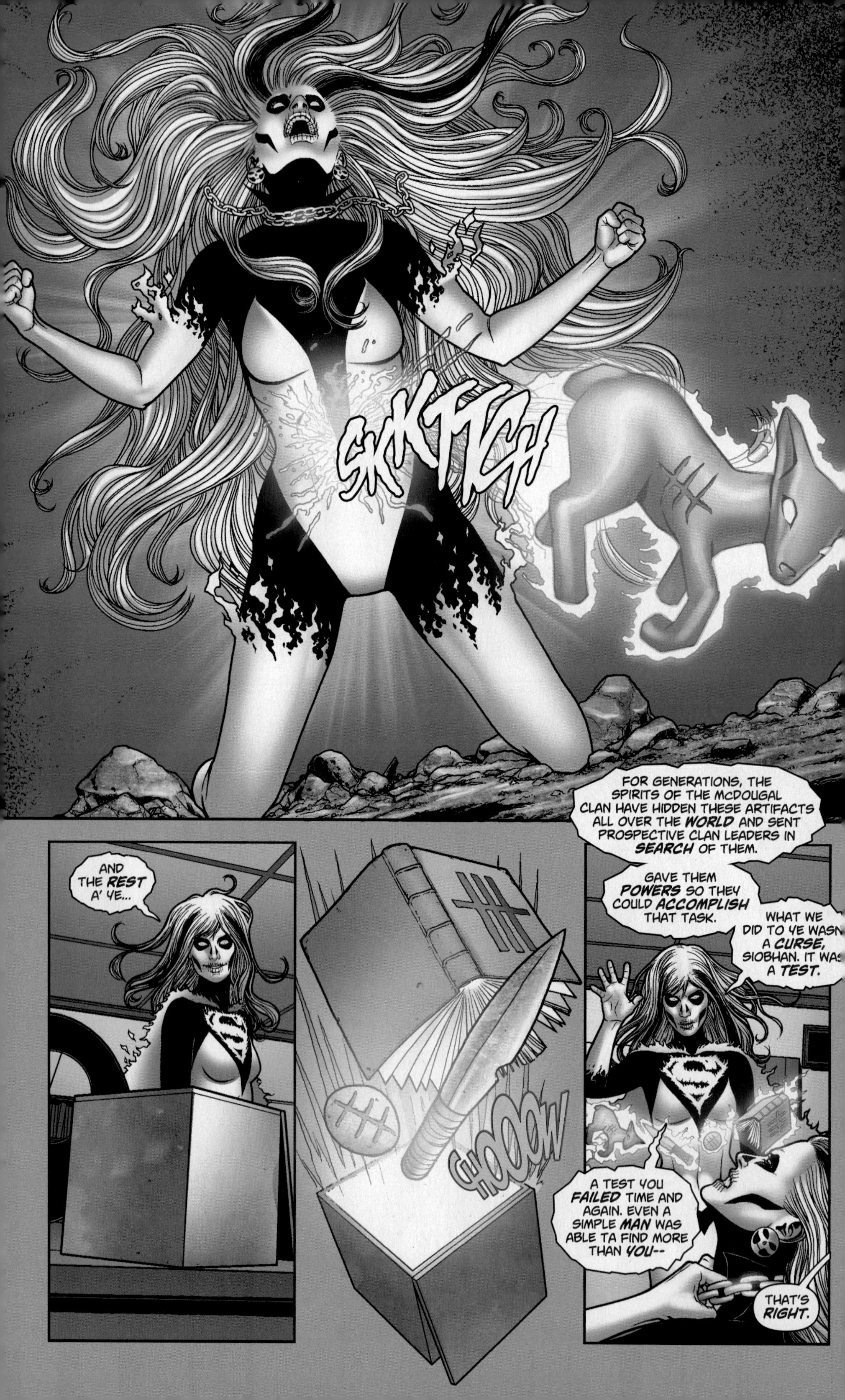
SKKTCH
FOR GENERATIONS, THE SPIRITS OF THE McDOUGAL CLAN HAVE HIDDEN THESE ARTIFACTS ALL OVER THE WORLD AND SENT PROSPECTIVE CLAN LEADERS IN SEARCH OF THEM.
AND THE REST A' YE...
CHOOOW
GAVE THEM POWERS SO THEY COULD ACCOMPLISH THAT TASK.
WHAT WE DID TO YE WASN A CURSE, SIOBHAN. IT WAS A TEST.
A TEST YOU FAILED TIME AND AGAIN. EVEN A SIMPLE MAN WAS ABLE TA FIND MORE THAN YOU--
THAT'S RIGHT.

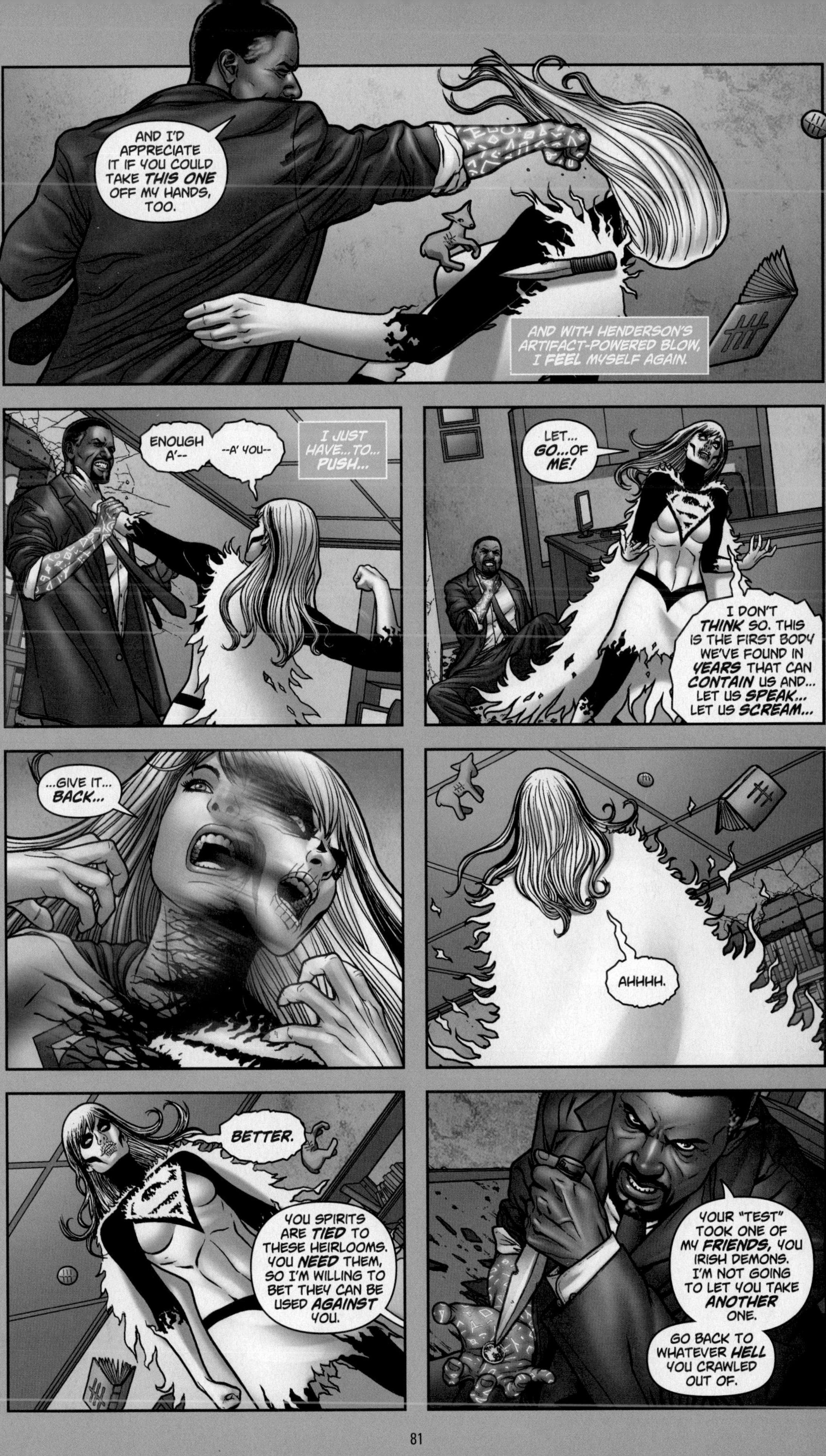
AND I'D APPRECIATE IT IF YOU COULD TAKE THIS ONE OFF MY HANDS, TOO.
AND WITH HENDERSON'S ARTIFACT-POWERED BLOW, I FEEL MYSELF AGAIN.
ENOUGH A'--
--A' YOU--
I JUST HAVE...TO... PUSH...
LET... GO...OF ME!
I DON'T THINK SO. THIS IS THE FIRST BODY WE'VE FOUND IN YEARS THAT CAN CONTAIN US AND... LET US SPEAK... LET US SCREAM...
...GIVE IT... BACK...
AHHHH.
BETTER.
YOU SPIRITS ARE TIED TO THESE HEIRLOOMS. YOU NEED THEM, SO I'M WILLING TO BET THEY CAN BE USED AGAINST YOU.
YOUR "TEST" TOOK ONE OF MY FRIENDS, YOU IRISH DEMONS. I'M NOT GOING TO LET YOU TAKE ANOTHER ONE.
GO BACK TO WHATEVER HELL YOU CRAWLED OUT OF.

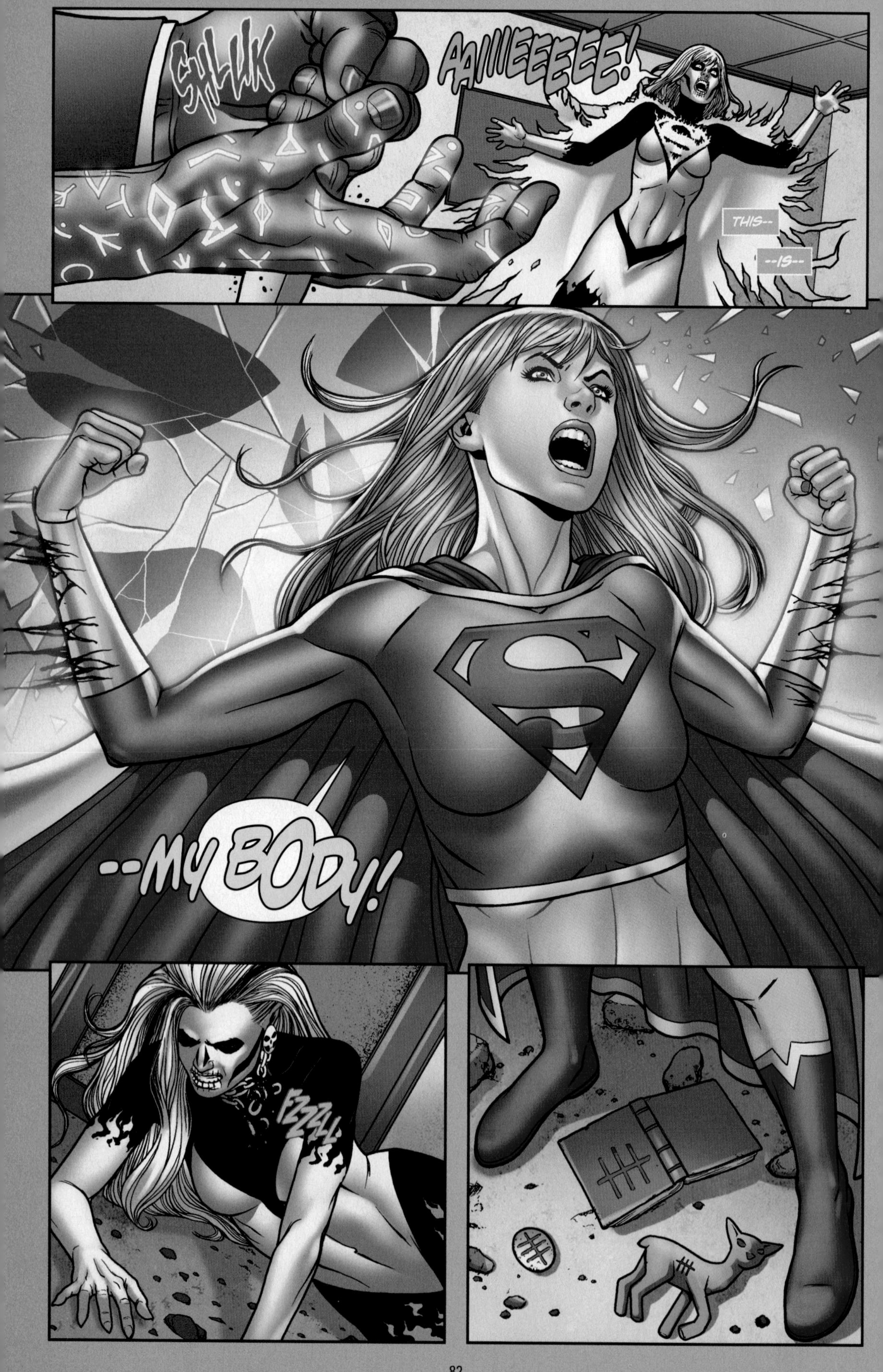

SHLUK
AAIIIEEEEEE!
THIS--
--IS--
--MY BODY!
FZZZLE

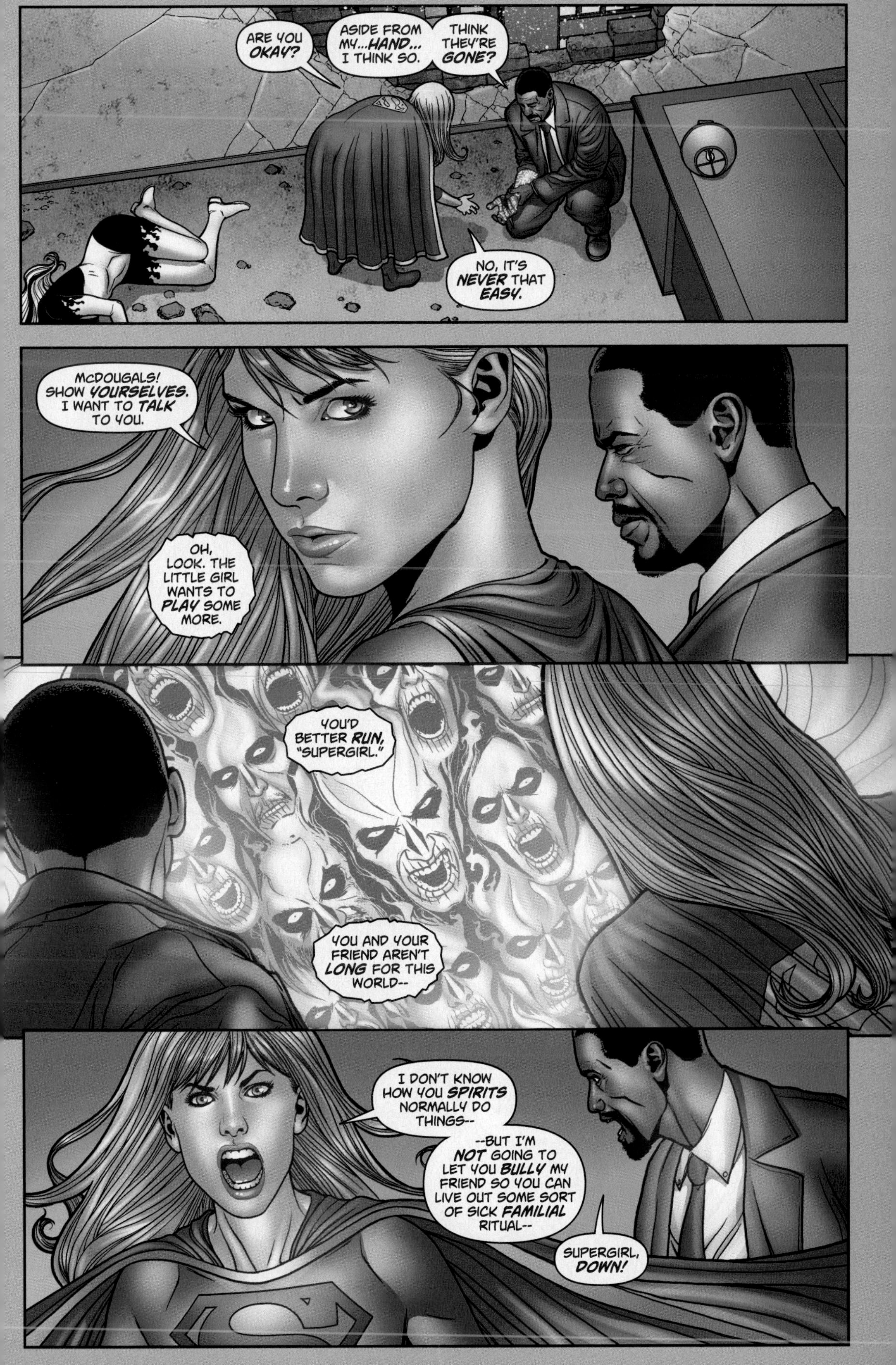
ARE YOU OKAY?
ASIDE FROM MY...HAND... I THINK SO.
THINK THEY'RE GONE?
NO, IT'S NEVER THAT EASY.
MCDOUGALS! SHOW YOURSELVES. I WANT TO TALK TO YOU.
OH, LOOK. THE LITTLE GIRL WANTS TO PLAY SOME MORE.
YOU'D BETTER RUN, "SUPERGIRL."
YOU AND YOUR FRIEND AREN'T LONG FOR THIS WORLD--
I DON'T KNOW HOW YOU SPIRITS NORMALLY DO THINGS--
--BUT I'M NOT GOING TO LET YOU BULLY MY FRIEND SO YOU CAN LIVE OUT SOME SORT OF SICK FAMILIAL RITUAL--
SUPERGIRL, DOWN!

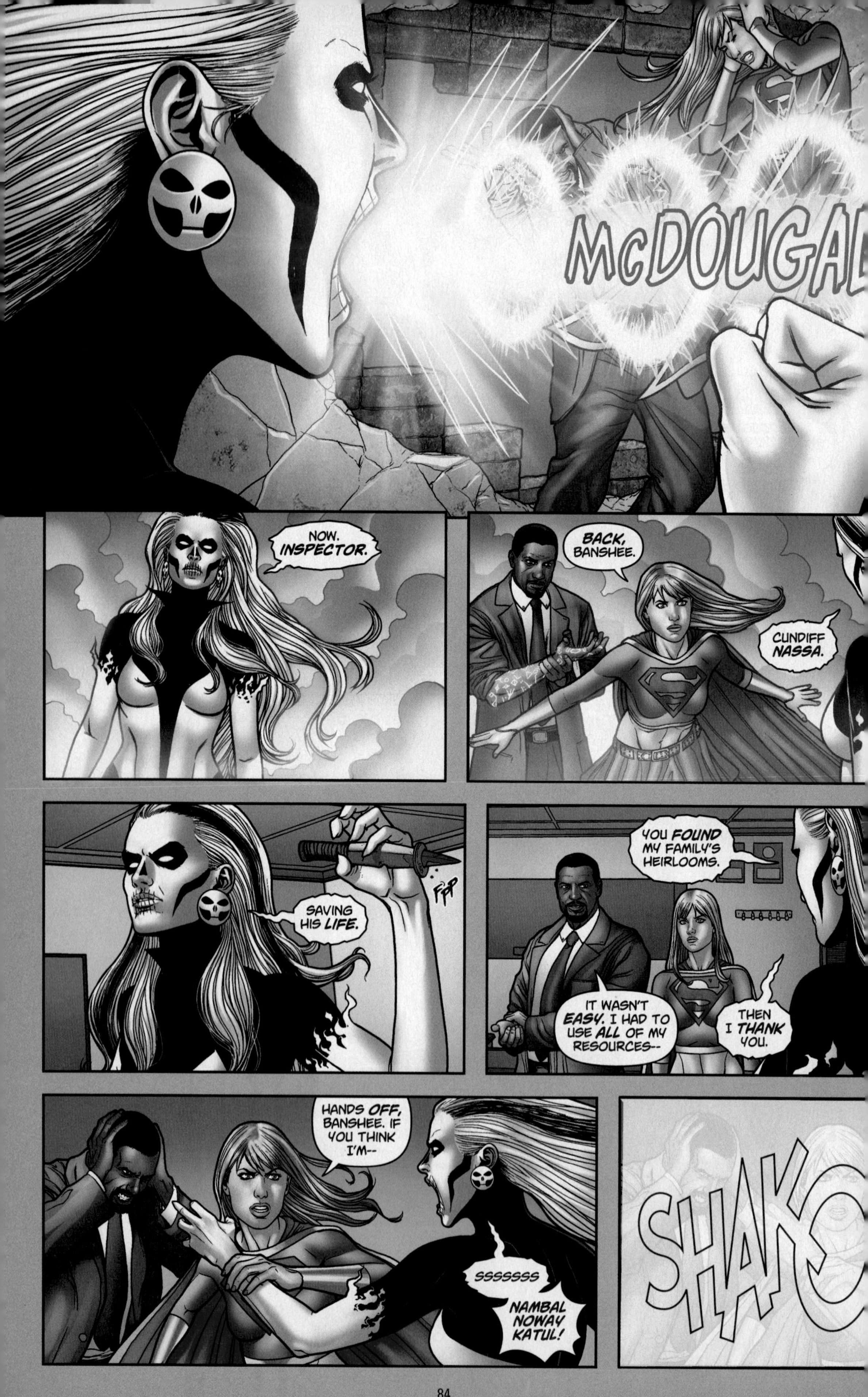
McDOUGAL
NOW. INSPECTOR.
BACK, BANSHEE.
CUNDIFF NASSA.
SAVING HIS LIFE.
FFP
YOU FOUND MY FAMILY'S HEIRLOOMS.
IT WASN'T EASY. I HAD TO USE ALL OF MY RESOURCES--
THEN I THANK YOU.
HANDS OFF, BANSHEE. IF YOU THINK I'M--
SSSSSSS
NAMBAL NOWAY KATUL!
SHAKO

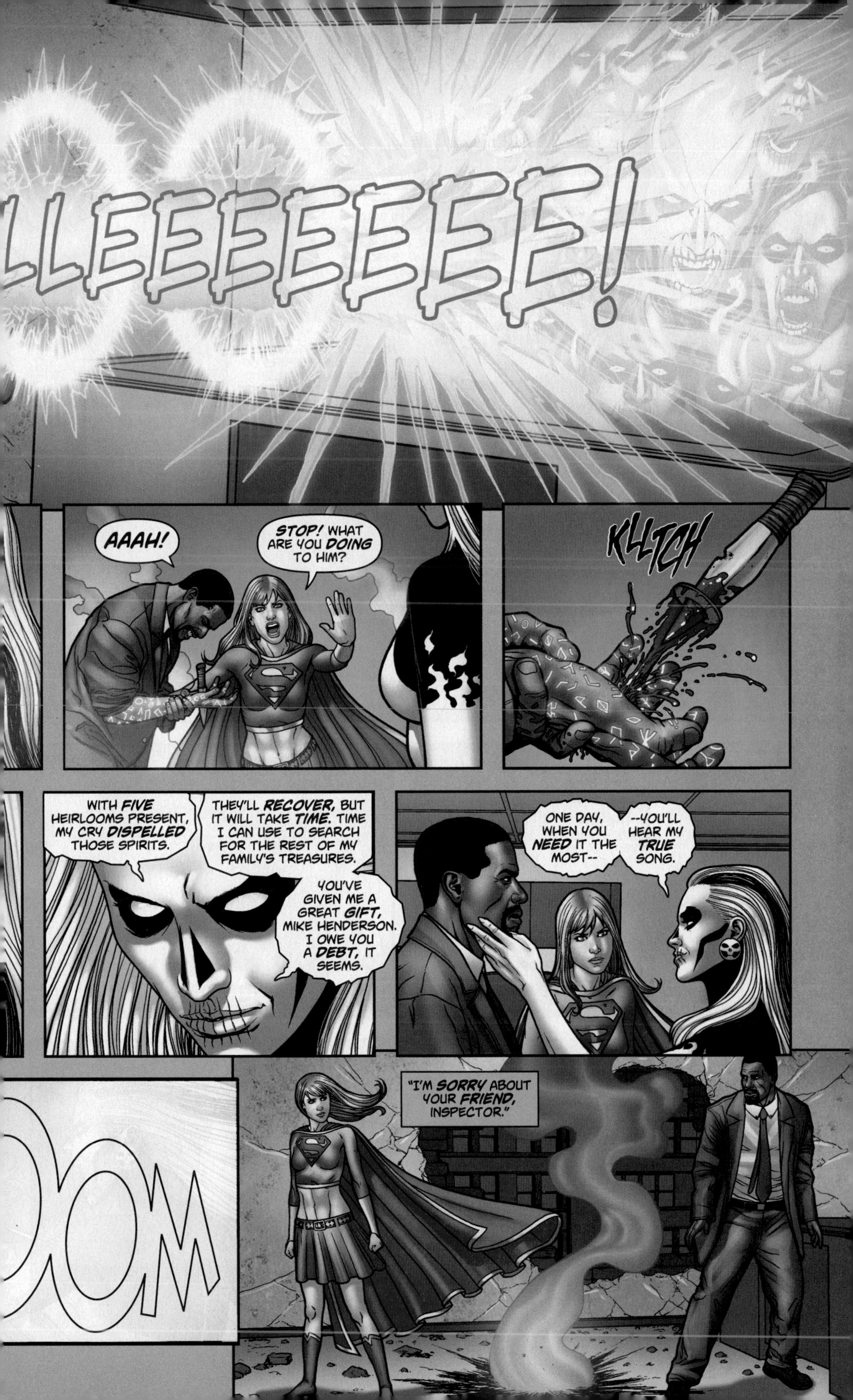
LLEEEEEEEE!
AAAH!
STOP! WHAT ARE YOU DOING TO HIM?
KLLTCH
WITH FIVE HEIRLOOMS PRESENT, MY CRY DISPELLED THOSE SPIRITS.
THEY'LL RECOVER, BUT IT WILL TAKE TIME. TIME I CAN USE TO SEARCH FOR THE REST OF MY FAMILY'S TREASURES.
YOU'VE GIVEN ME A GREAT GIFT, MIKE HENDERSON. I OWE YOU A DEBT, IT SEEMS.
ONE DAY, WHEN YOU NEED IT THE MOST--
--YOU'LL HEAR MY TRUE SONG.
OOM
"I'M SORRY ABOUT YOUR FRIEND, INSPECTOR."

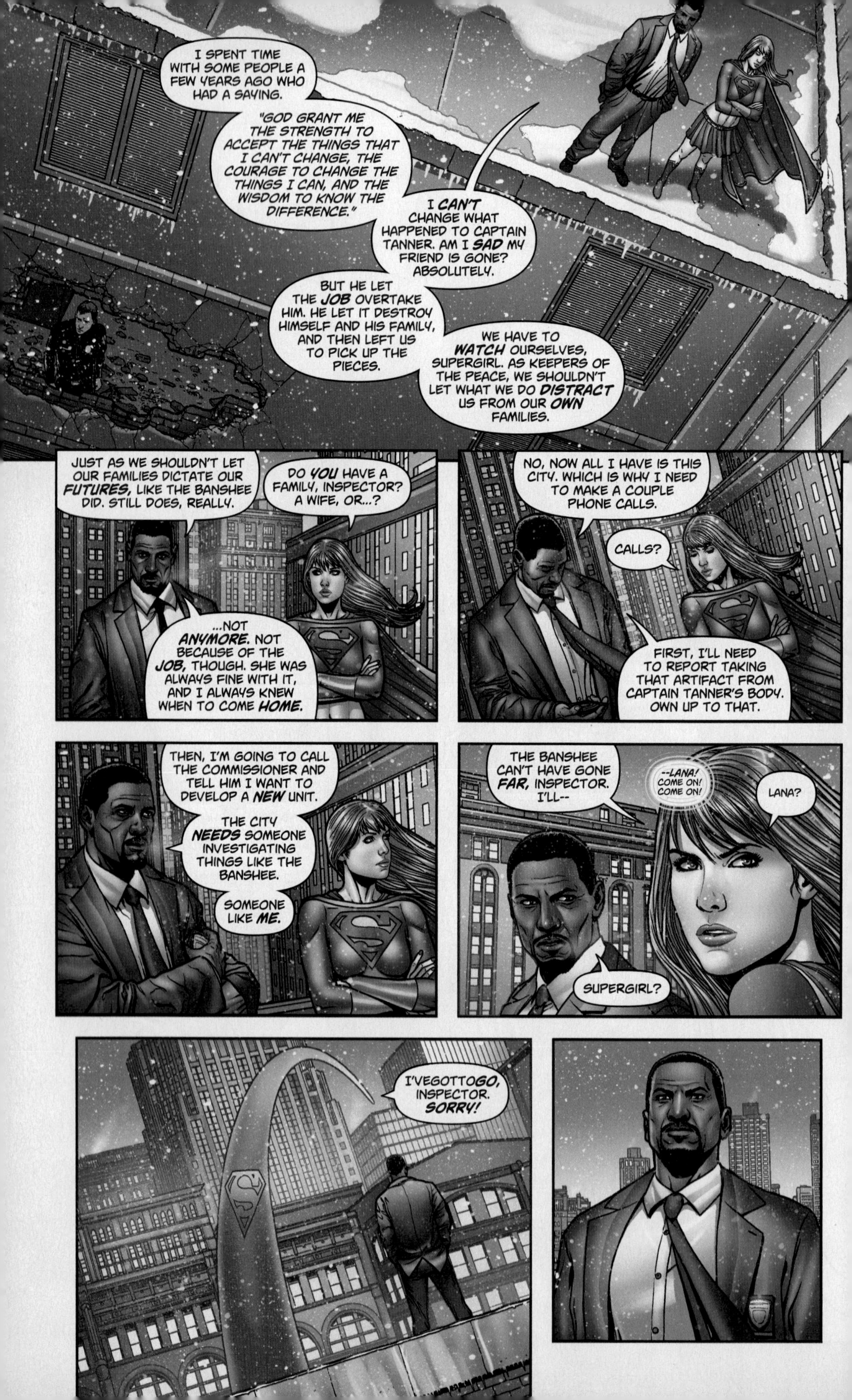

I SPENT TIME WITH SOME PEOPLE A FEW YEARS AGO WHO HAD A SAYING.
"GOD GRANT ME THE STRENGTH TO ACCEPT THE THINGS THAT I CAN'T CHANGE, THE COURAGE TO CHANGE THE THINGS I CAN, AND THE WISDOM TO KNOW THE DIFFERENCE."
I CAN'T CHANGE WHAT HAPPENED TO CAPTAIN TANNER. AM I SAD MY FRIEND IS GONE? ABSOLUTELY.
BUT HE LET THE JOB OVERTAKE HIM. HE LET IT DESTROY HIMSELF AND HIS FAMILY, AND THEN LEFT US TO PICK UP THE PIECES.
WE HAVE TO WATCH OURSELVES, SUPERGIRL. AS KEEPERS OF THE PEACE, WE SHOULDN'T LET WHAT WE DO DISTRACT US FROM OUR OWN FAMILIES.
JUST AS WE SHOULDN'T LET OUR FAMILIES DICTATE OUR FUTURES, LIKE THE BANSHEE DID. STILL DOES, REALLY.
DO YOU HAVE A FAMILY, INSPECTOR? A WIFE, OR...?
...NOT ANYMORE. NOT BECAUSE OF THE JOB, THOUGH. SHE WAS ALWAYS FINE WITH IT, AND I ALWAYS KNEW WHEN TO COME HOME.
NO, NOW ALL I HAVE IS THIS CITY. WHICH IS WHY I NEED TO MAKE A COUPLE PHONE CALLS.
CALLS?
FIRST, I'LL NEED TO REPORT TAKING THAT ARTIFACT FROM CAPTAIN TANNER'S BODY. OWN UP TO THAT.
THEN, I'M GOING TO CALL THE COMMISSIONER AND TELL HIM I WANT TO DEVELOP A NEW UNIT.
THE CITY NEEDS SOMEONE INVESTIGATING THINGS LIKE THE BANSHEE.
SOMEONE LIKE ME.
THE BANSHEE CAN'T HAVE GONE FAR, INSPECTOR. I'LL--
--LANA! COME ON! COME ON!
LANA?
SUPERGIRL?
I'VEGOTTOGO, INSPECTOR. SORRY!

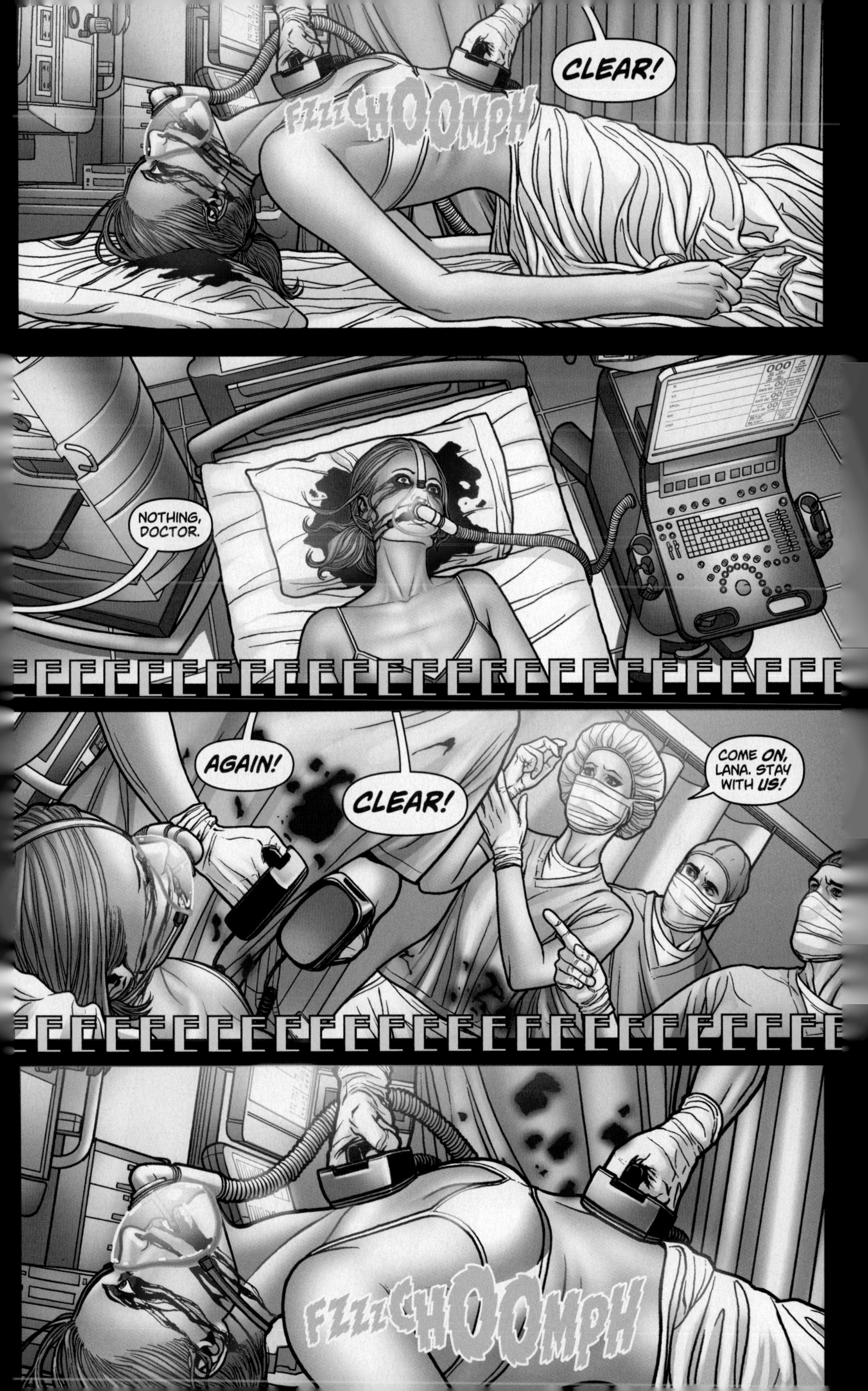
CLEAR!
FZZZCHOOOMPH
NOTHING, DOCTOR.
EEEEEEEEEEEEEEEEEEEEEEEEE
AGAIN!
CLEAR!
COME ON, LANA. STAY WITH US!
EEEEEEEEEEEEEEEEEEEEEEEEE
FZZZCHOOOMPH

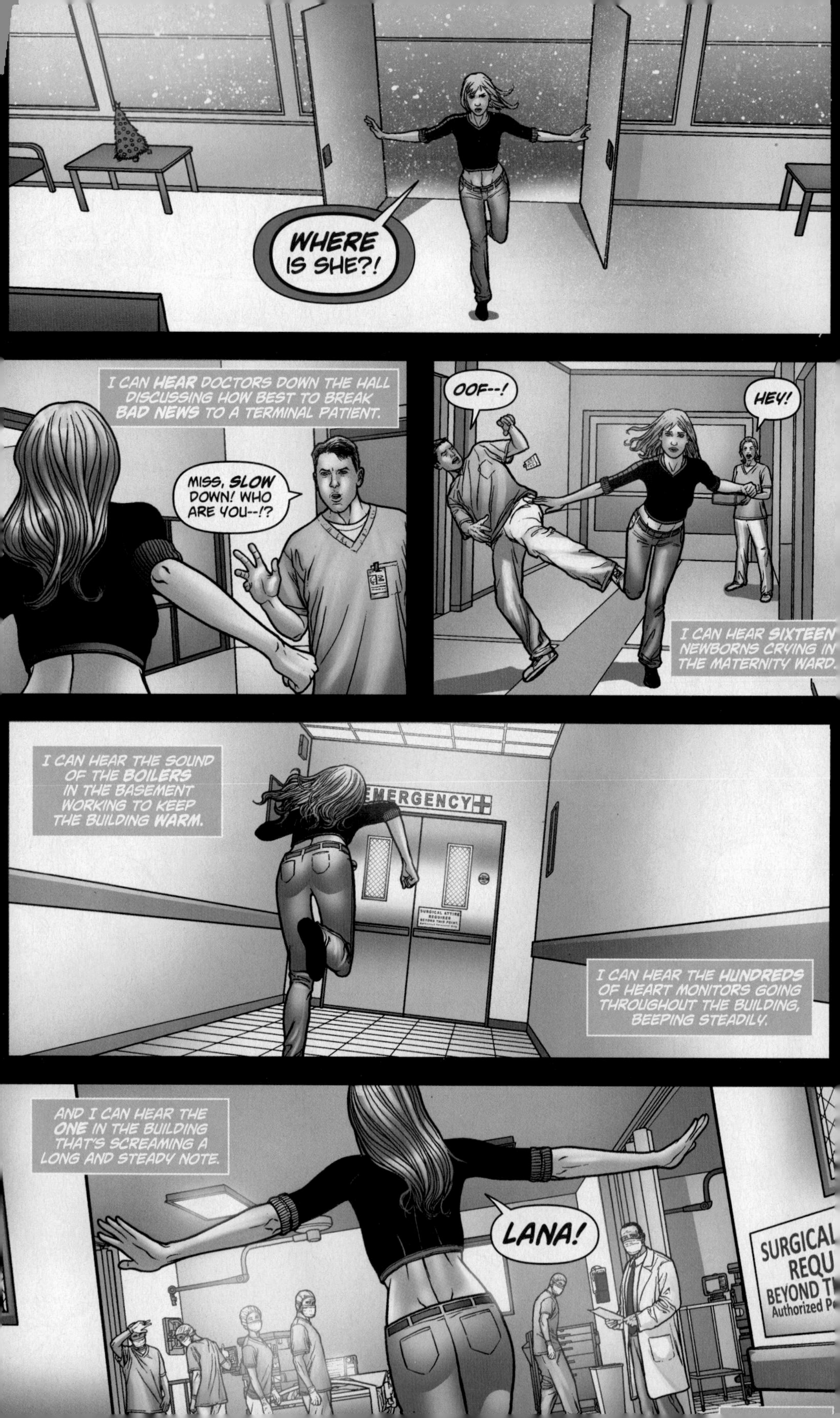
WHERE IS SHE?!
I CAN HEAR DOCTORS DOWN THE HALL DISCUSSING HOW BEST TO BREAK BAD NEWS TO A TERMINAL PATIENT.
MISS, SLOW DOWN! WHO ARE YOU--!?
OOF--!
HEY!
I CAN HEAR SIXTEEN NEWBORNS CRYING IN THE MATERNITY WARD.
I CAN HEAR THE SOUND OF THE BOILERS IN THE BASEMENT WORKING TO KEEP THE BUILDING WARM.
EMERGENCY
I CAN HEAR THE HUNDREDS OF HEART MONITORS GOING THROUGHOUT THE BUILDING, BEEPING STEADILY.
AND I CAN HEAR THE ONE IN THE BUILDING THAT'S SCREAMING A LONG AND STEADY NOTE.
LANA!
SURGICAL
REQU
BEYOND T
Authorized P

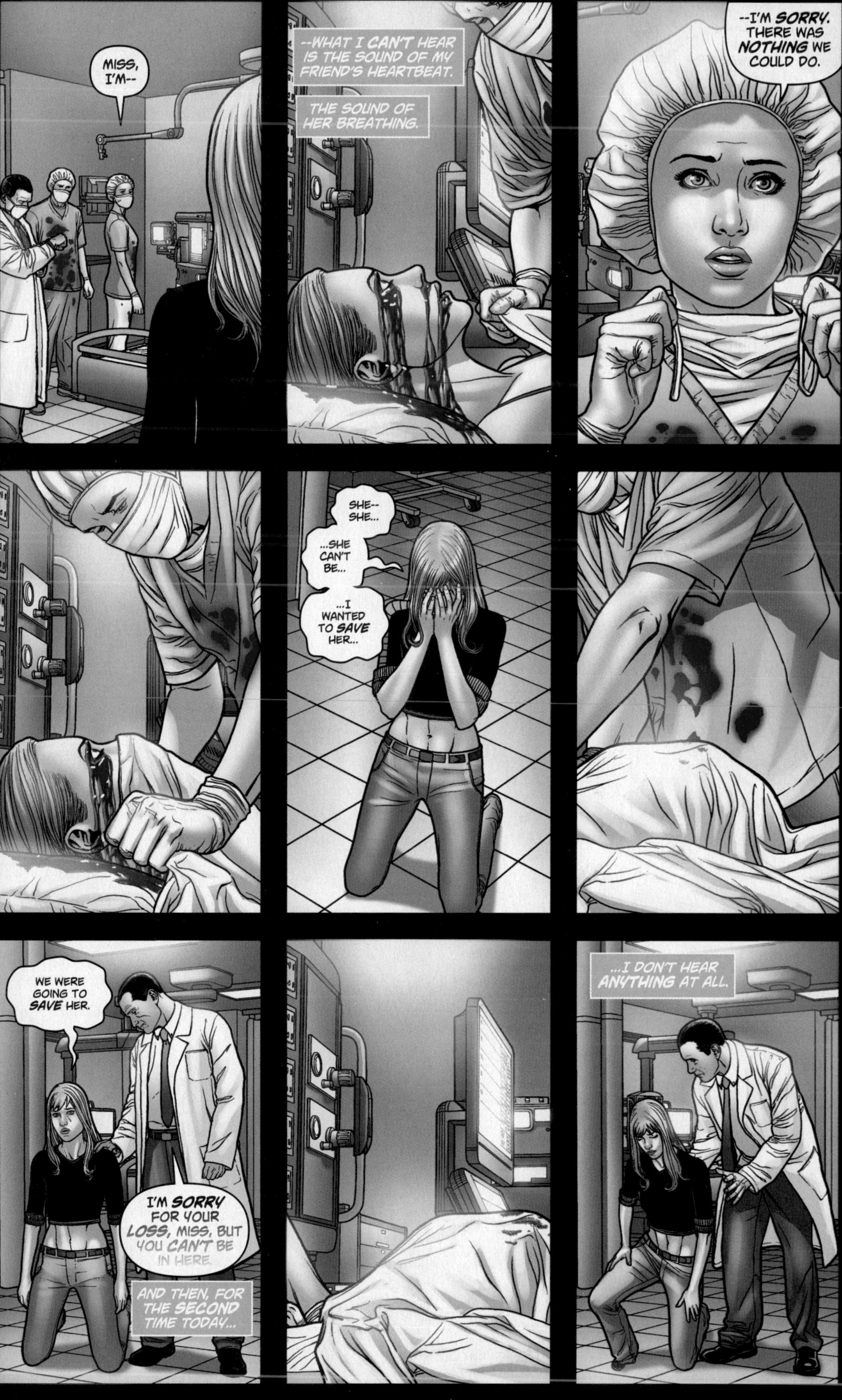

MISS, I'M--
--WHAT I CAN'T HEAR IS THE SOUND OF MY FRIEND'S HEARTBEAT.
THE SOUND OF HER BREATHING.
--I'M SORRY. THERE WAS NOTHING WE COULD DO.
SHE-- SHE...
...SHE CAN'T BE...
...I WANTED TO SAVE HER...
WE WERE GOING TO SAVE HER.
I'M SORRY FOR YOUR LOSS, MISS, BUT YOU CAN'T BE IN HERE.
AND THEN, FOR THE SECOND TIME TODAY...
...I DON'T HEAR ANYTHING AT ALL.

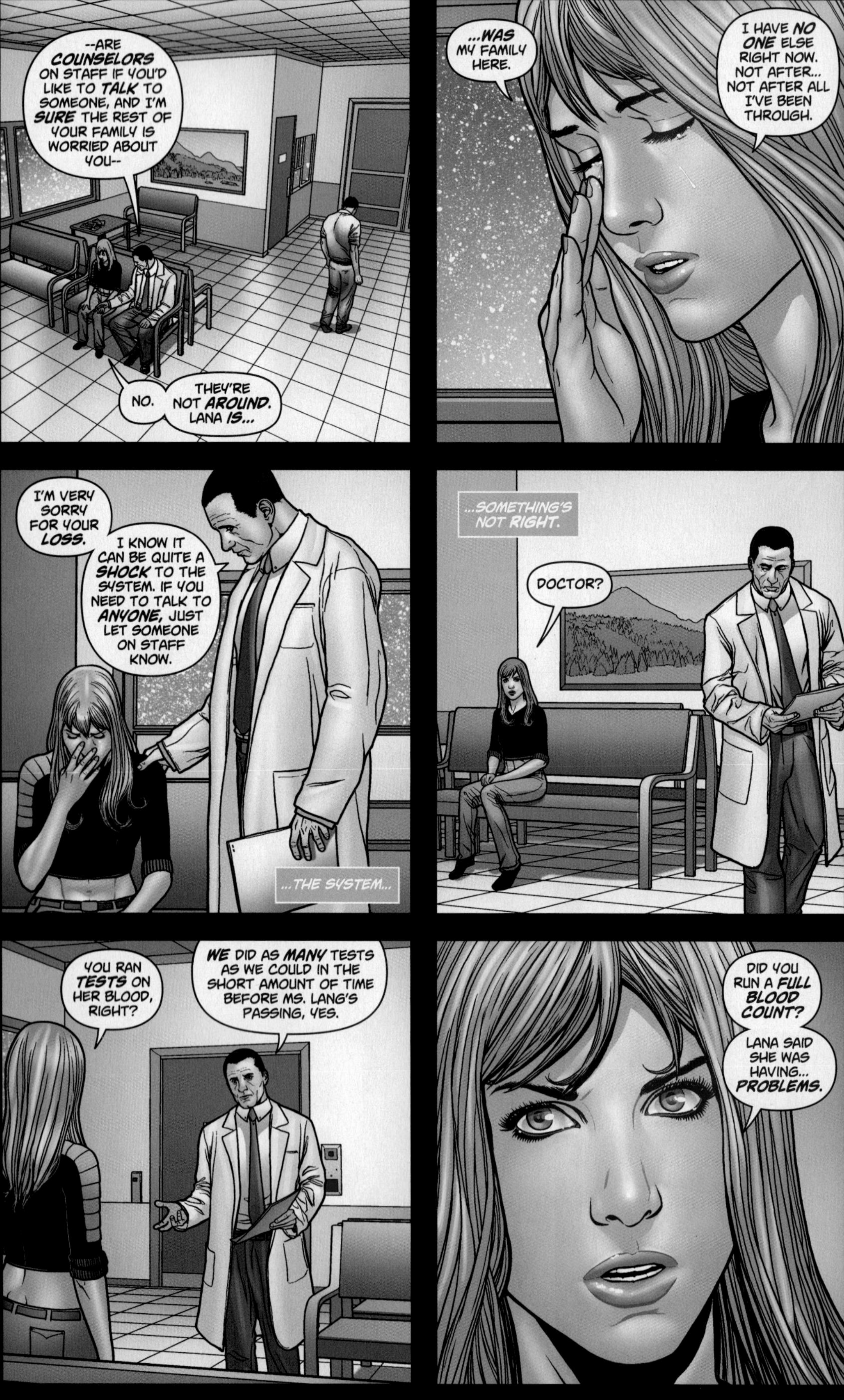
--ARE COUNSELORS ON STAFF IF YOU'D LIKE TO TALK TO SOMEONE, AND I'M SURE THE REST OF YOUR FAMILY IS WORRIED ABOUT YOU--
NO.
THEY'RE NOT AROUND. LANA IS...
...WAS MY FAMILY HERE.
I HAVE NO ONE ELSE RIGHT NOW. NOT AFTER... NOT AFTER ALL I'VE BEEN THROUGH.
I'M VERY SORRY FOR YOUR LOSS.
I KNOW IT CAN BE QUITE A SHOCK TO THE SYSTEM. IF YOU NEED TO TALK TO ANYONE, JUST LET SOMEONE ON STAFF KNOW.
...THE SYSTEM...
...SOMETHING'S NOT RIGHT.
DOCTOR?
YOU RAN TESTS ON HER BLOOD, RIGHT?
WE DID AS MANY TESTS AS WE COULD IN THE SHORT AMOUNT OF TIME BEFORE MS. LANG'S PASSING, YES.
DID YOU RUN A FULL BLOOD COUNT?
LANA SAID SHE WAS HAVING... PROBLEMS.

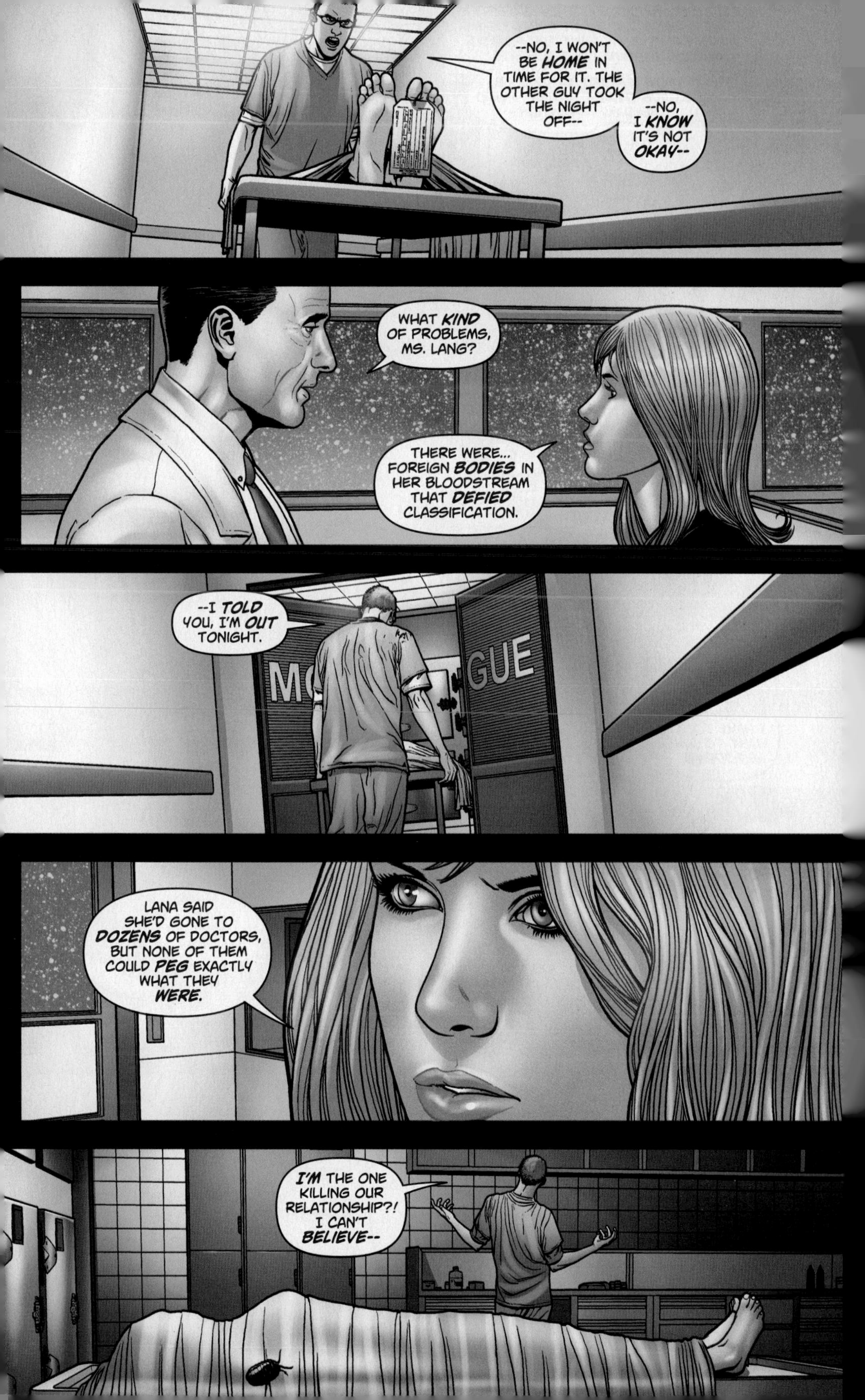

--NO, I WON'T BE HOME IN TIME FOR IT. THE OTHER GUY TOOK THE NIGHT OFF--
--NO, I KNOW IT'S NOT OKAY--
WHAT KIND OF PROBLEMS, MS. LANG?
THERE WERE... FOREIGN BODIES IN HER BLOODSTREAM THAT DEFIED CLASSIFICATION.
--I TOLD YOU, I'M OUT TONIGHT.
MORGUE
LANA SAID SHE'D GONE TO DOZENS OF DOCTORS, BUT NONE OF THEM COULD PEG EXACTLY WHAT THEY WERE.
I'M THE ONE KILLING OUR RELATIONSHIP?! I CAN'T BELIEVE--

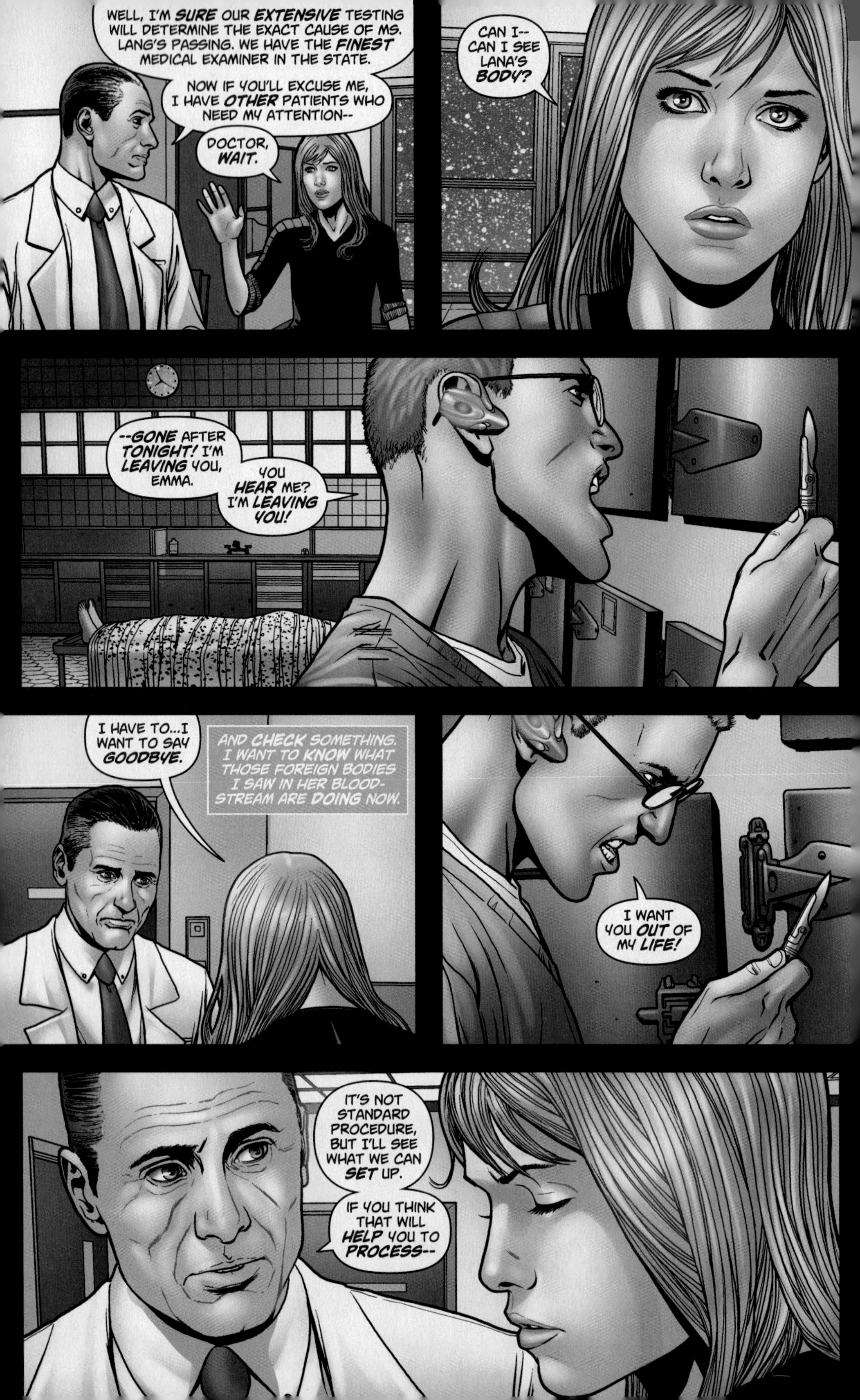
WELL, I'M SURE OUR EXTENSIVE TESTING WILL DETERMINE THE EXACT CAUSE OF MS. LANG'S PASSING. WE HAVE THE FINEST MEDICAL EXAMINER IN THE STATE.
NOW IF YOU'LL EXCUSE ME, I HAVE OTHER PATIENTS WHO NEED MY ATTENTION--
DOCTOR, WAIT.
CAN I-- CAN I SEE LANA'S BODY?
--GONE AFTER TONIGHT! I'M LEAVING YOU, EMMA.
YOU HEAR ME? I'M LEAVING YOU!
I HAVE TO...I WANT TO SAY GOODBYE.
AND CHECK SOMETHING. I WANT TO KNOW WHAT THOSE FOREIGN BODIES I SAW IN HER BLOOD-STREAM ARE DOING NOW.
I WANT YOU OUT OF MY LIFE!
IT'S NOT STANDARD PROCEDURE, BUT I'LL SEE WHAT WE CAN SET UP.
IF YOU THINK THAT WILL HELP YOU TO PROCESS--

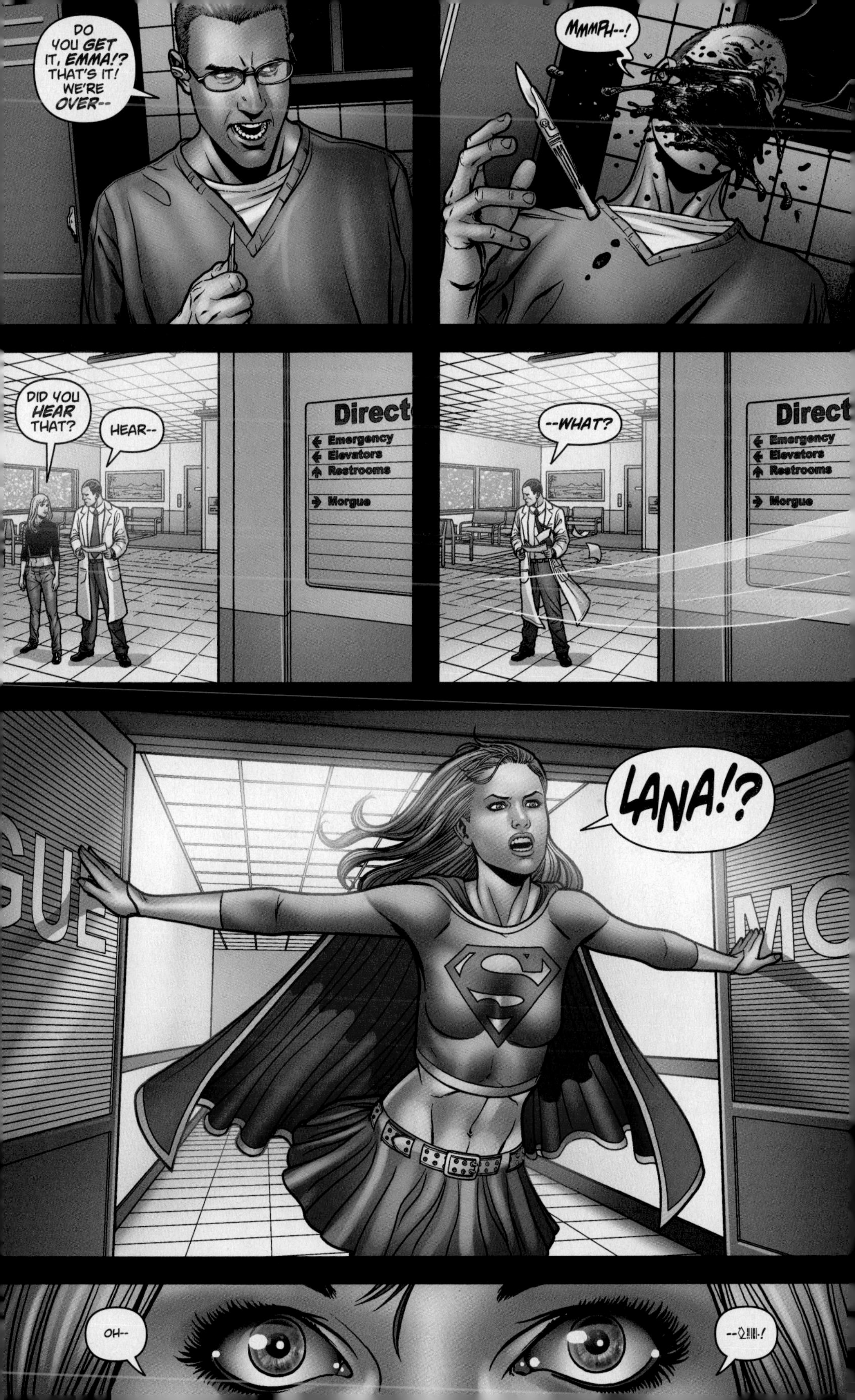
DO YOU GET IT, EMMA!? THAT'S IT! WE'RE OVER--
MMMPH--!
DID YOU HEAR THAT?
HEAR--
Directo
Emergency
Elevators
Restrooms
Morgue
--WHAT?
LANA!?
GUE
MO
OH--

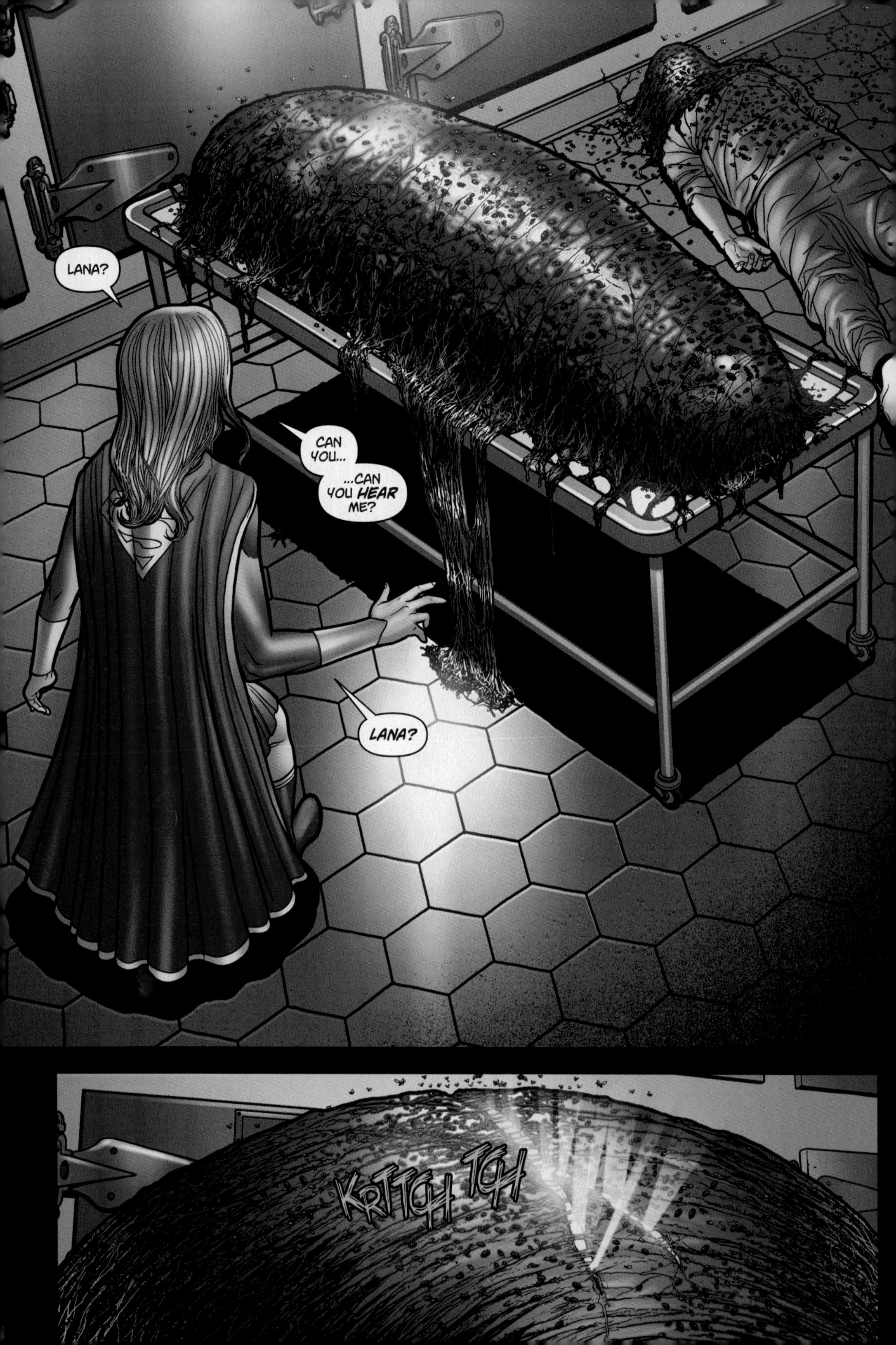
LANA?
CAN YOU...
...CAN YOU HEAR ME?
LANA?
KRTTCH TCH

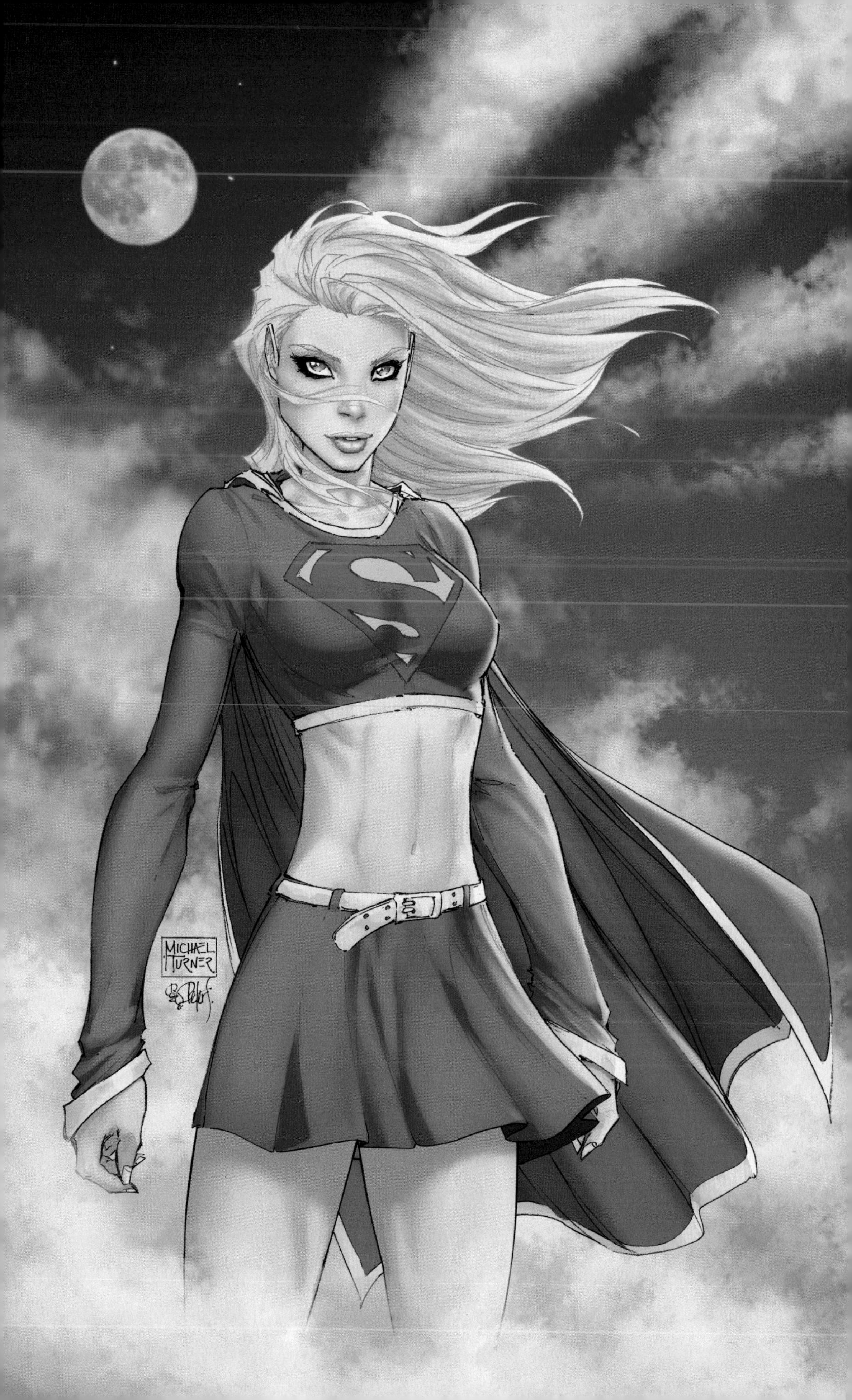
MICHAEL TURNER

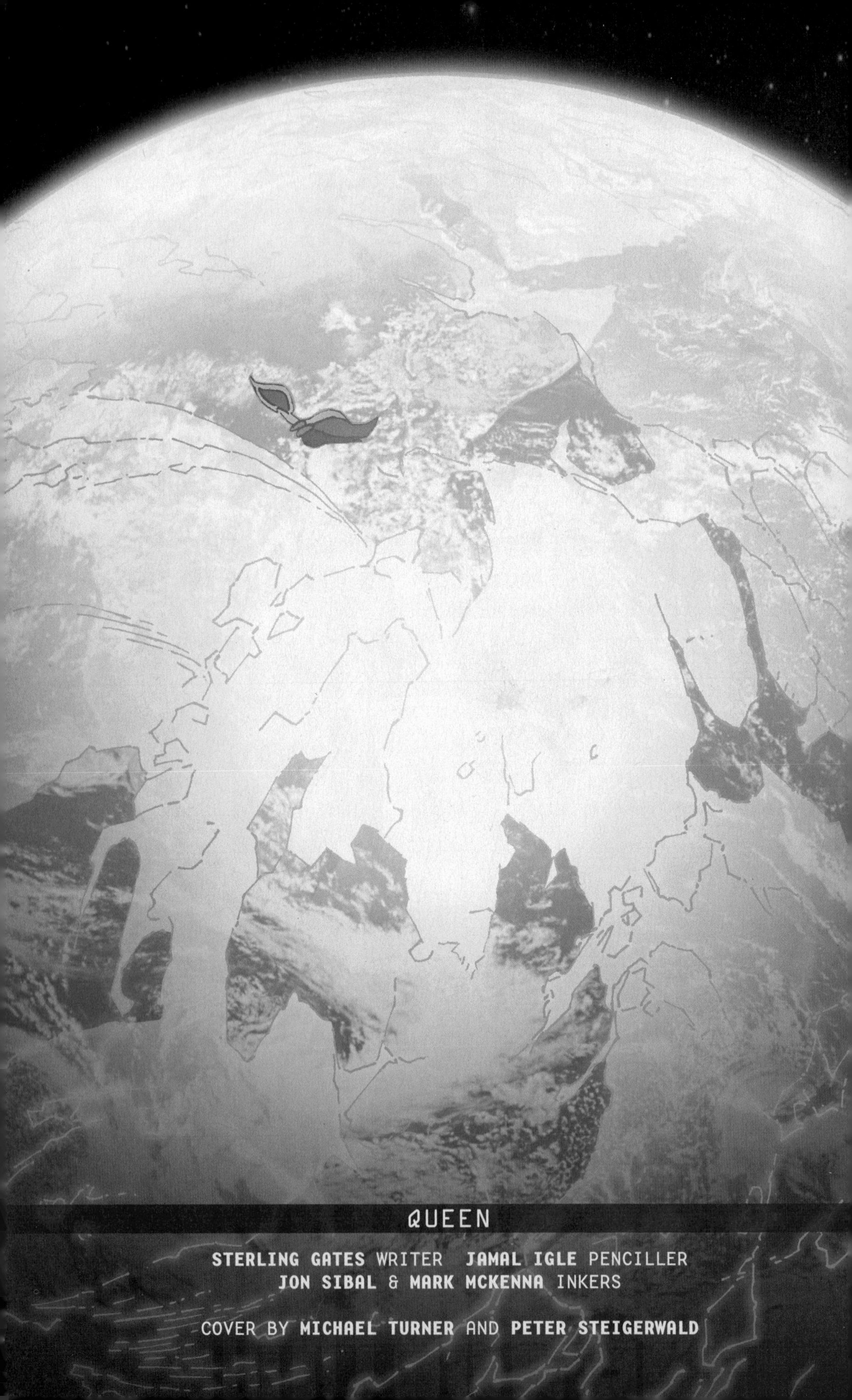
QUEEN
STERLING GATES WRITER JAMAL IGLE PENCILLER
JON SIBAL & MARK MCKENNA INKERS
COVER BY MICHAEL TURNER AND PETER STEIGERWALD

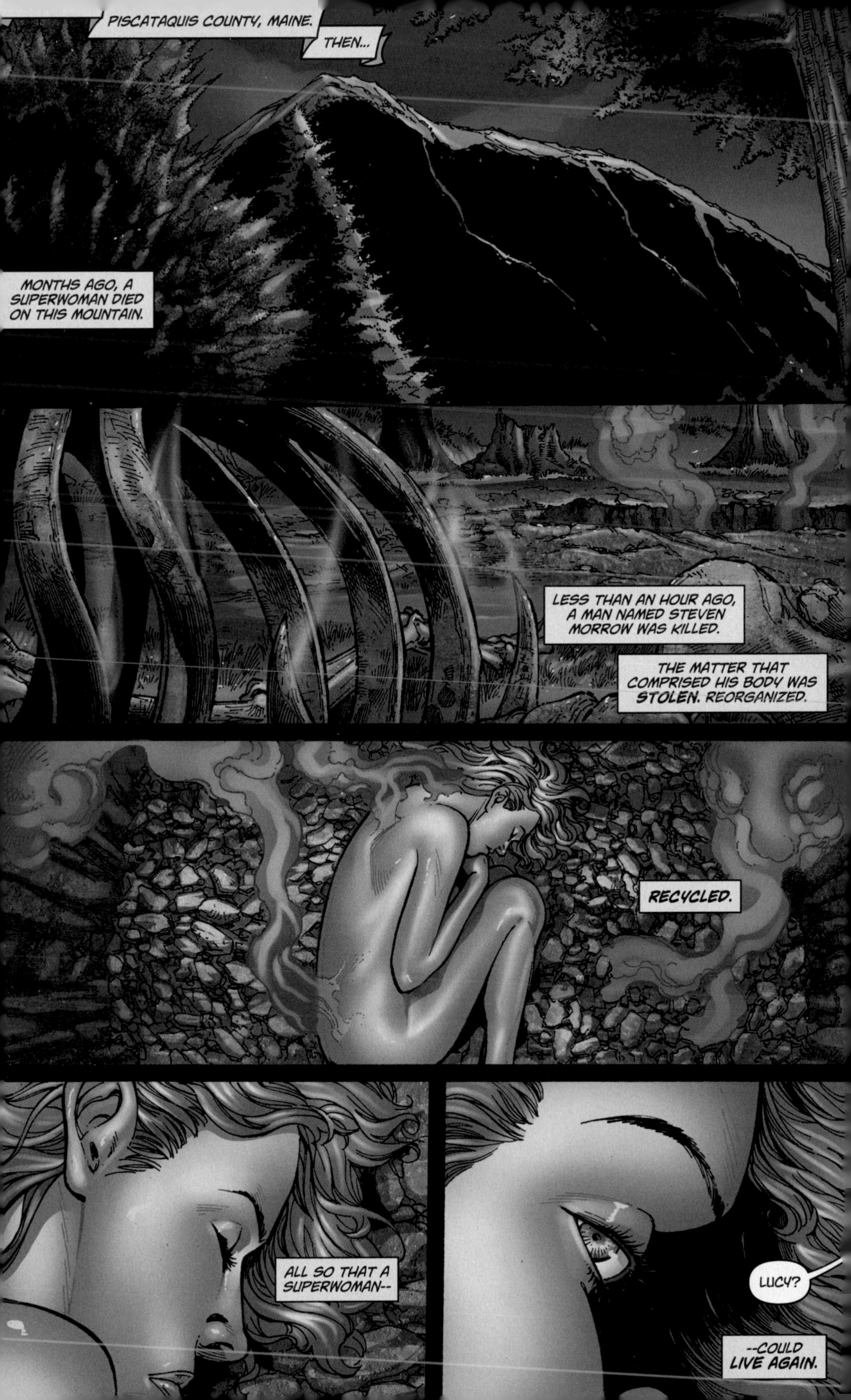
PISCATAQUIS COUNTY, MAINE.
THEN...
MONTHS AGO, A SUPERWOMAN DIED ON THIS MOUNTAIN.
LESS THAN AN HOUR AGO, A MAN NAMED STEVEN MORROW WAS KILLED.
THE MATTER THAT COMPRISED HIS BODY WAS STOLEN. REORGANIZED.
RECYCLED.
ALL SO THAT A SUPERWOMAN--
LUCY?
--COULD LIVE AGAIN.

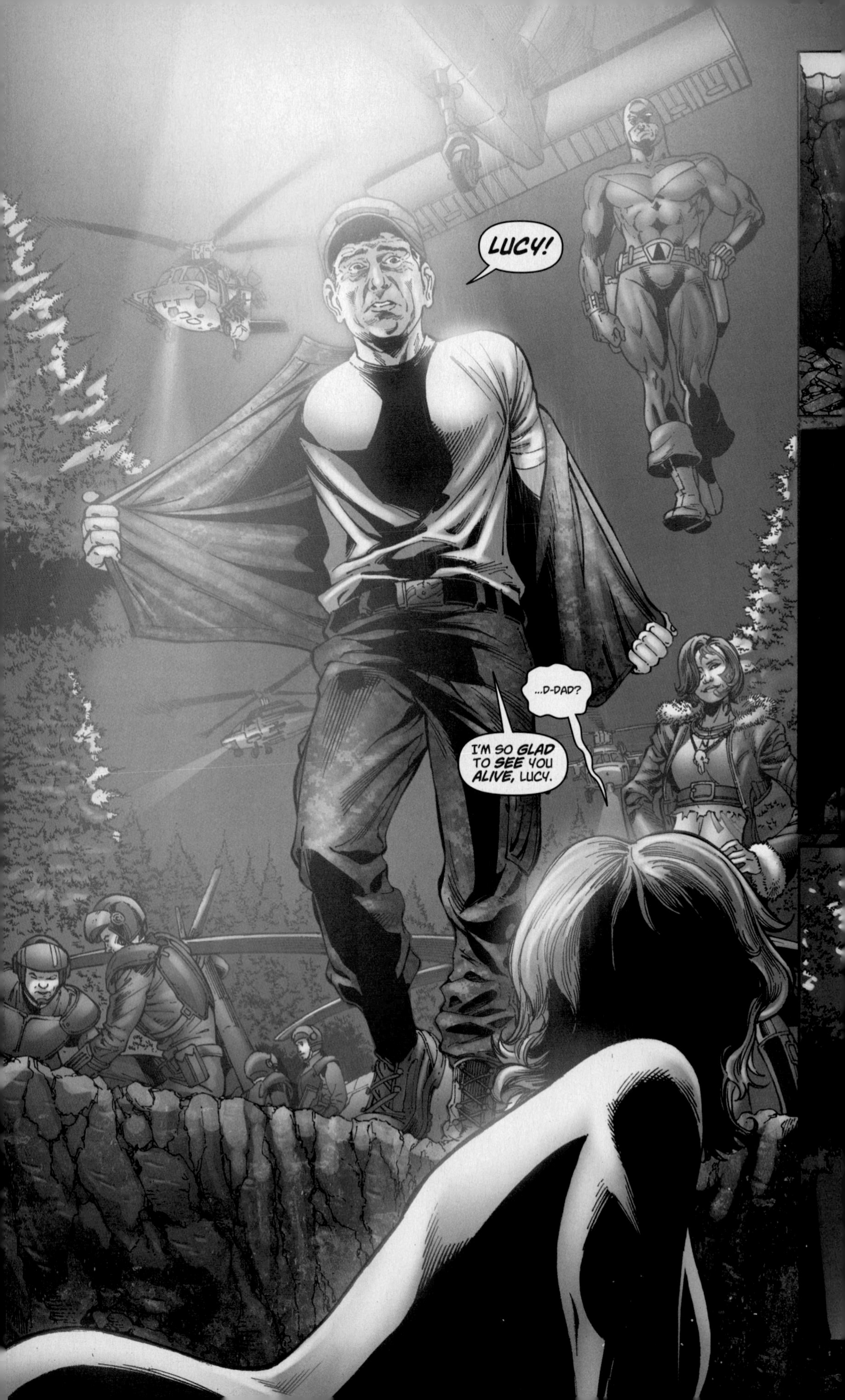
LUCY!
...D-DAD?
I'M SO GLAD TO SEE YOU ALIVE, LUCY.

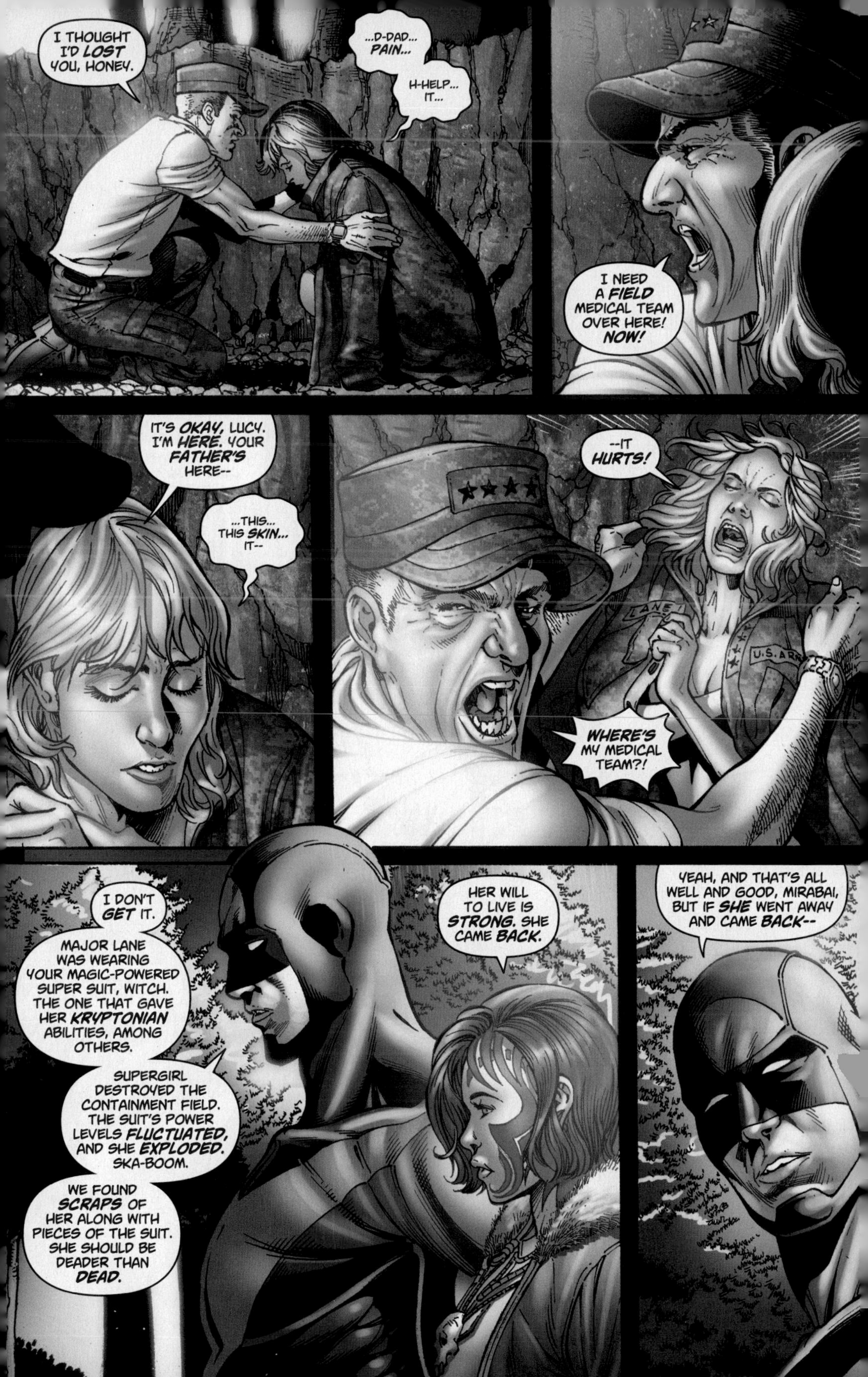
I THOUGHT I'D LOST YOU, HONEY.
...D-DAD... PAIN...
H-HELP... IT...
I NEED A FIELD MEDICAL TEAM OVER HERE! NOW!
IT'S OKAY, LUCY. I'M HERE. YOUR FATHER'S HERE--
...THIS... THIS SKIN... IT--
--IT HURTS!
WHERE'S MY MEDICAL TEAM?!
I DON'T GET IT.
MAJOR LANE WAS WEARING YOUR MAGIC-POWERED SUPER SUIT, WITCH. THE ONE THAT GAVE HER KRYPTONIAN ABILITIES, AMONG OTHERS.
SUPERGIRL DESTROYED THE CONTAINMENT FIELD. THE SUIT'S POWER LEVELS FLUCTUATED, AND SHE EXPLODED. SKA-BOOM.
WE FOUND SCRAPS OF HER ALONG WITH PIECES OF THE SUIT. SHE SHOULD BE DEADER THAN DEAD.
HER WILL TO LIVE IS STRONG. SHE CAME BACK.
YEAH, AND THAT'S ALL WELL AND GOOD, MIRABAI, BUT IF SHE WENT AWAY AND CAME BACK--

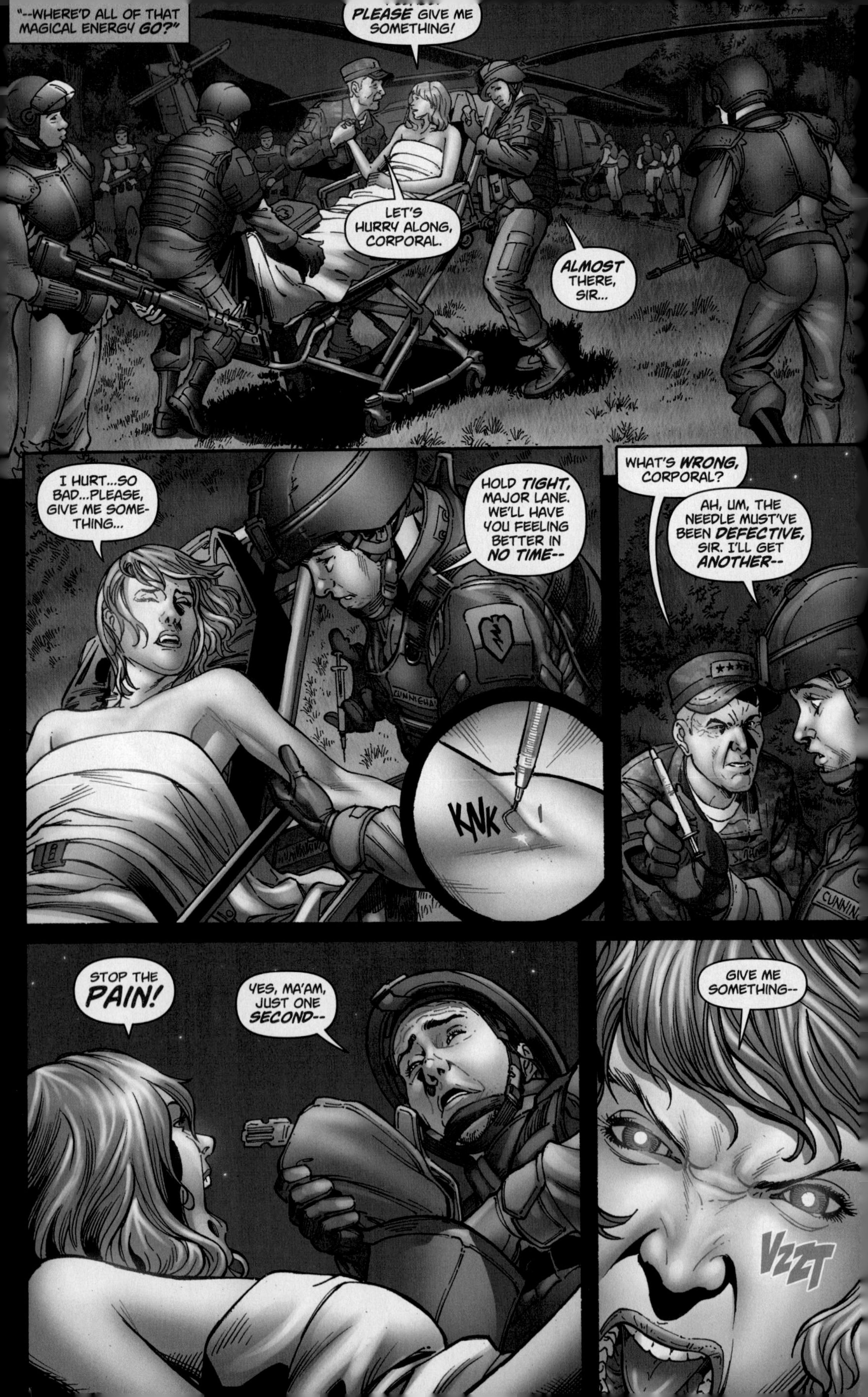
"--WHERE'D ALL OF THAT MAGICAL ENERGY GO?"
PLEASE GIVE ME SOMETHING!
LET'S HURRY ALONG, CORPORAL.
ALMOST THERE, SIR...
I HURT...SO BAD...PLEASE, GIVE ME SOMETHING...
HOLD TIGHT, MAJOR LANE. WE'LL HAVE YOU FEELING BETTER IN NO TIME--
KNK
WHAT'S WRONG, CORPORAL?
AH, UM, THE NEEDLE MUST'VE BEEN DEFECTIVE, SIR. I'LL GET ANOTHER--
STOP THE PAIN!
YES, MA'AM, JUST ONE SECOND--
GIVE ME SOMETHING--
VZZT

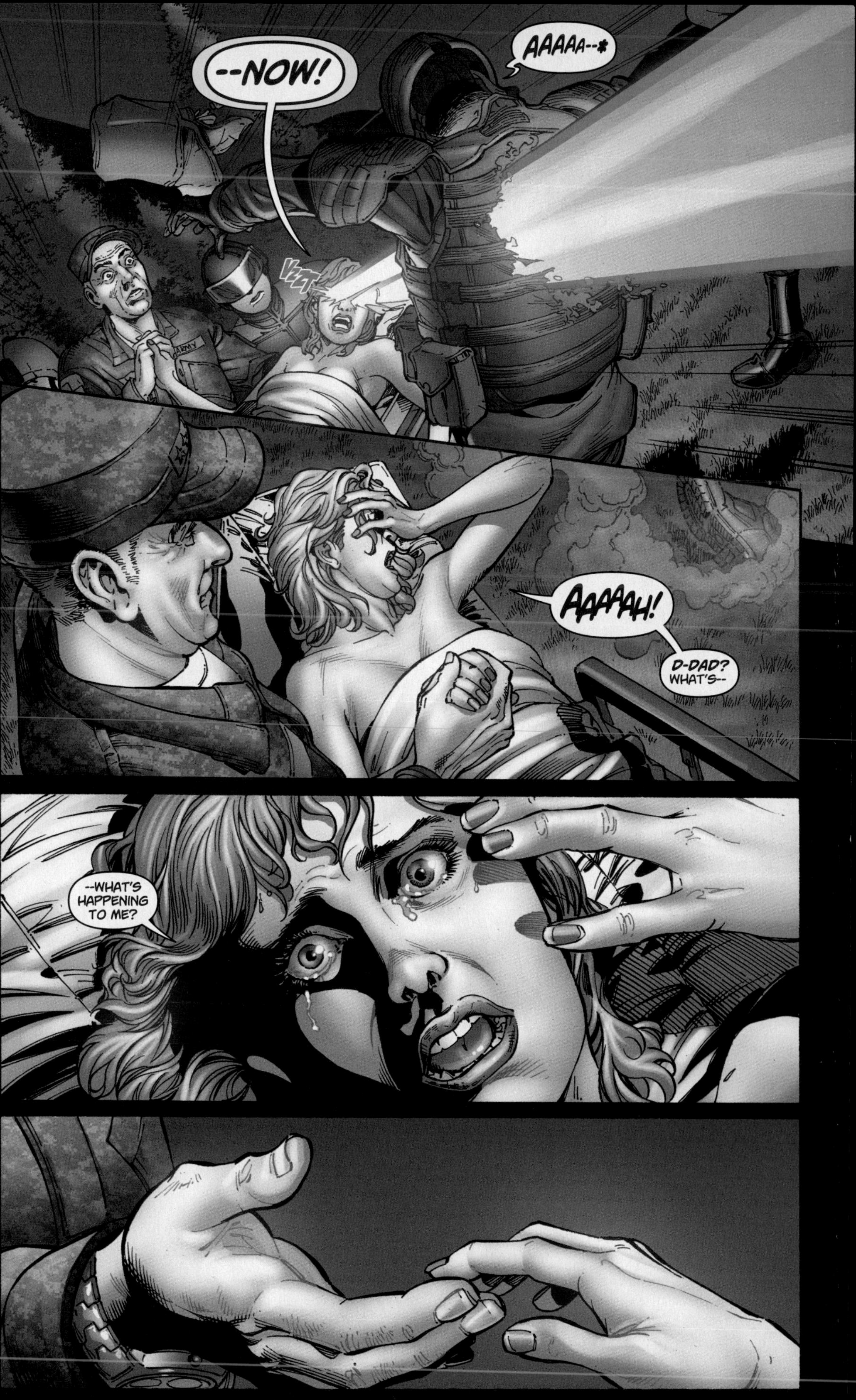
--NOW!
AAAAA--*
VZT
AAAAAH!
D-DAD? WHAT'S--
--WHAT'S HAPPENING TO ME?

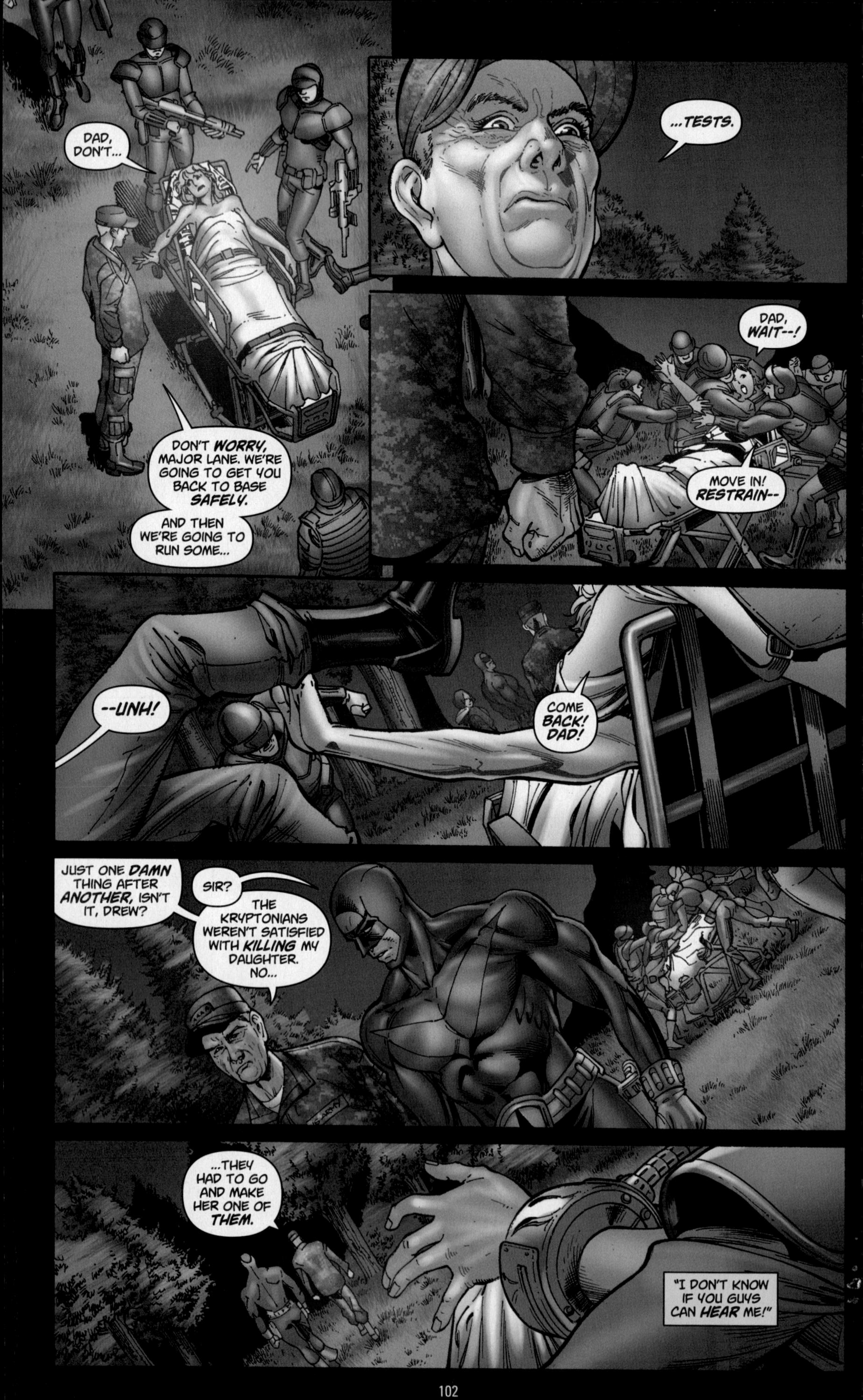
DAD, DON'T...
DON'T WORRY, MAJOR LANE. WE'RE GOING TO GET YOU BACK TO BASE SAFELY.
AND THEN WE'RE GOING TO RUN SOME...
...TESTS.
DAD, WAIT--!
MOVE IN! RESTRAIN--
--UNH!
COME BACK! DAD!
JUST ONE DAMN THING AFTER ANOTHER, ISN'T IT, DREW?
SIR?
THE KRYPTONIANS WEREN'T SATISFIED WITH KILLING MY DAUGHTER. NO...
...THEY HAD TO GO AND MAKE HER ONE OF THEM.
"I DON'T KNOW IF YOU GUYS CAN HEAR ME!"

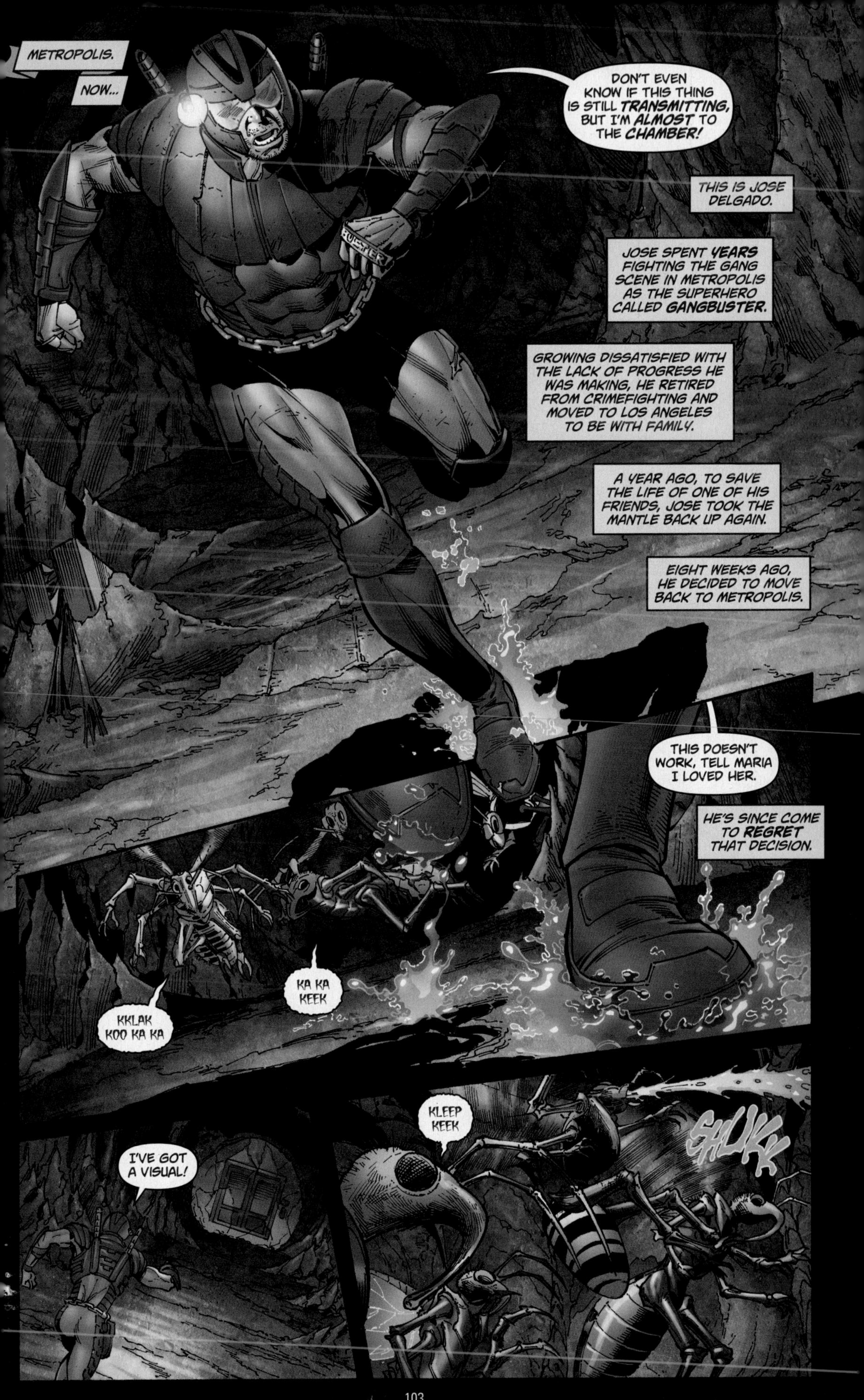
METROPOLIS.
NOW...
DON'T EVEN KNOW IF THIS THING IS STILL TRANSMITTING, BUT I'M ALMOST TO THE CHAMBER!
THIS IS JOSE DELGADO.
JOSE SPENT YEARS FIGHTING THE GANG SCENE IN METROPOLIS AS THE SUPERHERO CALLED GANGBUSTER.
GROWING DISSATISFIED WITH THE LACK OF PROGRESS HE WAS MAKING, HE RETIRED FROM CRIMEFIGHTING AND MOVED TO LOS ANGELES TO BE WITH FAMILY.
A YEAR AGO, TO SAVE THE LIFE OF ONE OF HIS FRIENDS, JOSE TOOK THE MANTLE BACK UP AGAIN.
EIGHT WEEKS AGO, HE DECIDED TO MOVE BACK TO METROPOLIS.
THIS DOESN'T WORK, TELL MARIA I LOVED HER.
HE'S SINCE COME TO REGRET THAT DECISION.
KA KA KEEK
KKLAK KOO KA KA
I'VE GOT A VISUAL!
KLEEP KEEK
SHLIKK

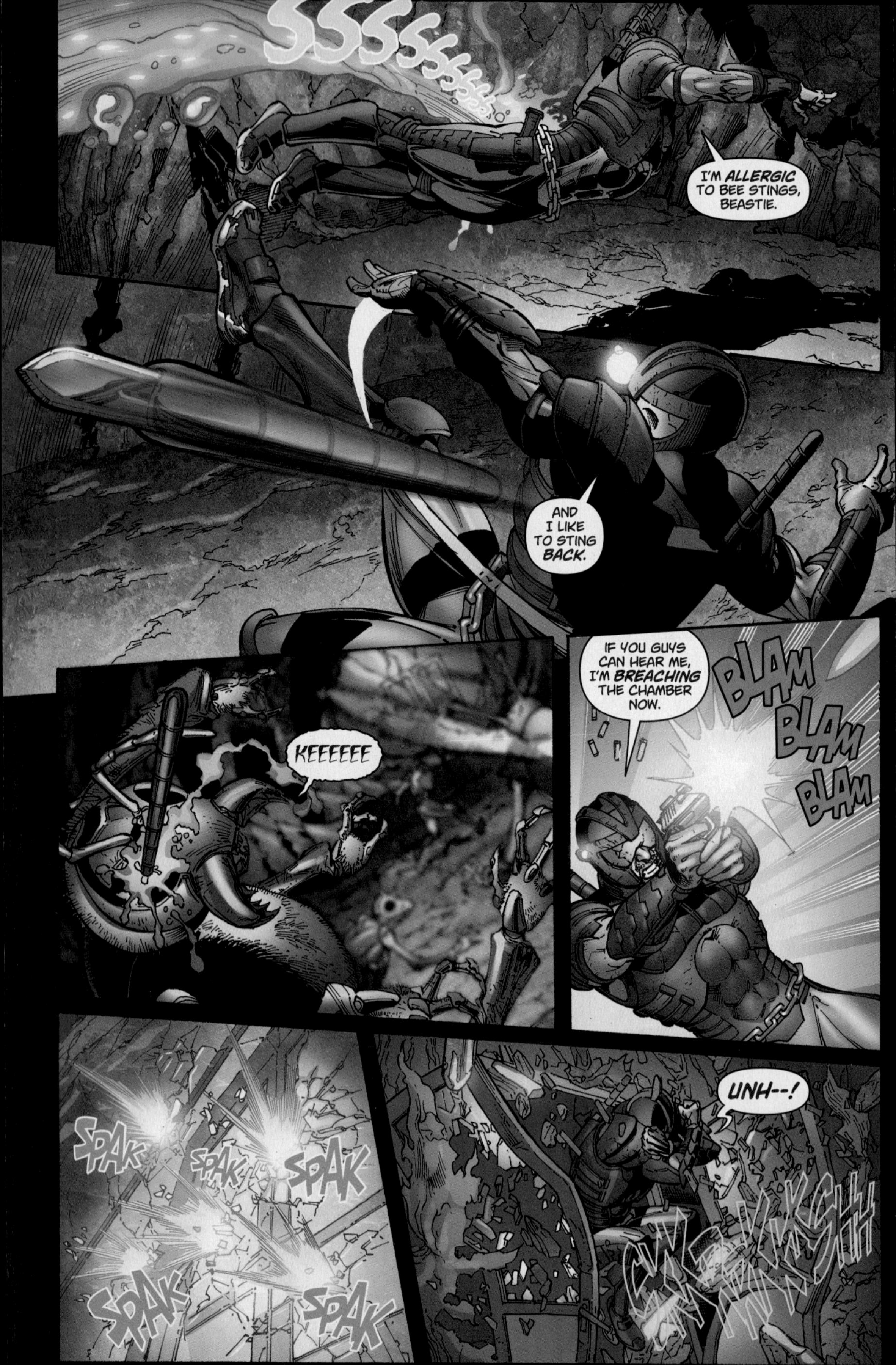
SSSSSSSSS
I'M ALLERGIC TO BEE STINGS, BEASTIE.
AND I LIKE TO STING BACK.
KEEEEEE
IF YOU GUYS CAN HEAR ME, I'M BREACHING THE CHAMBER NOW.
BLAM
BLAM
BLAM
SPAK
SPAK
SPAK
SPAK
SPAK
UNH--!
CKRAKKSH

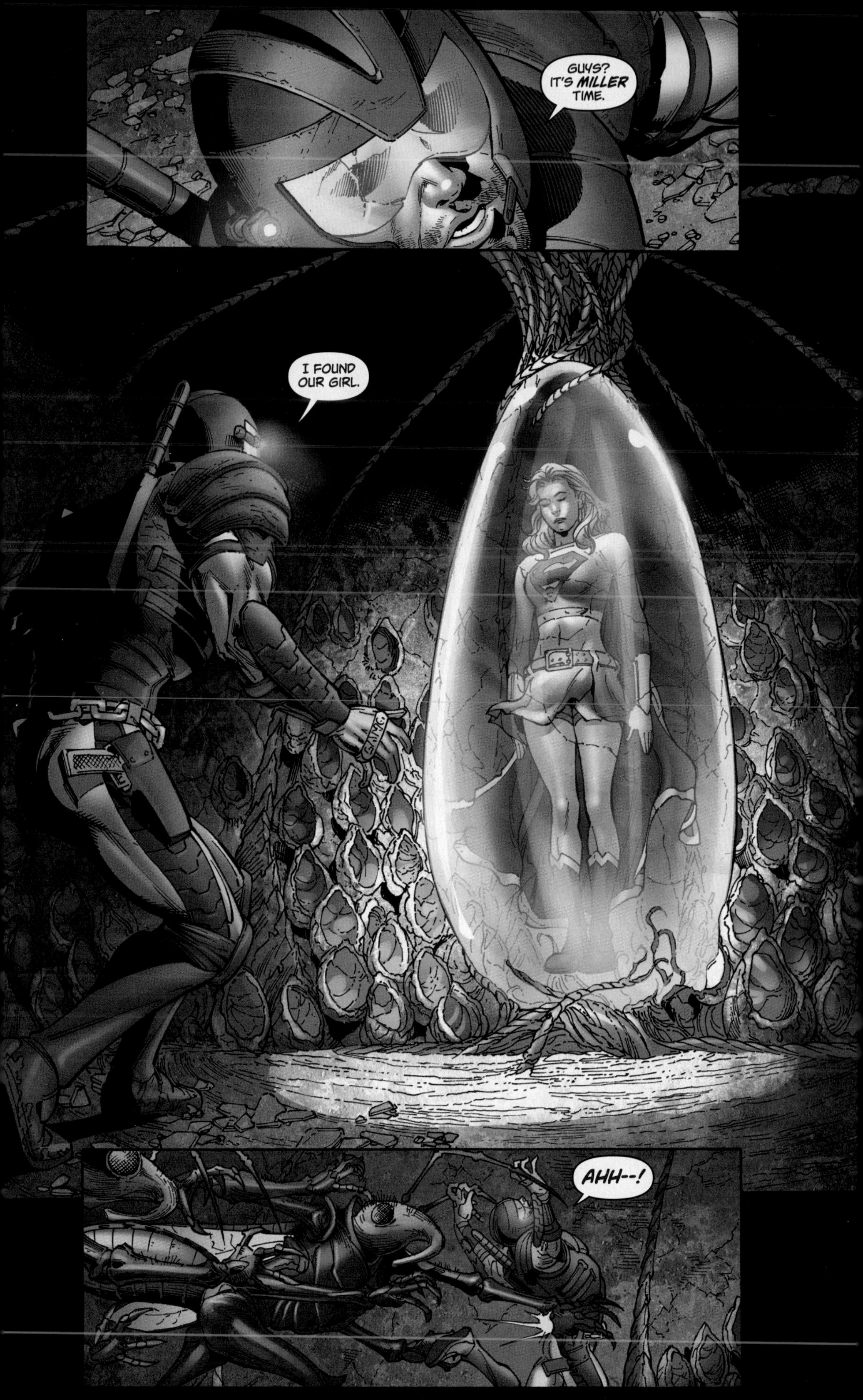
GUYS? IT'S MILLER TIME.
I FOUND OUR GIRL.
AHH--!

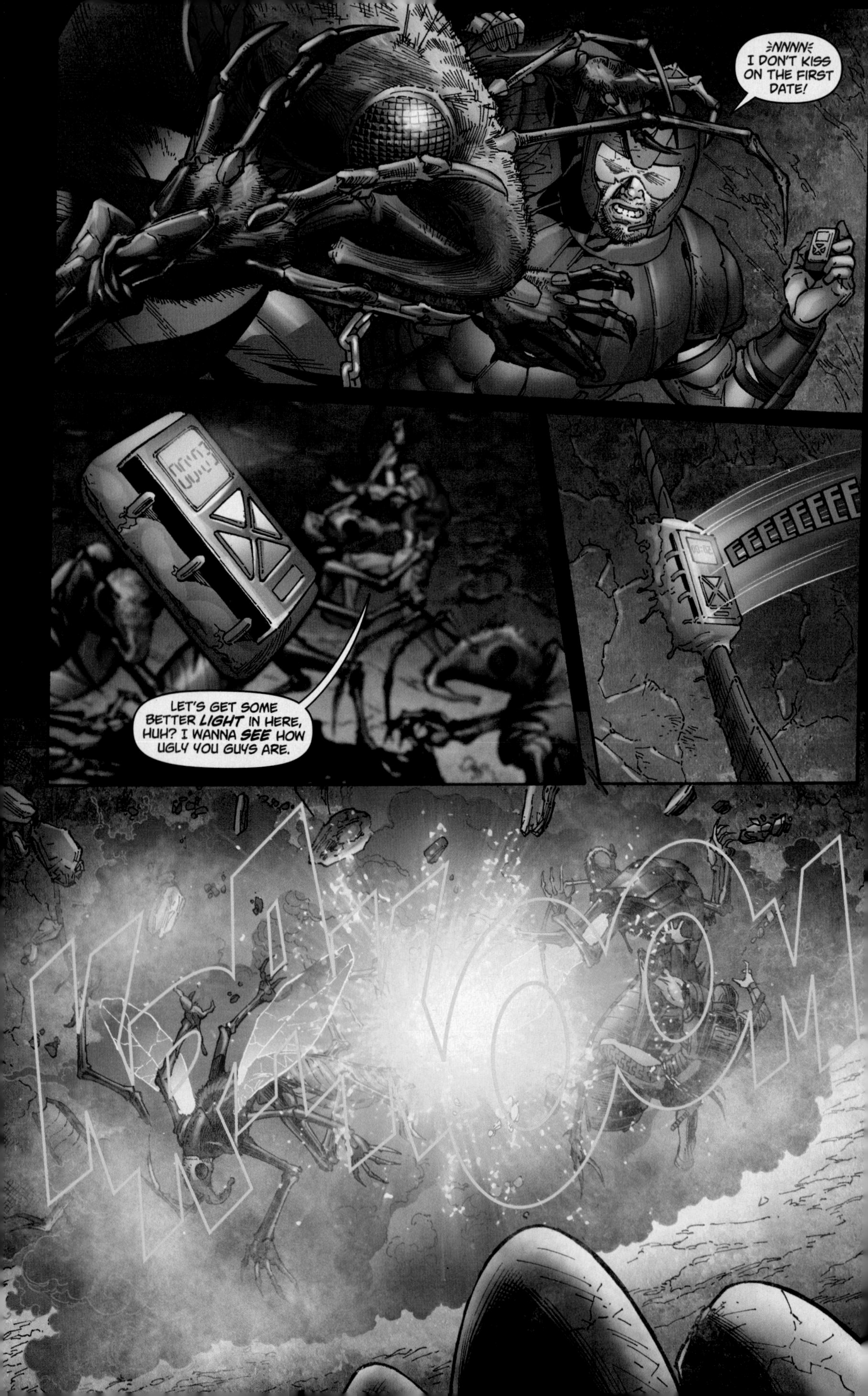

=NNNN= I DON'T KISS ON THE FIRST DATE!
LET'S GET SOME BETTER *LIGHT* IN HERE, HUH? I WANNA *SEE* HOW UGLY YOU GUYS ARE.
EEEEEEEE
KWHHOOOM

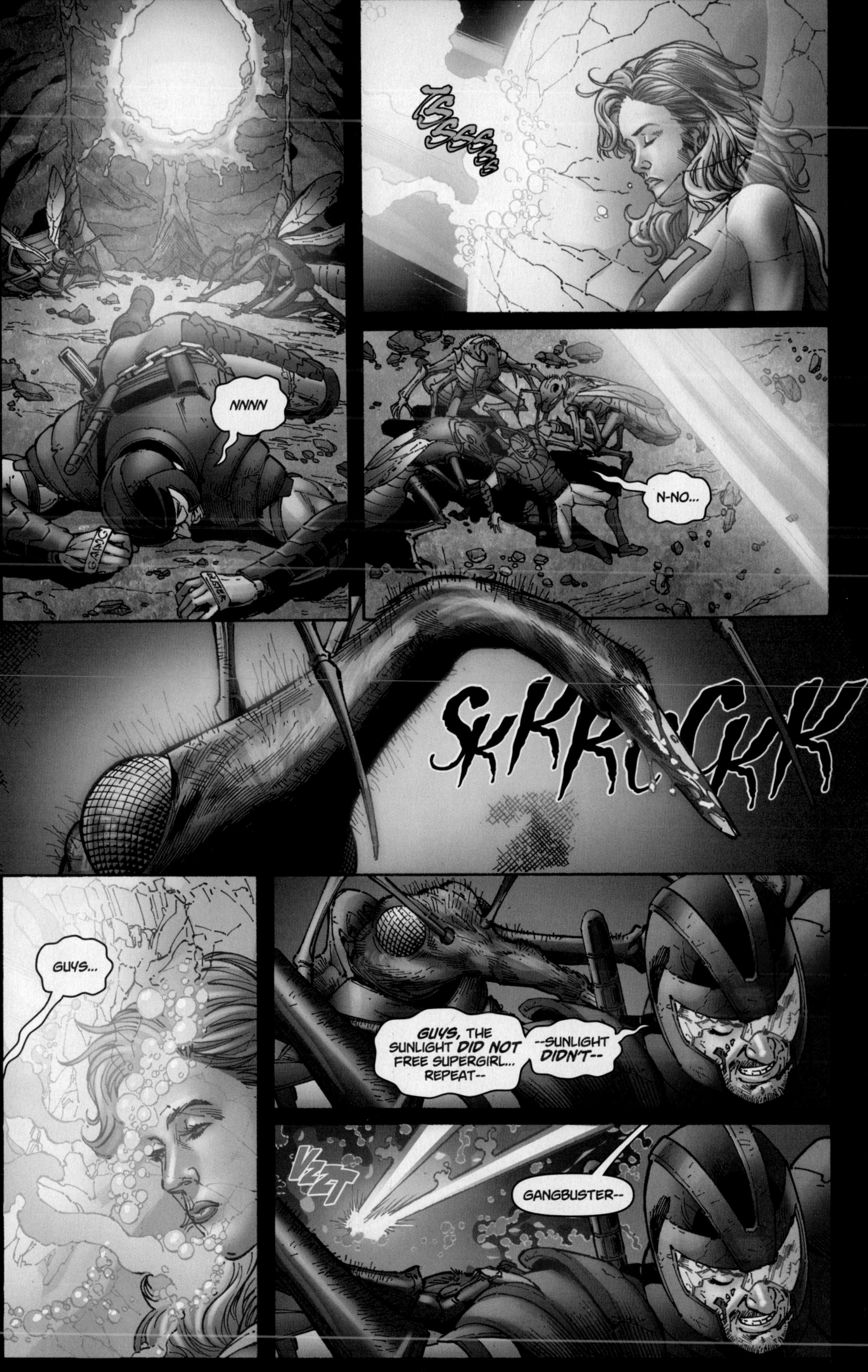
TSSSSSS
NNNN
N-NO...
SKKRCKK
GUYS...
GUYS, THE SUNLIGHT DID NOT FREE SUPERGIRL... REPEAT--
--SUNLIGHT DIDN'T--
VZZT
GANGBUSTER--

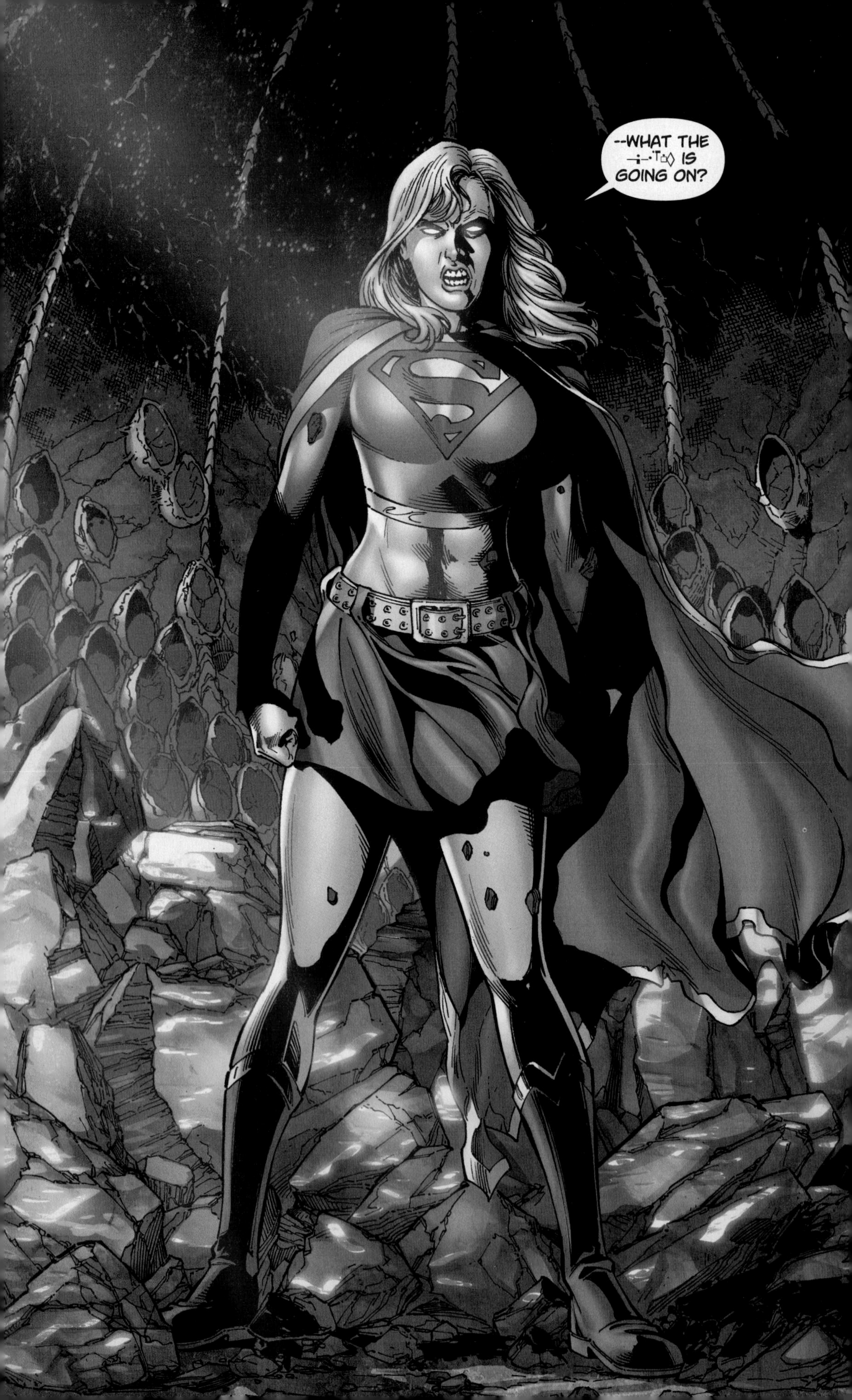
--WHAT THE
IS
GOING ON?

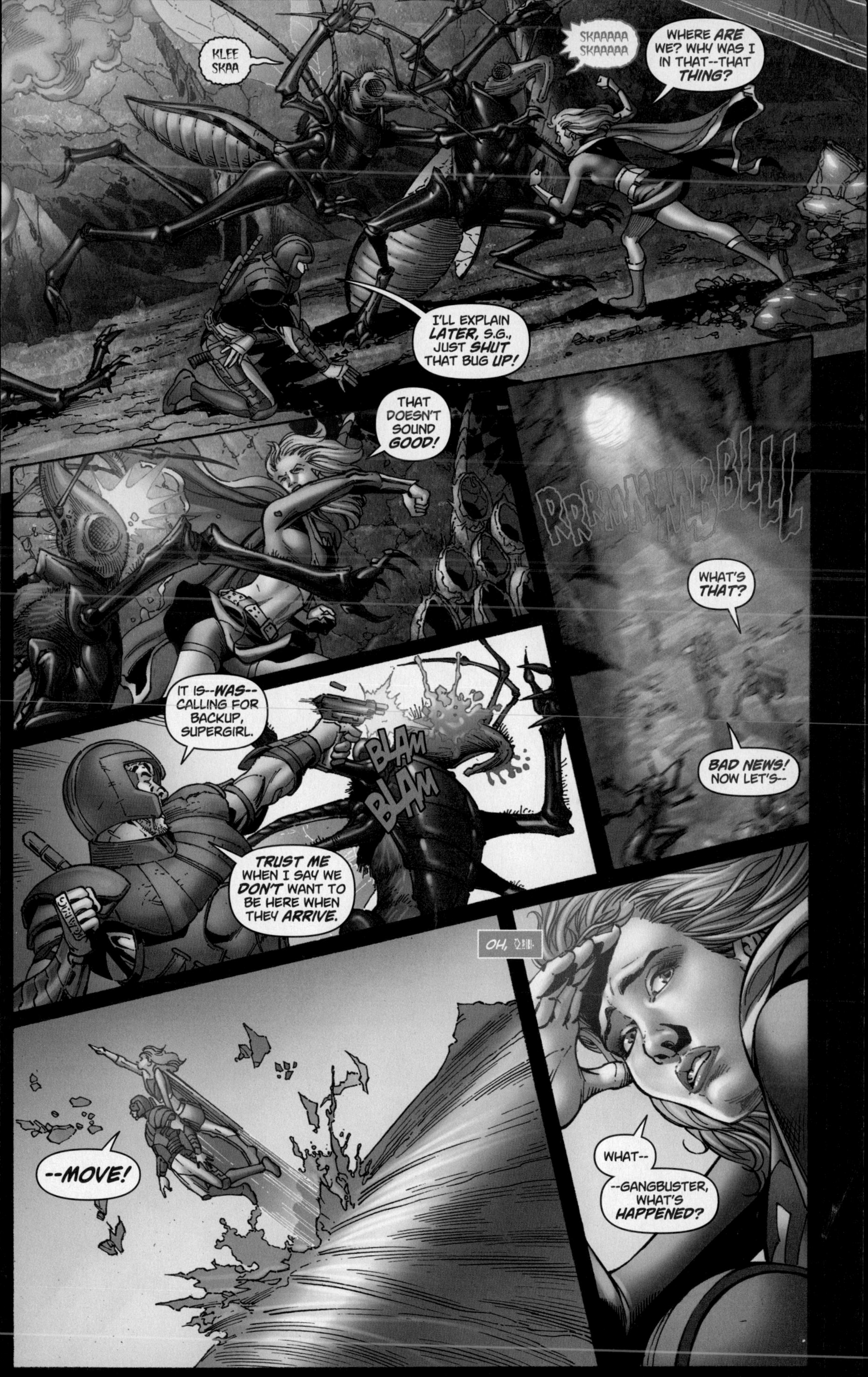

KLEE SKAA
SKAAAAA SKAAAAA
WHERE ARE WE? WHY WAS I IN THAT--THAT THING?
I'LL EXPLAIN LATER, S.G., JUST SHUT THAT BUG UP!
THAT DOESN'T SOUND GOOD!
RRRMMMMBLLL
WHAT'S THAT?
BAD NEWS! NOW LET'S--
IT IS--WAS--CALLING FOR BACKUP, SUPERGIRL.
BLAM
BLAM
TRUST ME WHEN I SAY WE DON'T WANT TO BE HERE WHEN THEY ARRIVE.
--MOVE!
WHAT--
--GANGBUSTER, WHAT'S HAPPENED?

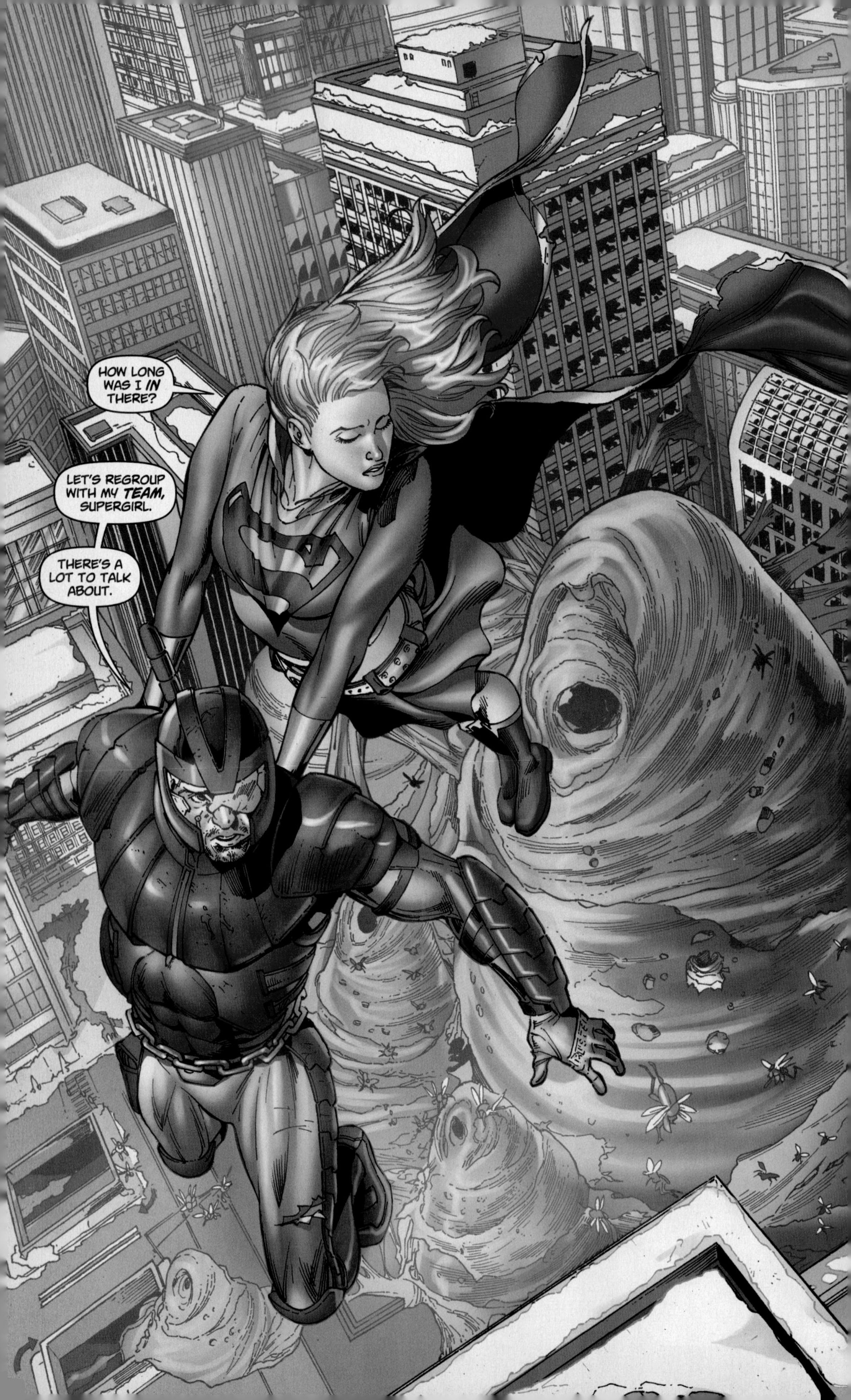
HOW LONG WAS I *IN* THERE?
LET'S REGROUP WITH MY **TEAM,** SUPERGIRL.
THERE'S A LOT TO TALK ABOUT.

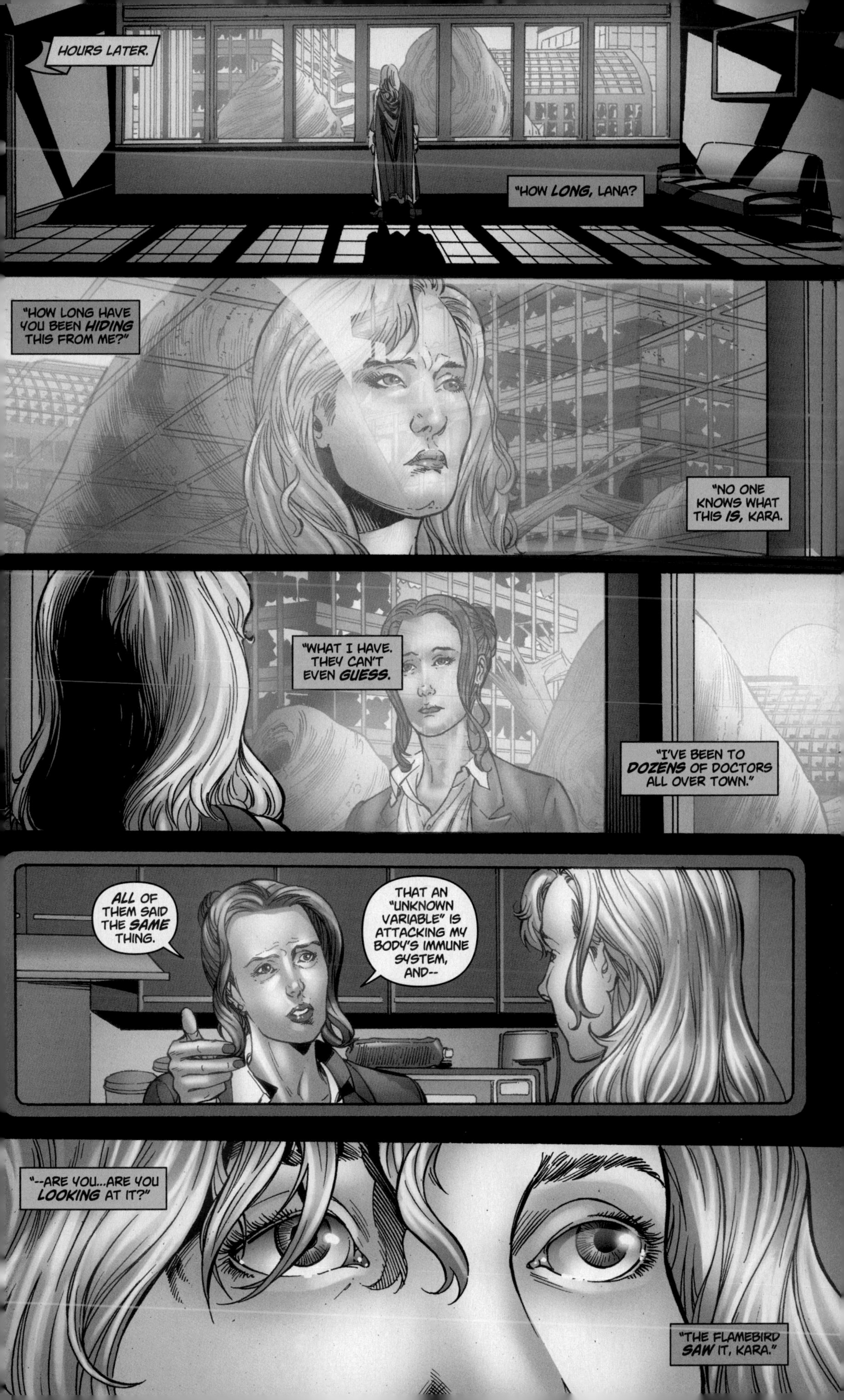
HOURS LATER.
"HOW LONG, LANA?
"HOW LONG HAVE YOU BEEN HIDING THIS FROM ME?"
"NO ONE KNOWS WHAT THIS IS, KARA.
"WHAT I HAVE. THEY CAN'T EVEN GUESS.
"I'VE BEEN TO DOZENS OF DOCTORS ALL OVER TOWN."
ALL OF THEM SAID THE SAME THING.
THAT AN "UNKNOWN VARIABLE" IS ATTACKING MY BODY'S IMMUNE SYSTEM, AND--
"--ARE YOU...ARE YOU LOOKING AT IT?"
"THE FLAMEBIRD SAW IT, KARA."

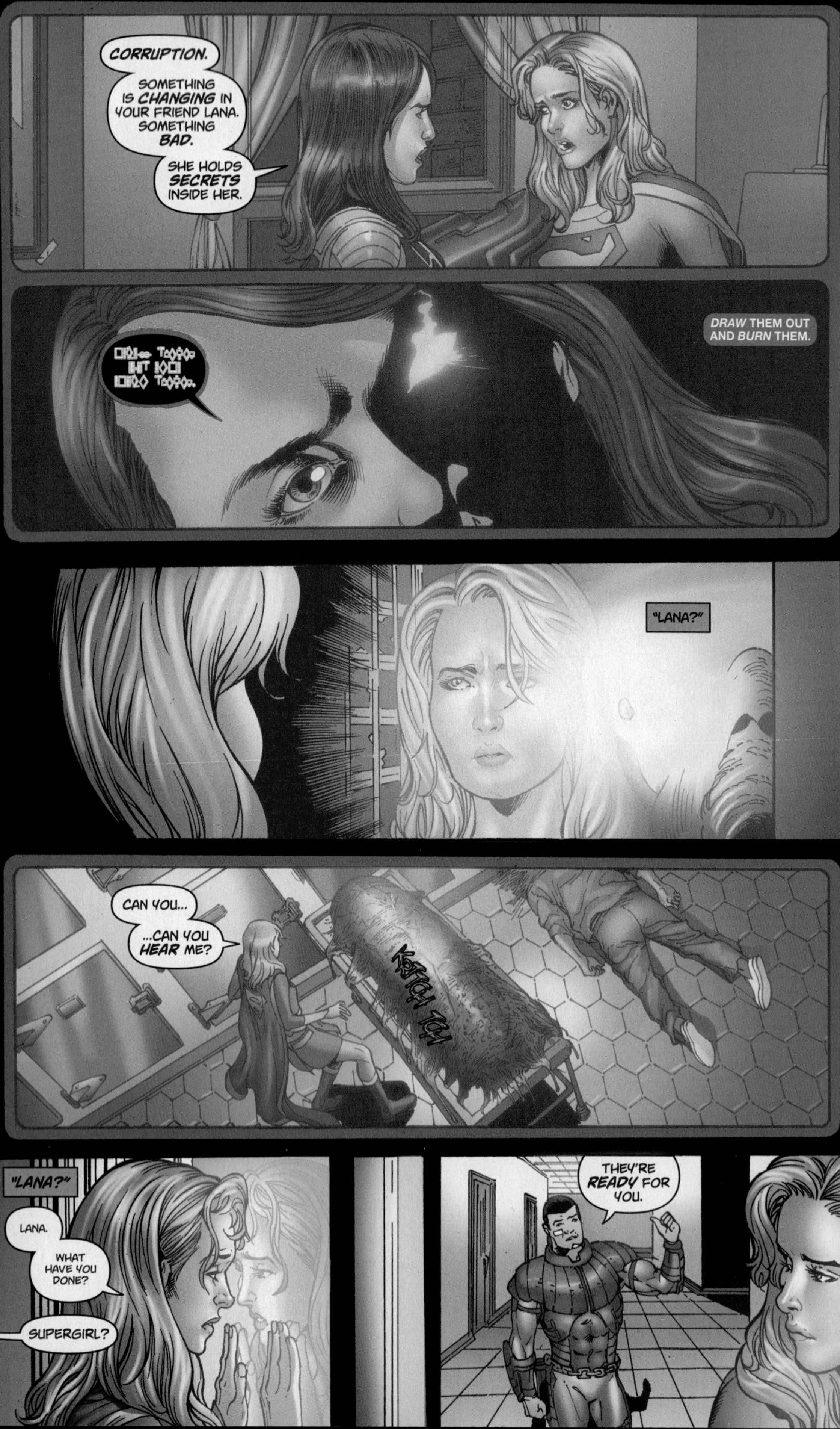

CORRUPTION.
SOMETHING IS CHANGING IN YOUR FRIEND LANA. SOMETHING BAD.
SHE HOLDS SECRETS INSIDE HER.
DRAW THEM OUT AND BURN THEM.
"LANA?"
CAN YOU...
...CAN YOU HEAR ME?
"LANA?"
LANA.
WHAT HAVE YOU DONE?
SUPERGIRL?
THEY'RE READY FOR YOU.

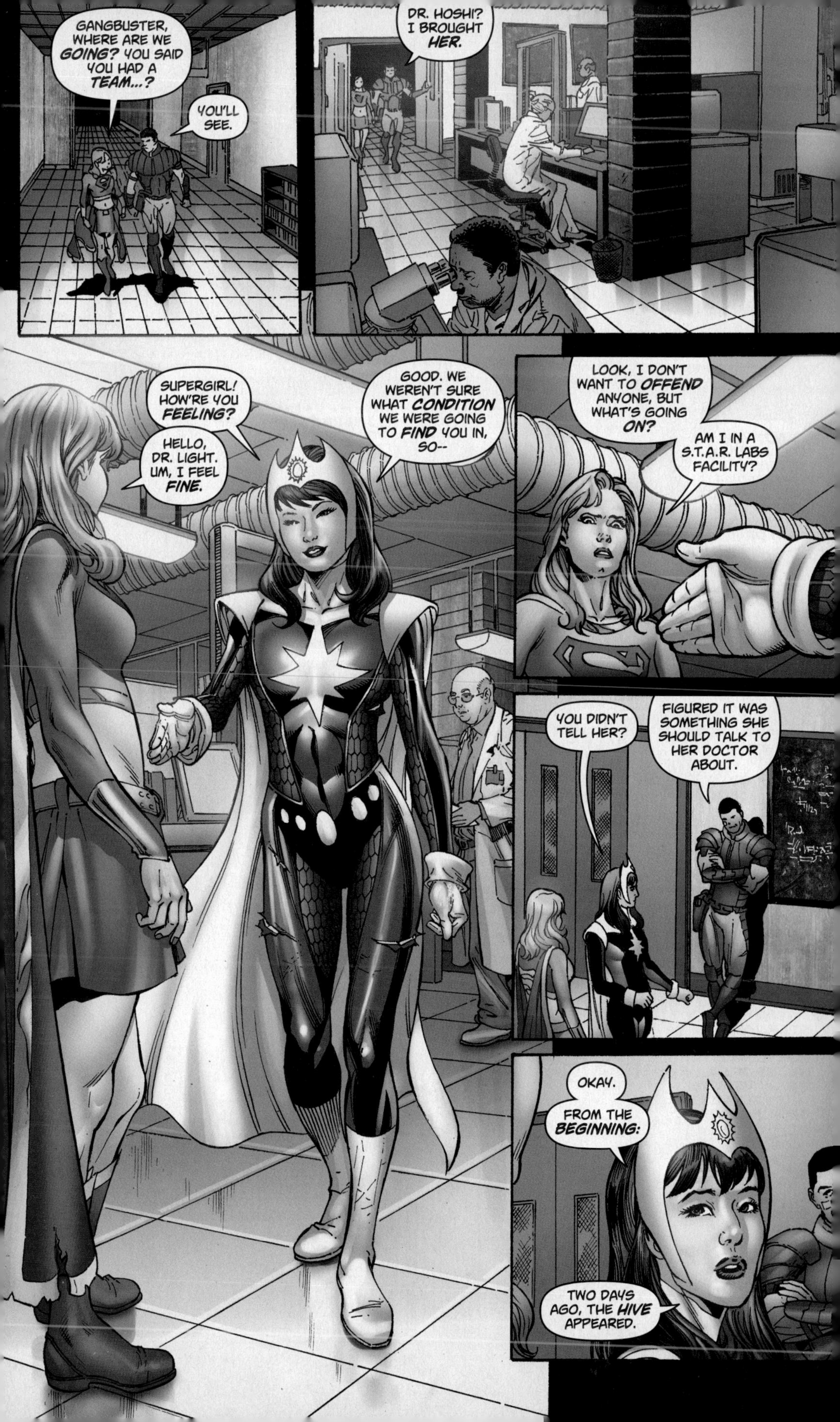
GANGBUSTER, WHERE ARE WE GOING? YOU SAID YOU HAD A TEAM...?
YOU'LL SEE.
DR. HOSHI? I BROUGHT HER.
SUPERGIRL! HOW'RE YOU FEELING?
HELLO, DR. LIGHT. UM, I FEEL FINE.
GOOD. WE WEREN'T SURE WHAT CONDITION WE WERE GOING TO FIND YOU IN, SO--
LOOK, I DON'T WANT TO OFFEND ANYONE, BUT WHAT'S GOING ON?
AM I IN A S.T.A.R. LABS FACILITY?
YOU DIDN'T TELL HER?
FIGURED IT WAS SOMETHING SHE SHOULD TALK TO HER DOCTOR ABOUT.
OKAY.
FROM THE BEGINNING:
TWO DAYS AGO, THE HIVE APPEARED.

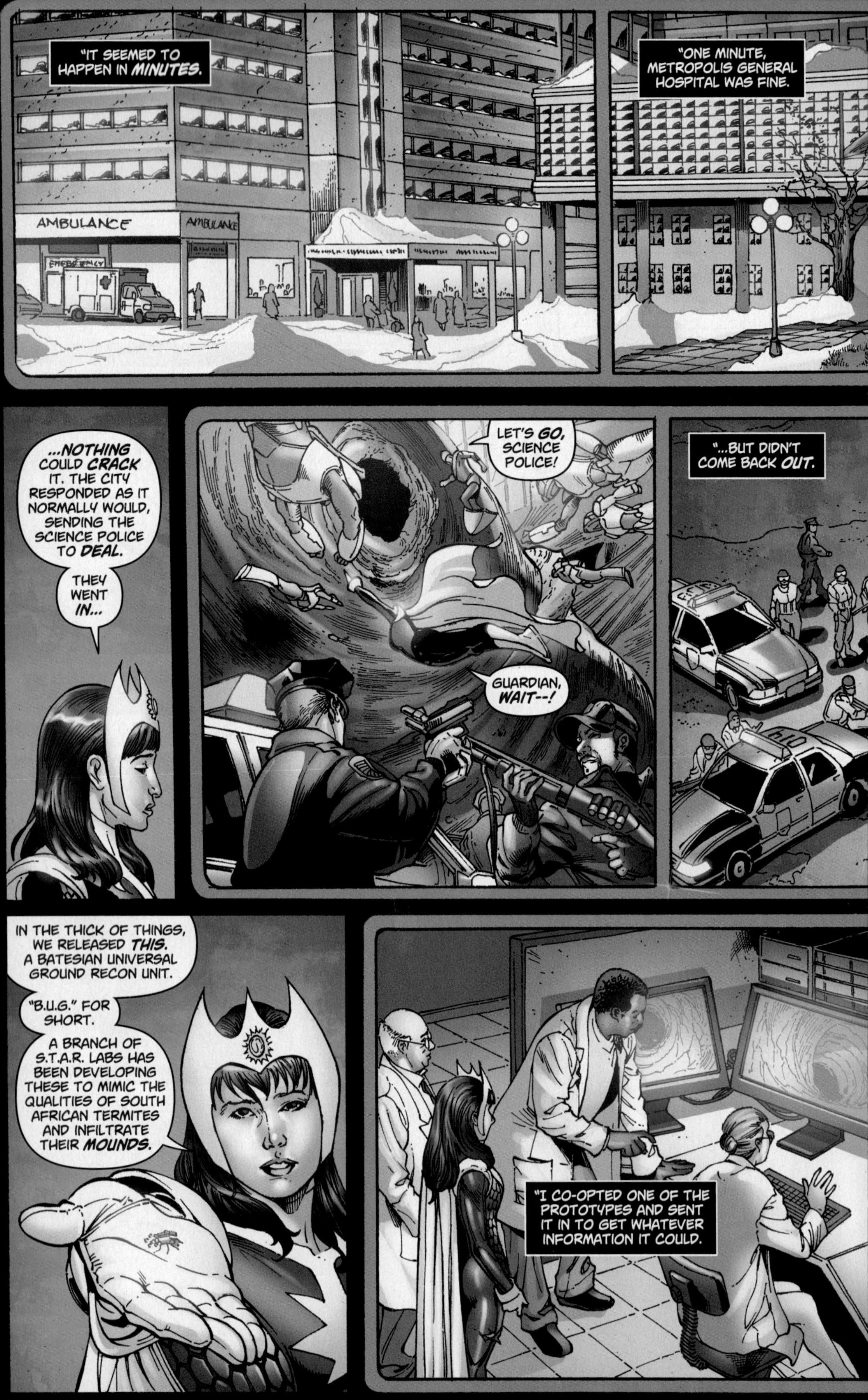
"IT SEEMED TO HAPPEN IN MINUTES.
"ONE MINUTE, METROPOLIS GENERAL HOSPITAL WAS FINE.
AMBULANCE
AMBULANCE
...NOTHING COULD CRACK IT. THE CITY RESPONDED AS IT NORMALLY WOULD, SENDING THE SCIENCE POLICE TO DEAL.
THEY WENT IN...
LET'S GO, SCIENCE POLICE!
GUARDIAN, WAIT--!
"...BUT DIDN'T COME BACK OUT.
IN THE THICK OF THINGS, WE RELEASED THIS. A BATESIAN UNIVERSAL GROUND RECON UNIT.
"B.U.G." FOR SHORT.
A BRANCH OF S.T.A.R. LABS HAS BEEN DEVELOPING THESE TO MIMIC THE QUALITIES OF SOUTH AFRICAN TERMITES AND INFILTRATE THEIR MOUNDS.
"I CO-OPTED ONE OF THE PROTOTYPES AND SENT IT IN TO GET WHATEVER INFORMATION IT COULD.

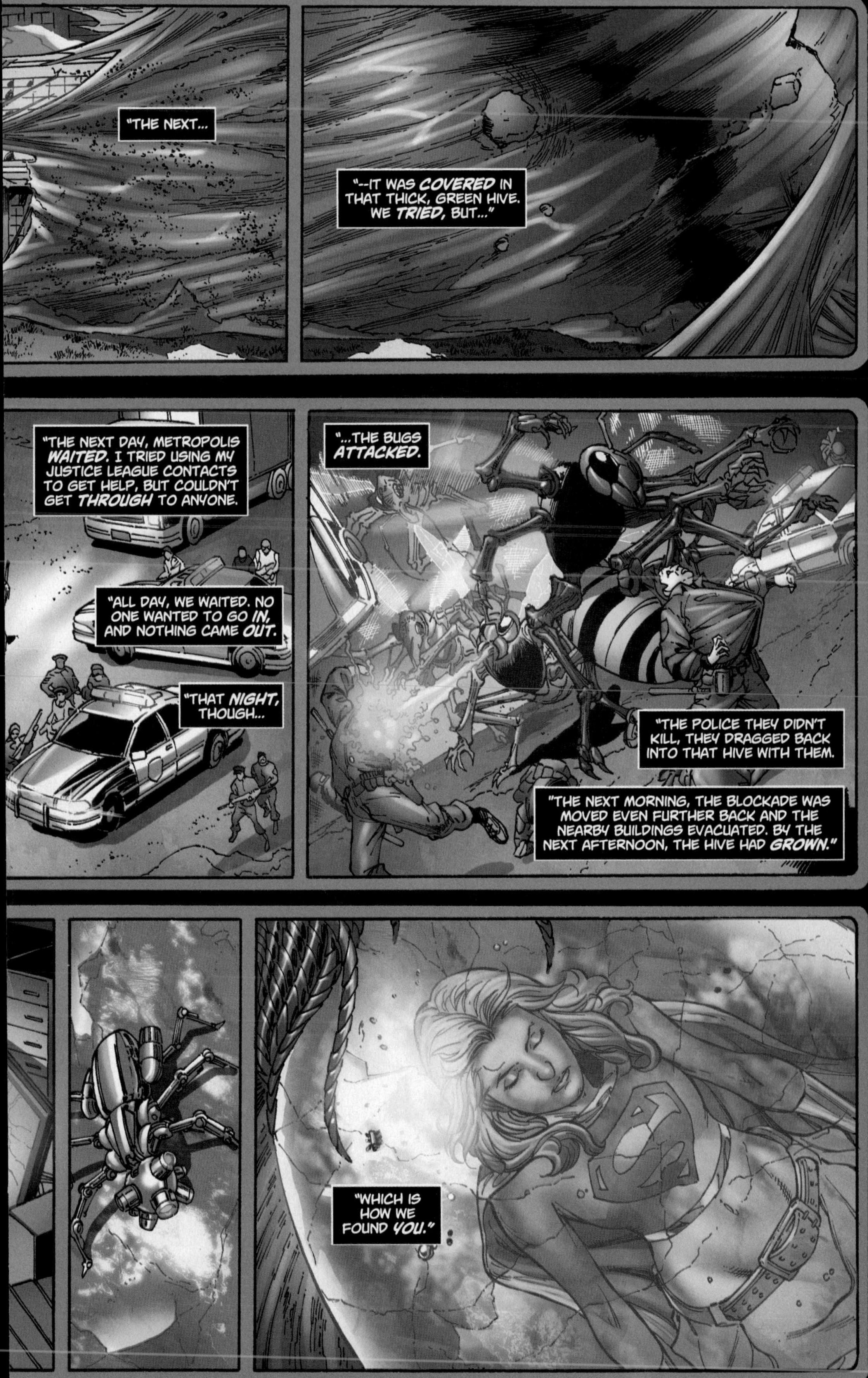
"THE NEXT...
"--IT WAS COVERED IN THAT THICK, GREEN HIVE. WE TRIED, BUT..."
"THE NEXT DAY, METROPOLIS WAITED. I TRIED USING MY JUSTICE LEAGUE CONTACTS TO GET HELP, BUT COULDN'T GET THROUGH TO ANYONE.
"ALL DAY, WE WAITED. NO ONE WANTED TO GO IN, AND NOTHING CAME OUT.
"THAT NIGHT, THOUGH...
"...THE BUGS ATTACKED.
"THE POLICE THEY DIDN'T KILL, THEY DRAGGED BACK INTO THAT HIVE WITH THEM.
"THE NEXT MORNING, THE BLOCKADE WAS MOVED EVEN FURTHER BACK AND THE NEARBY BUILDINGS EVACUATED. BY THE NEXT AFTERNOON, THE HIVE HAD GROWN."
"WHICH IS HOW WE FOUND YOU."

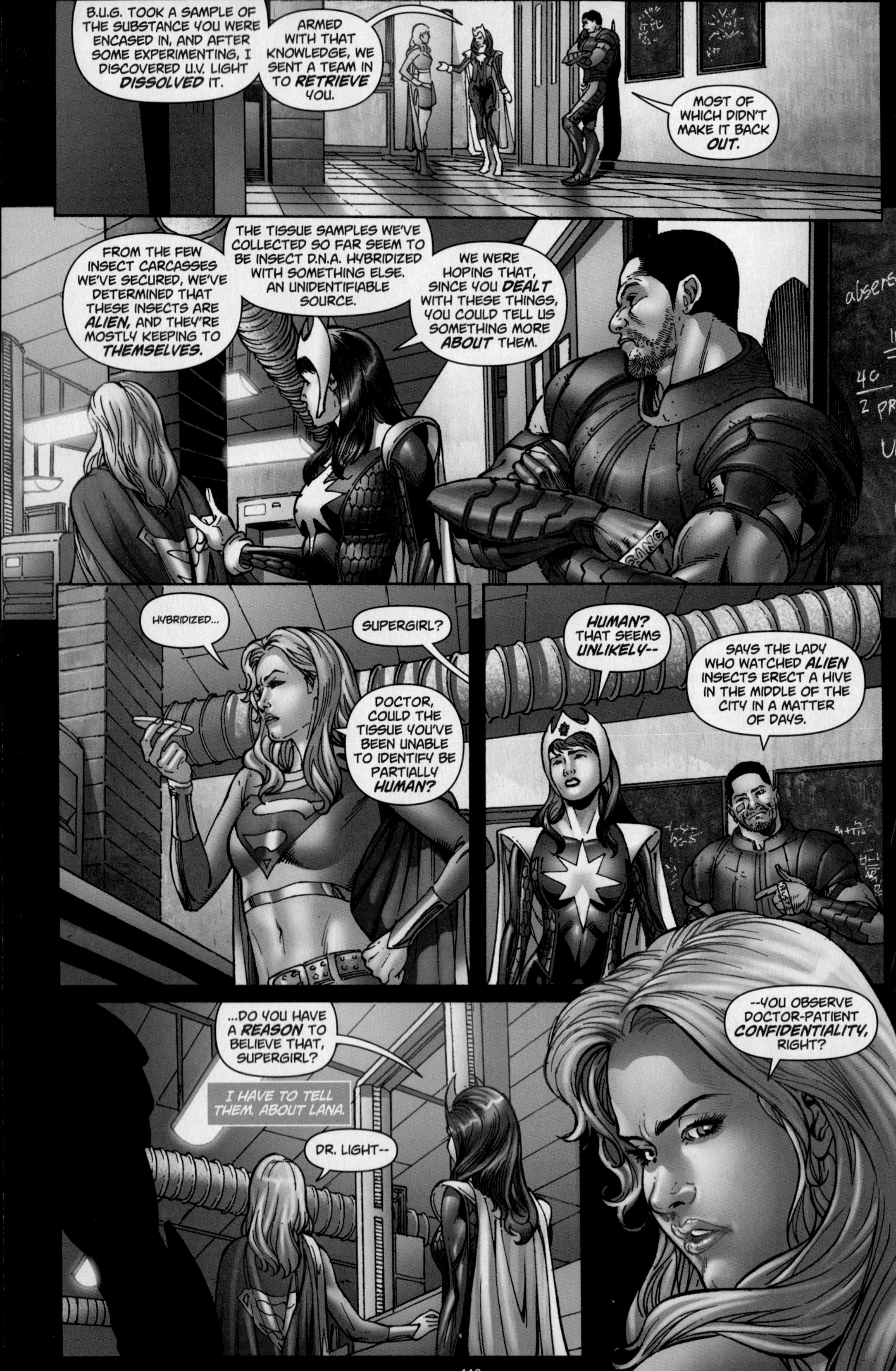
B.U.G. TOOK A SAMPLE OF THE SUBSTANCE YOU WERE ENCASED IN, AND AFTER SOME EXPERIMENTING, I DISCOVERED U.V. LIGHT DISSOLVED IT.
ARMED WITH THAT KNOWLEDGE, WE SENT A TEAM IN TO RETRIEVE YOU.
MOST OF WHICH DIDN'T MAKE IT BACK OUT.
FROM THE FEW INSECT CARCASSES WE'VE SECURED, WE'VE DETERMINED THAT THESE INSECTS ARE ALIEN, AND THEY'RE MOSTLY KEEPING TO THEMSELVES.
THE TISSUE SAMPLES WE'VE COLLECTED SO FAR SEEM TO BE INSECT D.N.A. HYBRIDIZED WITH SOMETHING ELSE. AN UNIDENTIFIABLE SOURCE.
WE WERE HOPING THAT, SINCE YOU DEALT WITH THESE THINGS, YOU COULD TELL US SOMETHING MORE ABOUT THEM.
HYBRIDIZED...
SUPERGIRL?
DOCTOR, COULD THE TISSUE YOU'VE BEEN UNABLE TO IDENTIFY BE PARTIALLY HUMAN?
HUMAN? THAT SEEMS UNLIKELY--
SAYS THE LADY WHO WATCHED ALIEN INSECTS ERECT A HIVE IN THE MIDDLE OF THE CITY IN A MATTER OF DAYS.
...DO YOU HAVE A REASON TO BELIEVE THAT, SUPERGIRL?
I HAVE TO TELL THEM. ABOUT LANA.
DR. LIGHT--
--YOU OBSERVE DOCTOR-PATIENT CONFIDENTIALITY, RIGHT?

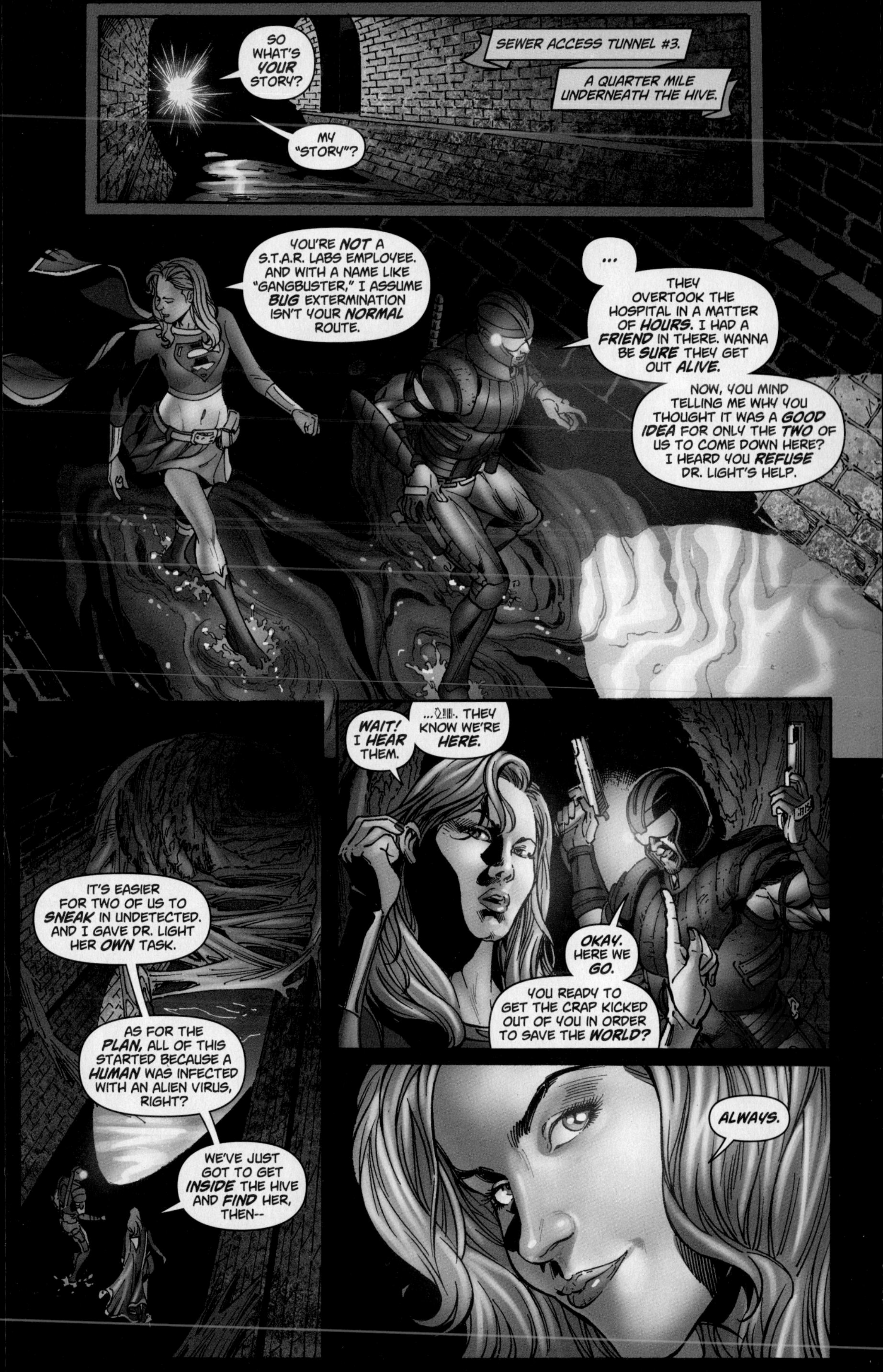
SO WHAT'S YOUR STORY?
SEWER ACCESS TUNNEL #3.
A QUARTER MILE UNDERNEATH THE HIVE.
MY "STORY"?
YOU'RE NOT A S.T.A.R. LABS EMPLOYEE. AND WITH A NAME LIKE "GANGBUSTER," I ASSUME BUG EXTERMINATION ISN'T YOUR NORMAL ROUTE.
...
THEY OVERTOOK THE HOSPITAL IN A MATTER OF HOURS. I HAD A FRIEND IN THERE. WANNA BE SURE THEY GET OUT ALIVE.
NOW, YOU MIND TELLING ME WHY YOU THOUGHT IT WAS A GOOD IDEA FOR ONLY THE TWO OF US TO COME DOWN HERE? I HEARD YOU REFUSE DR. LIGHT'S HELP.
IT'S EASIER FOR TWO OF US TO SNEAK IN UNDETECTED. AND I GAVE DR. LIGHT HER OWN TASK.
AS FOR THE PLAN, ALL OF THIS STARTED BECAUSE A HUMAN WAS INFECTED WITH AN ALIEN VIRUS, RIGHT?
WE'VE JUST GOT TO GET INSIDE THE HIVE AND FIND HER, THEN--
WAIT! I HEAR THEM.
... THEY KNOW WE'RE HERE.
OKAY. HERE WE GO.
YOU READY TO GET THE CRAP KICKED OUT OF YOU IN ORDER TO SAVE THE WORLD?
ALWAYS.

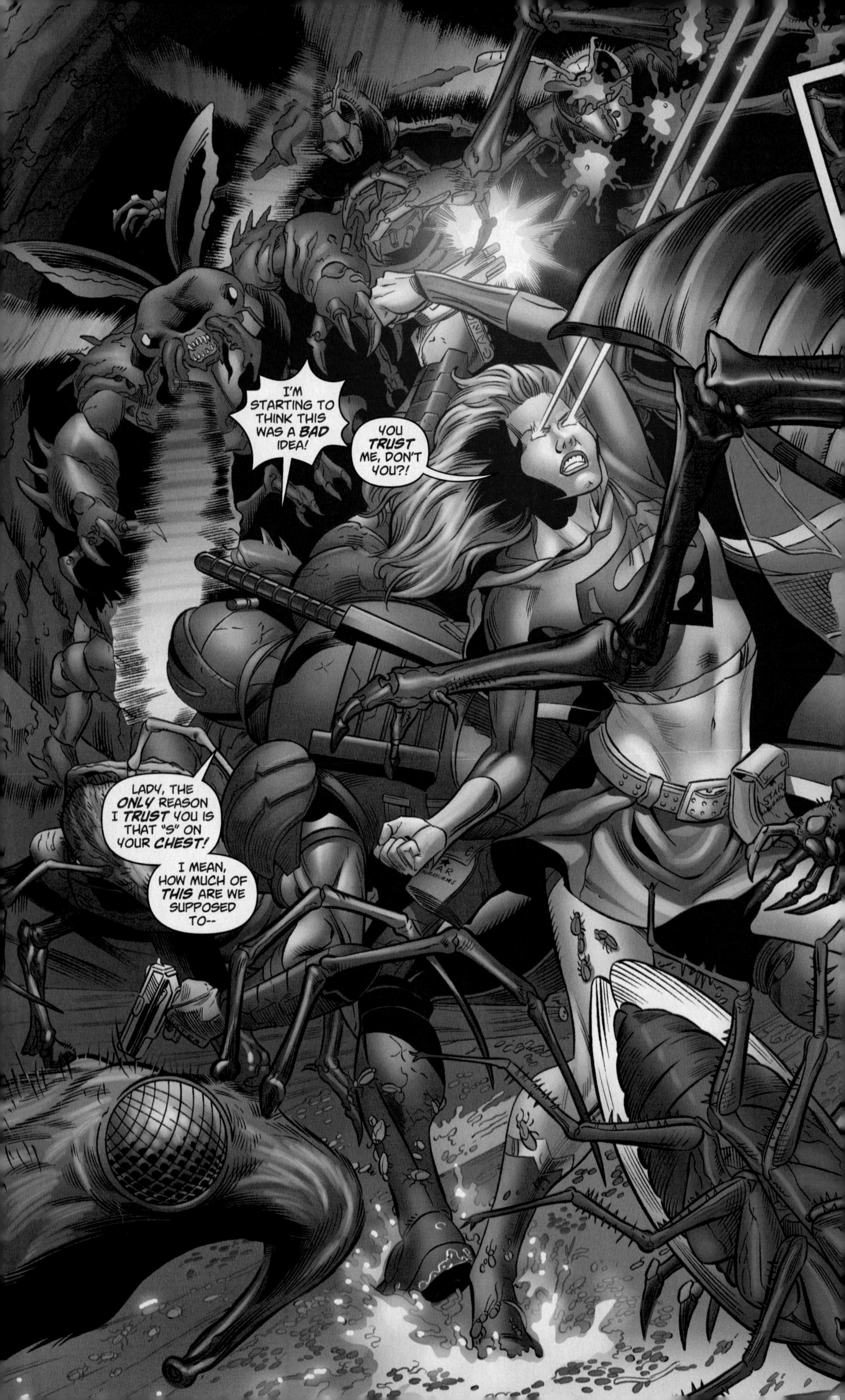
I'M STARTING TO THINK THIS WAS A BAD IDEA!
YOU TRUST ME, DON'T YOU?!
LADY, THE ONLY REASON I TRUST YOU IS THAT "S" ON YOUR CHEST!
I MEAN, HOW MUCH OF THIS ARE WE SUPPOSED TO--

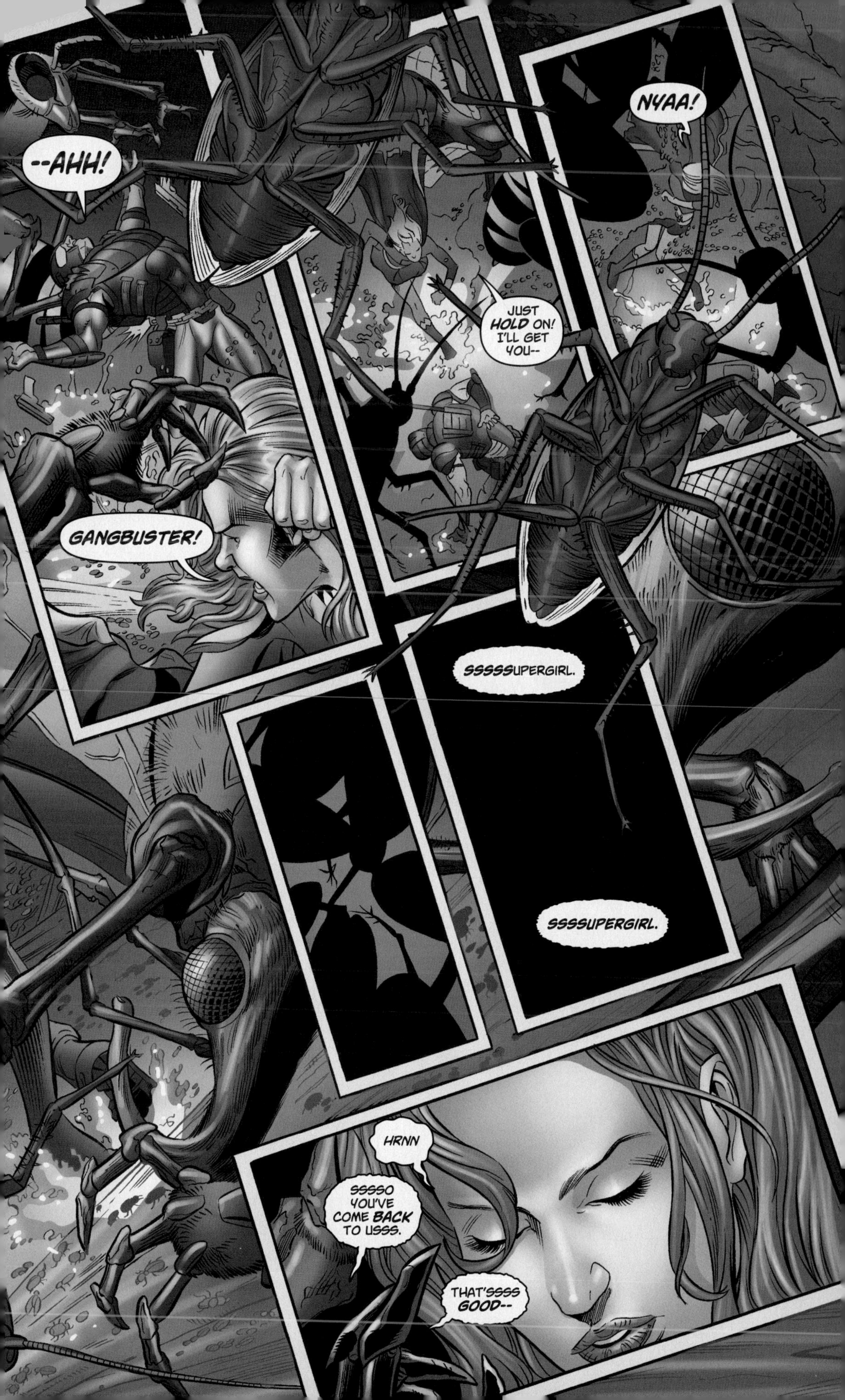
--AHH!
NYAA!
JUST HOLD ON! I'LL GET YOU--
GANGBUSTER!
SSSSSUPERGIRL.
SSSSUPERGIRL.
HRNN
SSSSO YOU'VE COME BACK TO USSS.
THAT'SSSS GOOD--

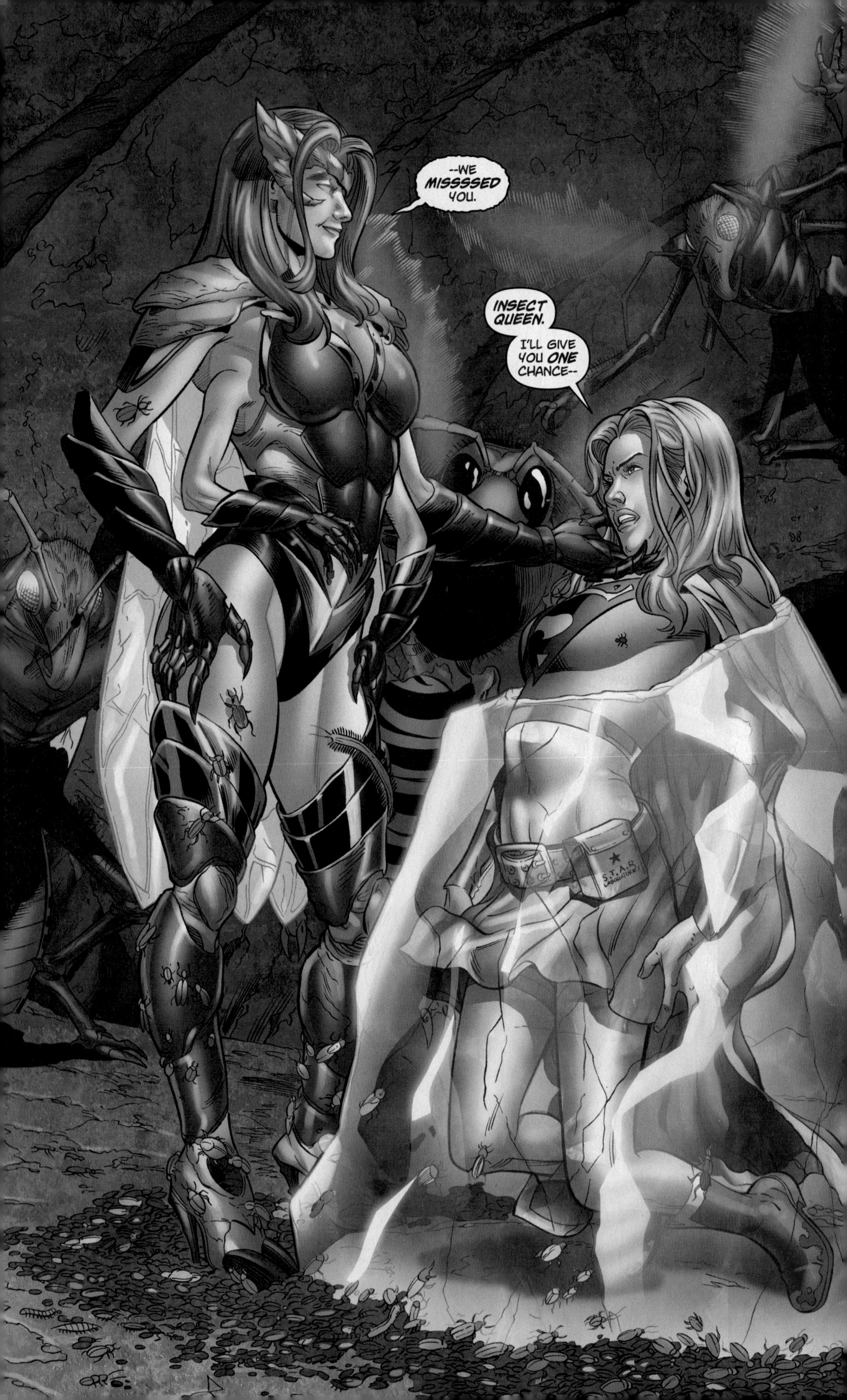
--WE MISSSSED YOU.
INSECT QUEEN.
I'LL GIVE YOU ONE CHANCE--

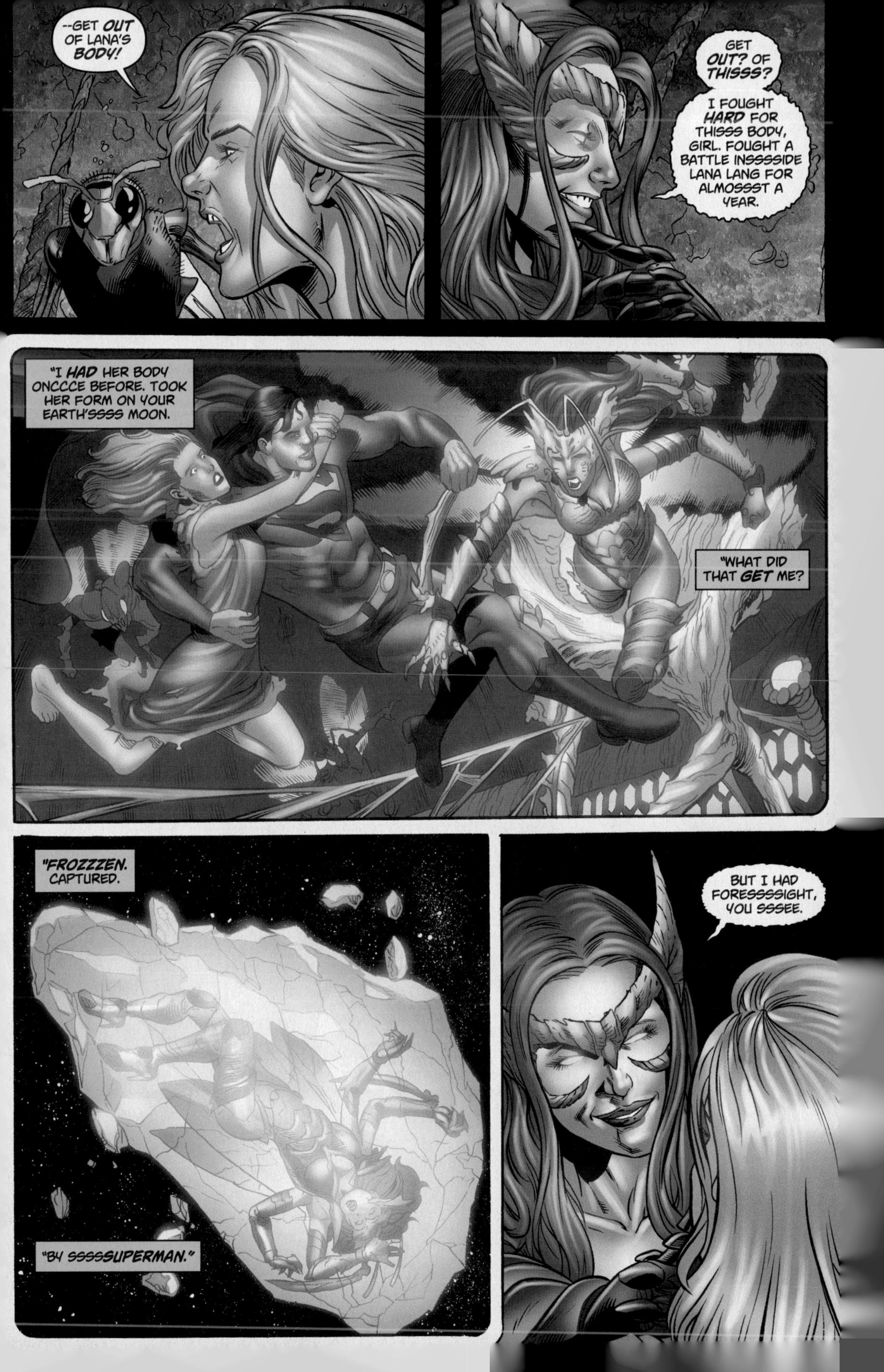
--GET OUT OF LANA'S BODY!
GET OUT? OF THISSS?
I FOUGHT HARD FOR THISSS BODY, GIRL. FOUGHT A BATTLE INSSSSIDE LANA LANG FOR ALMOSSST A YEAR.
"I HAD HER BODY ONCCCE BEFORE. TOOK HER FORM ON YOUR EARTH'SSSS MOON.
"WHAT DID THAT GET ME?
"FROZZZEN. CAPTURED.
"BY SSSSSUPERMAN."
BUT I HAD FORESSSSIGHT, YOU SSSEE.

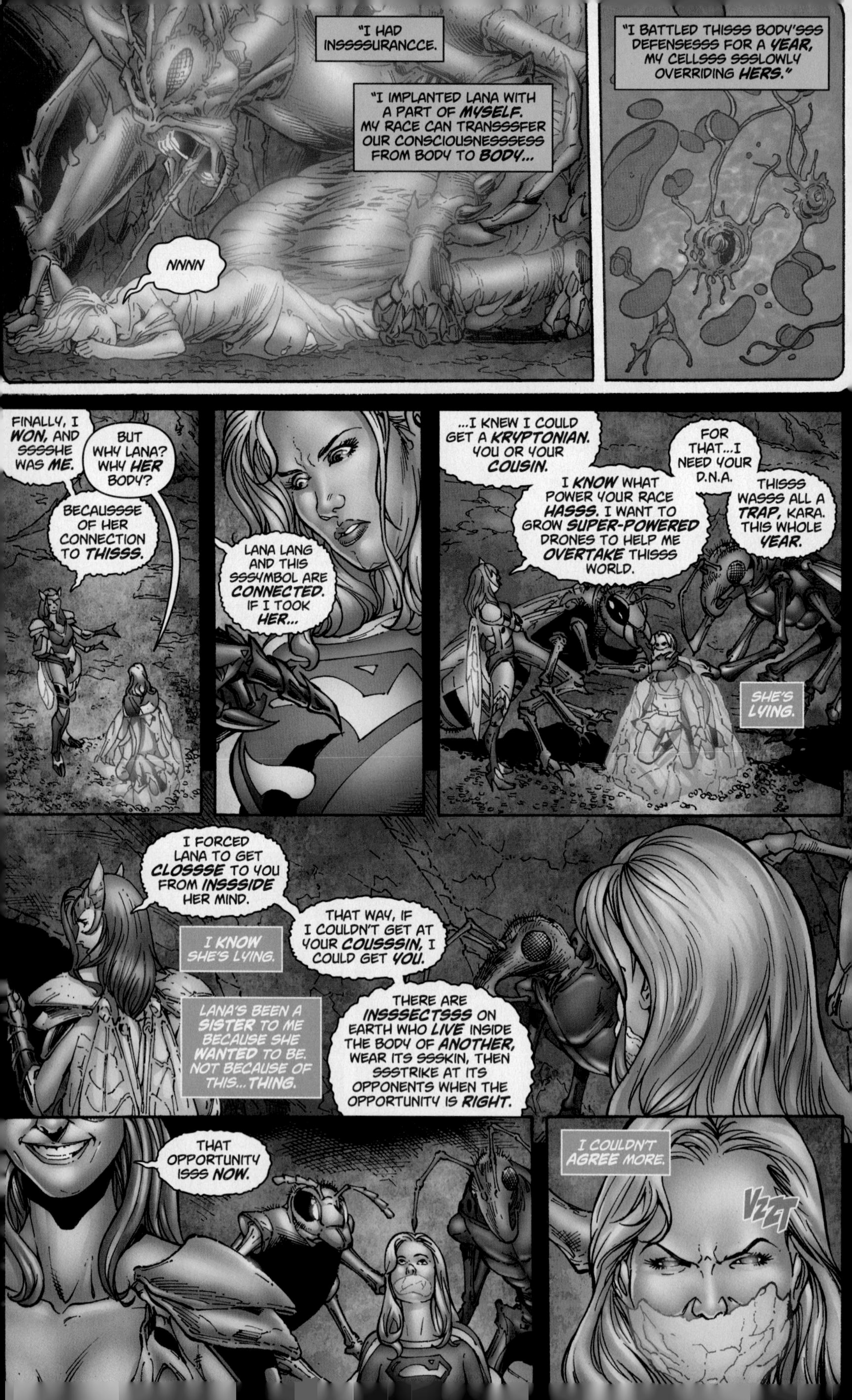
"I HAD INSSSSURANCCE.
"I IMPLANTED LANA WITH A PART OF MYSELF. MY RACE CAN TRANSSSFER OUR CONSCIOUSNESSSESS FROM BODY TO BODY...
NNNN
"I BATTLED THISSS BODY'SSS DEFENSESSS FOR A YEAR, MY CELLSSS SSSLOWLY OVERRIDING HERS."
FINALLY, I WON, AND SSSSHE WAS ME.
BUT WHY LANA? WHY HER BODY?
BECAUSSSE OF HER CONNECTION TO THISSS.
LANA LANG AND THIS SSSYMBOL ARE CONNECTED. IF I TOOK HER...
...I KNEW I COULD GET A KRYPTONIAN. YOU OR YOUR COUSIN.
I KNOW WHAT POWER YOUR RACE HASSS. I WANT TO GROW SUPER-POWERED DRONES TO HELP ME OVERTAKE THISSS WORLD.
FOR THAT...I NEED YOUR D.N.A.
THISSS WASSS ALL A TRAP, KARA. THIS WHOLE YEAR.
SHE'S LYING.
I FORCED LANA TO GET CLOSSSE TO YOU FROM INSSSIDE HER MIND.
I KNOW SHE'S LYING.
THAT WAY, IF I COULDN'T GET AT YOUR COUSSSIN, I COULD GET YOU.
LANA'S BEEN A SISTER TO ME BECAUSE SHE WANTED TO BE. NOT BECAUSE OF THIS...THING.
THERE ARE INSSSECTSSS ON EARTH WHO LIVE INSIDE THE BODY OF ANOTHER, WEAR ITS SSSKIN, THEN SSSTRIKE AT ITS OPPONENTS WHEN THE OPPORTUNITY IS RIGHT.
THAT OPPORTUNITY ISSS NOW.
I COULDN'T AGREE MORE.
VZZT

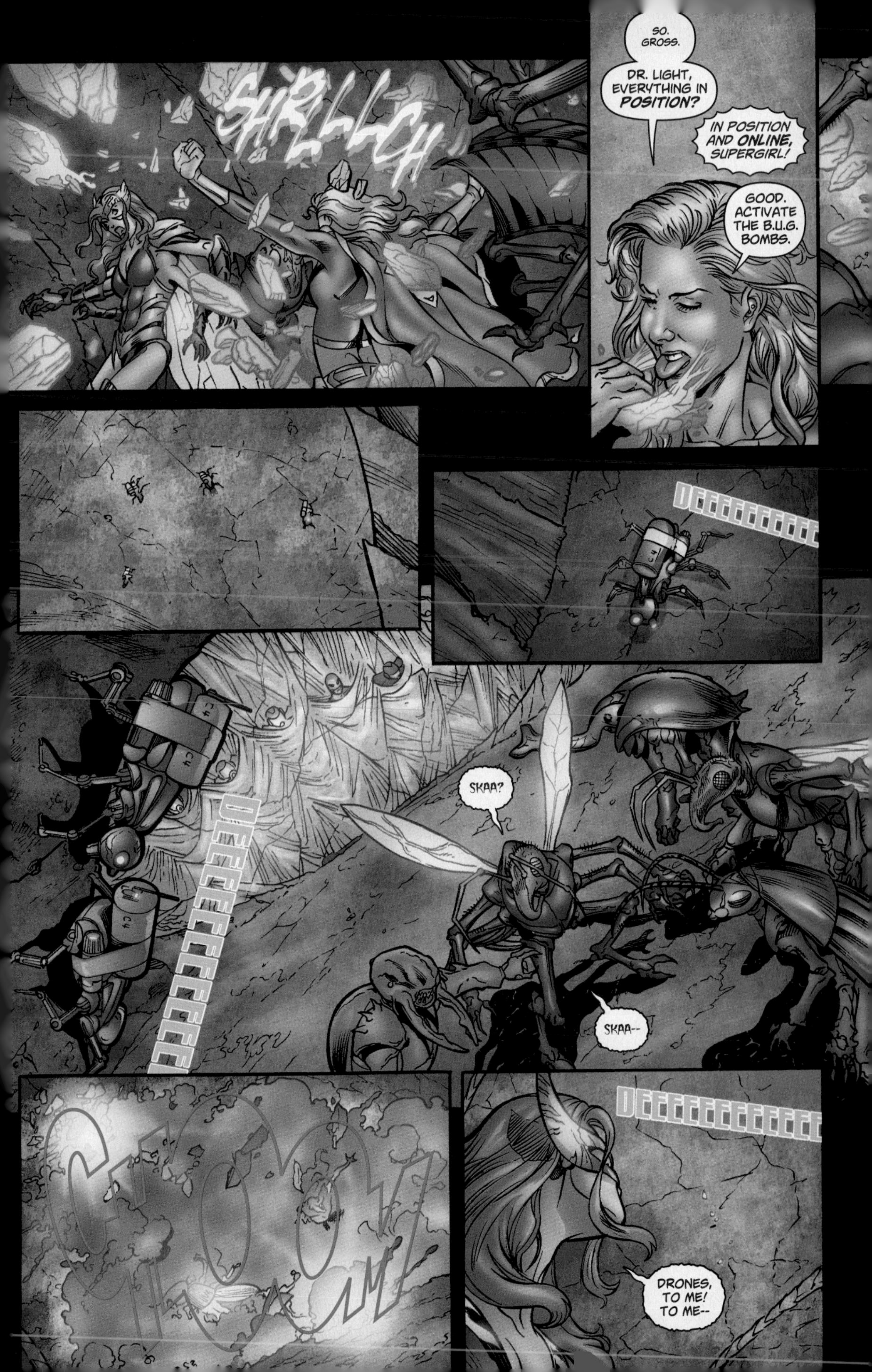
SHRLLLCH
SO. GROSS.
DR. LIGHT, EVERYTHING IN POSITION?
IN POSITION AND ONLINE, SUPERGIRL!
GOOD. ACTIVATE THE B.U.G. BOMBS.
DEEEEEEEEEEE
DEEEEEEEEEEEEEE
SKAA?
SKAA--
CHOOM
DEEEEEEEEEEEE
DRONES, TO ME! TO ME--

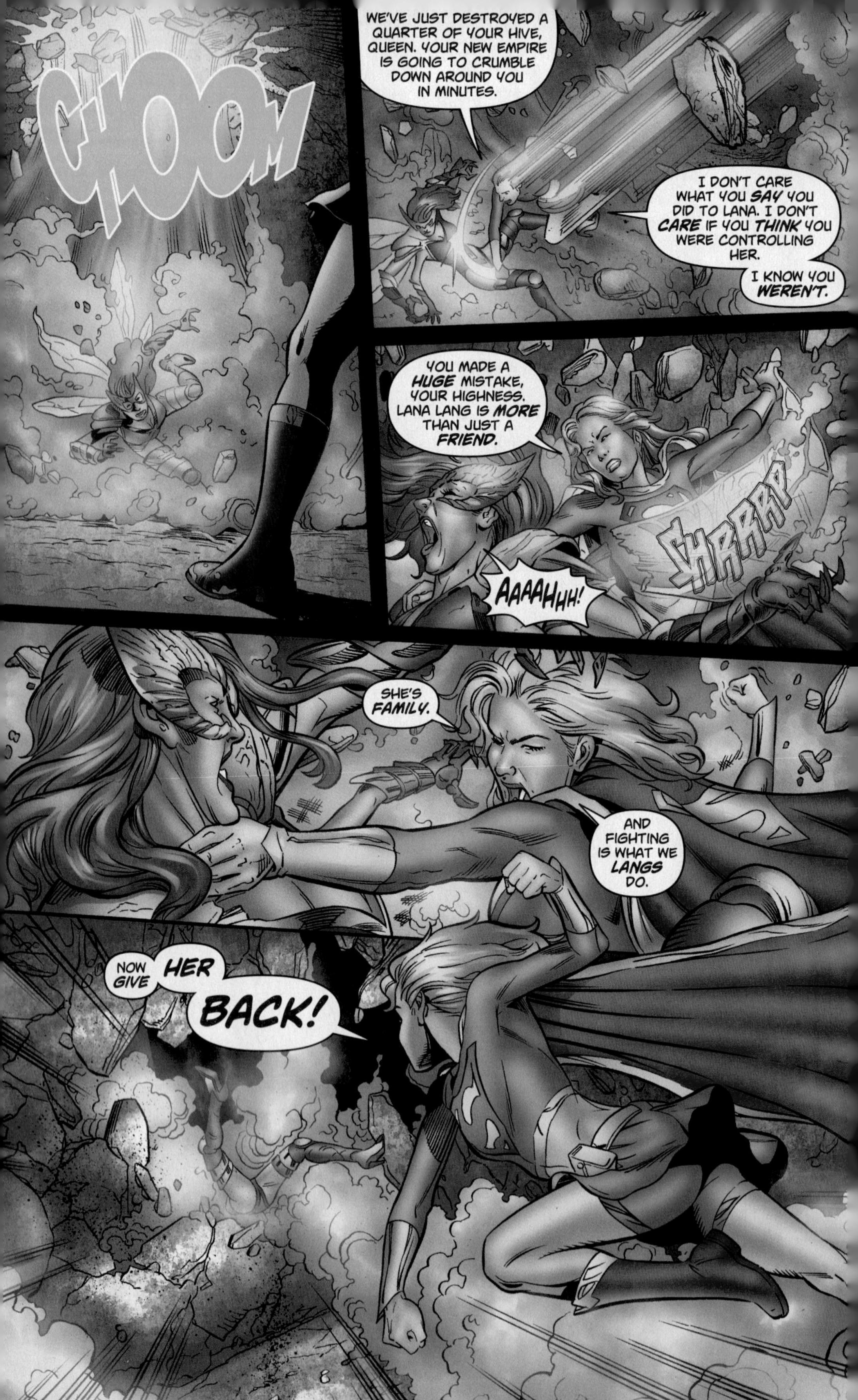
CHOOM
WE'VE JUST DESTROYED A QUARTER OF YOUR HIVE, QUEEN. YOUR NEW EMPIRE IS GOING TO CRUMBLE DOWN AROUND YOU IN MINUTES.
I DON'T CARE WHAT YOU SAY YOU DID TO LANA. I DON'T CARE IF YOU THINK YOU WERE CONTROLLING HER.
I KNOW YOU WEREN'T.
YOU MADE A HUGE MISTAKE, YOUR HIGHNESS. LANA LANG IS MORE THAN JUST A FRIEND.
SHRRRP
AAAAHHH!
SHE'S FAMILY.
AND FIGHTING IS WHAT WE LANGS DO.
NOW GIVE HER BACK!

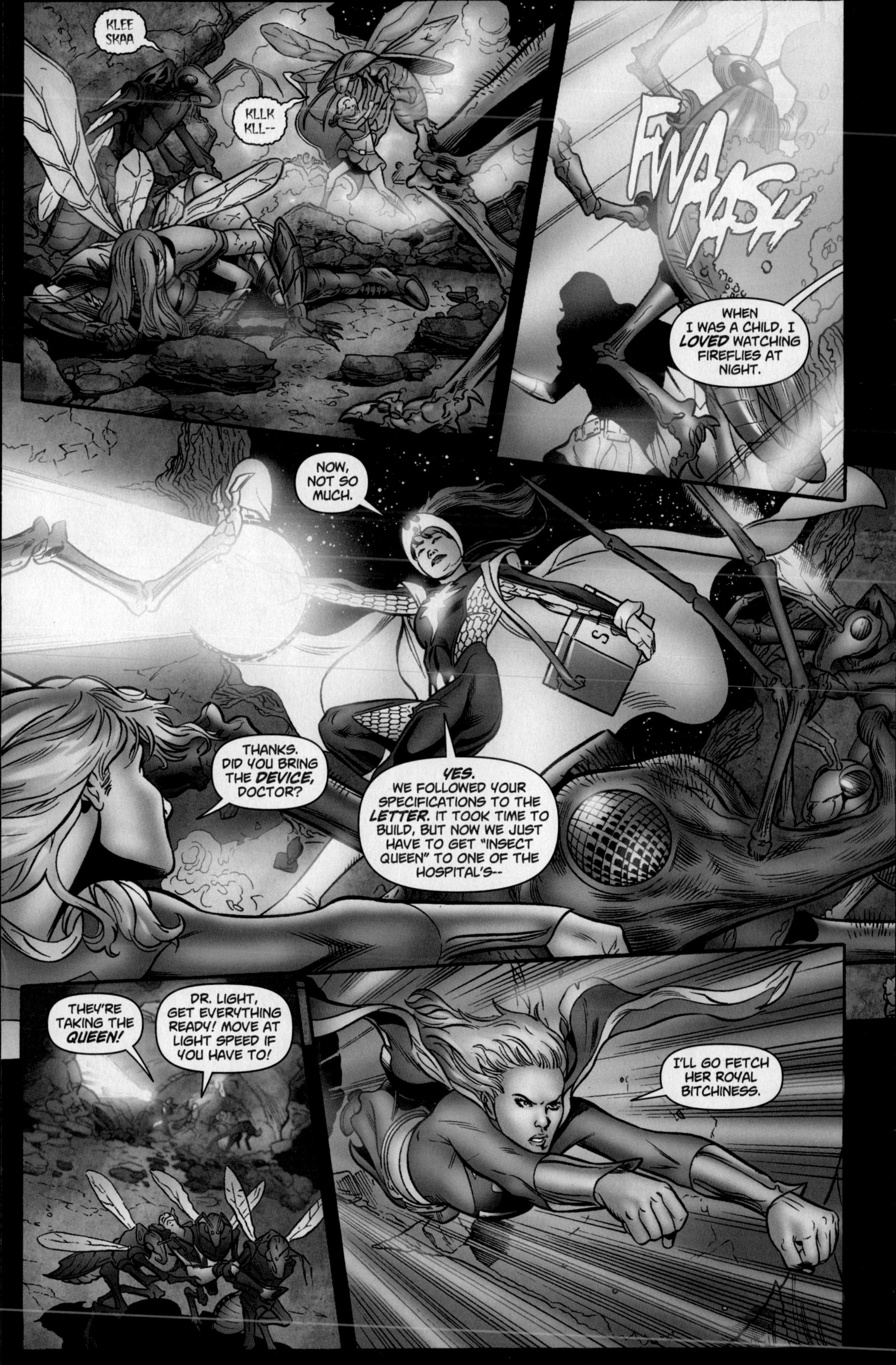

KLEE SKAA
KLLK KLL--
FWASH
WHEN I WAS A CHILD, I LOVED WATCHING FIREFLIES AT NIGHT.
NOW, NOT SO MUCH.
THANKS. DID YOU BRING THE DEVICE, DOCTOR?
YES. WE FOLLOWED YOUR SPECIFICATIONS TO THE LETTER. IT TOOK TIME TO BUILD, BUT NOW WE JUST HAVE TO GET "INSECT QUEEN" TO ONE OF THE HOSPITAL'S--
THEY'RE TAKING THE QUEEN!
DR. LIGHT, GET EVERYTHING READY! MOVE AT LIGHT SPEED IF YOU HAVE TO!
I'LL GO FETCH HER ROYAL BITCHINESS.

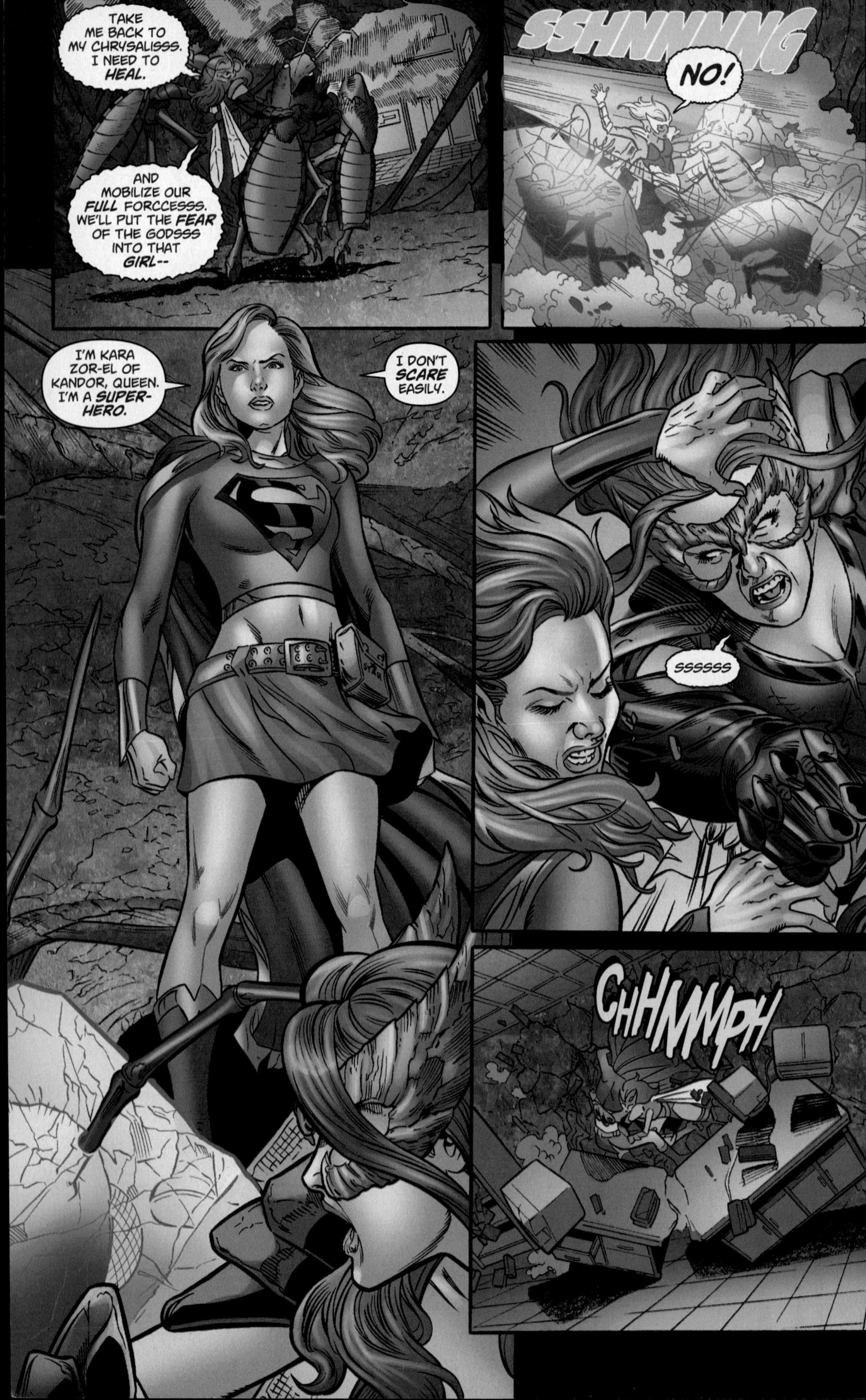
TAKE ME BACK TO MY CHRYSALISSS. I NEED TO HEAL.
AND MOBILIZE OUR FULL FORCCESSS. WE'LL PUT THE FEAR OF THE GODSSS INTO THAT GIRL--
SSHNNNNG
NO!
I'M KARA ZOR-EL OF KANDOR, QUEEN. I'M A SUPER-HERO.
I DON'T SCARE EASILY.
SSSSSS
CHHMMPH

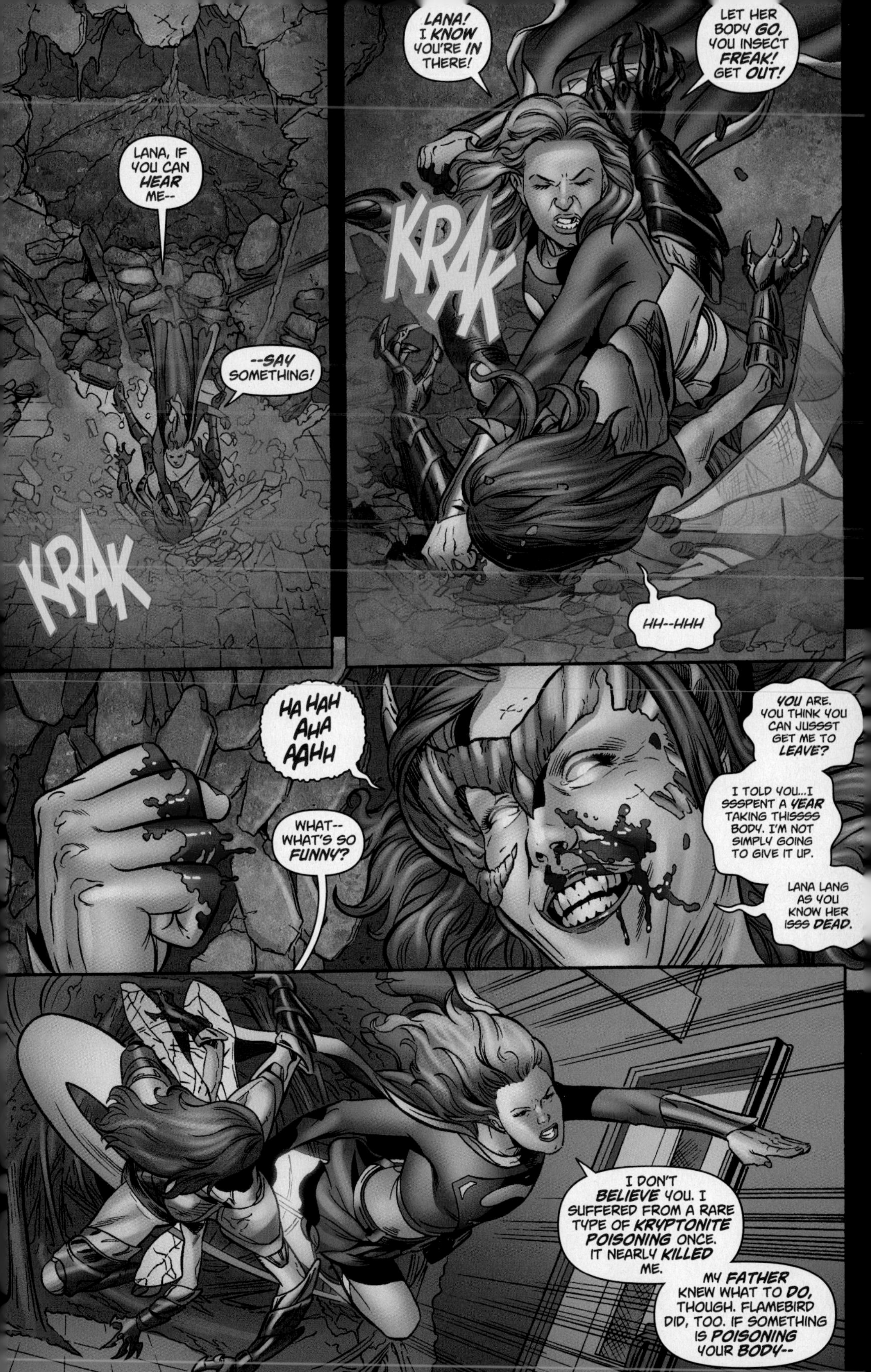
LANA, IF YOU CAN HEAR ME--
--SAY SOMETHING!
KRAK
LANA! I KNOW YOU'RE IN THERE!
LET HER BODY GO, YOU INSECT FREAK! GET OUT!
KRAK
HH--HHH
HA HAH AHA AAHH
WHAT--WHAT'S SO FUNNY?
YOU ARE. YOU THINK YOU CAN JUSSST GET ME TO LEAVE?
I TOLD YOU...I SSSPENT A YEAR TAKING THISSSS BODY. I'M NOT SIMPLY GOING TO GIVE IT UP.
LANA LANG AS YOU KNOW HER ISSS DEAD.
I DON'T BELIEVE YOU. I SUFFERED FROM A RARE TYPE OF KRYPTONITE POISONING ONCE. IT NEARLY KILLED ME.
MY FATHER KNEW WHAT TO DO, THOUGH. FLAMEBIRD DID, TOO. IF SOMETHING IS POISONING YOUR BODY--

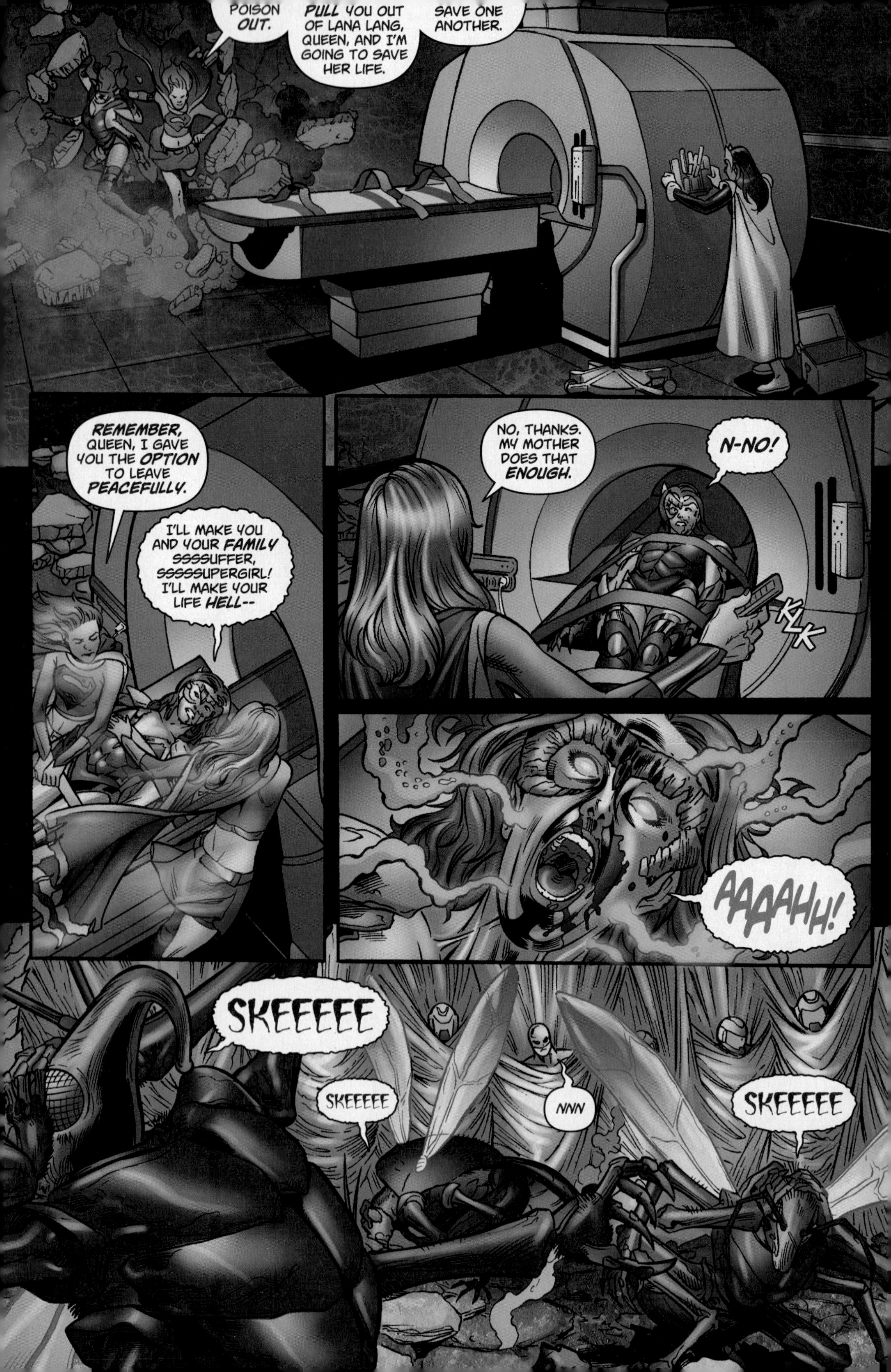
POISON OUT.
PULL YOU OUT OF LANA LANG, QUEEN, AND I'M GOING TO SAVE HER LIFE.
SAVE ONE ANOTHER.
REMEMBER, QUEEN, I GAVE YOU THE OPTION TO LEAVE PEACEFULLY.
I'LL MAKE YOU AND YOUR FAMILY SSSSUFFER, SSSSSUPERGIRL! I'LL MAKE YOUR LIFE HELL--
NO, THANKS. MY MOTHER DOES THAT ENOUGH.
N-NO!
KLIK
AAAAHH!
SKEEEEE
SKEEEEE
NNN
SKEEEEE

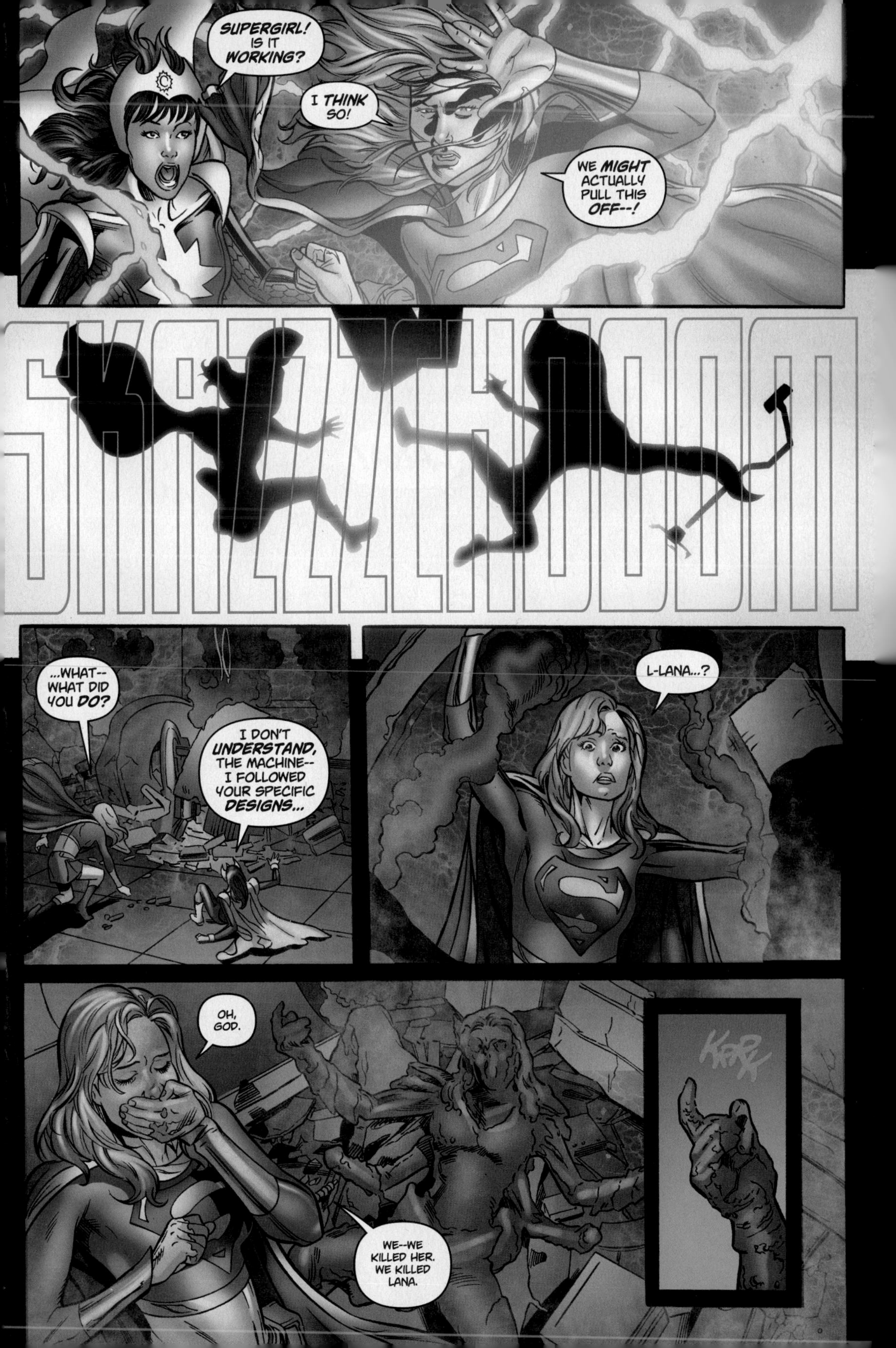
SUPERGIRL! IS IT WORKING?
I THINK SO!
WE MIGHT ACTUALLY PULL THIS OFF--!
SKRZZZZCHOOOM
...WHAT-- WHAT DID YOU DO?
I DON'T UNDERSTAND, THE MACHINE-- I FOLLOWED YOUR SPECIFIC DESIGNS...
L-LANA...?
OH, GOD.
WE--WE KILLED HER. WE KILLED LANA.
KRRK

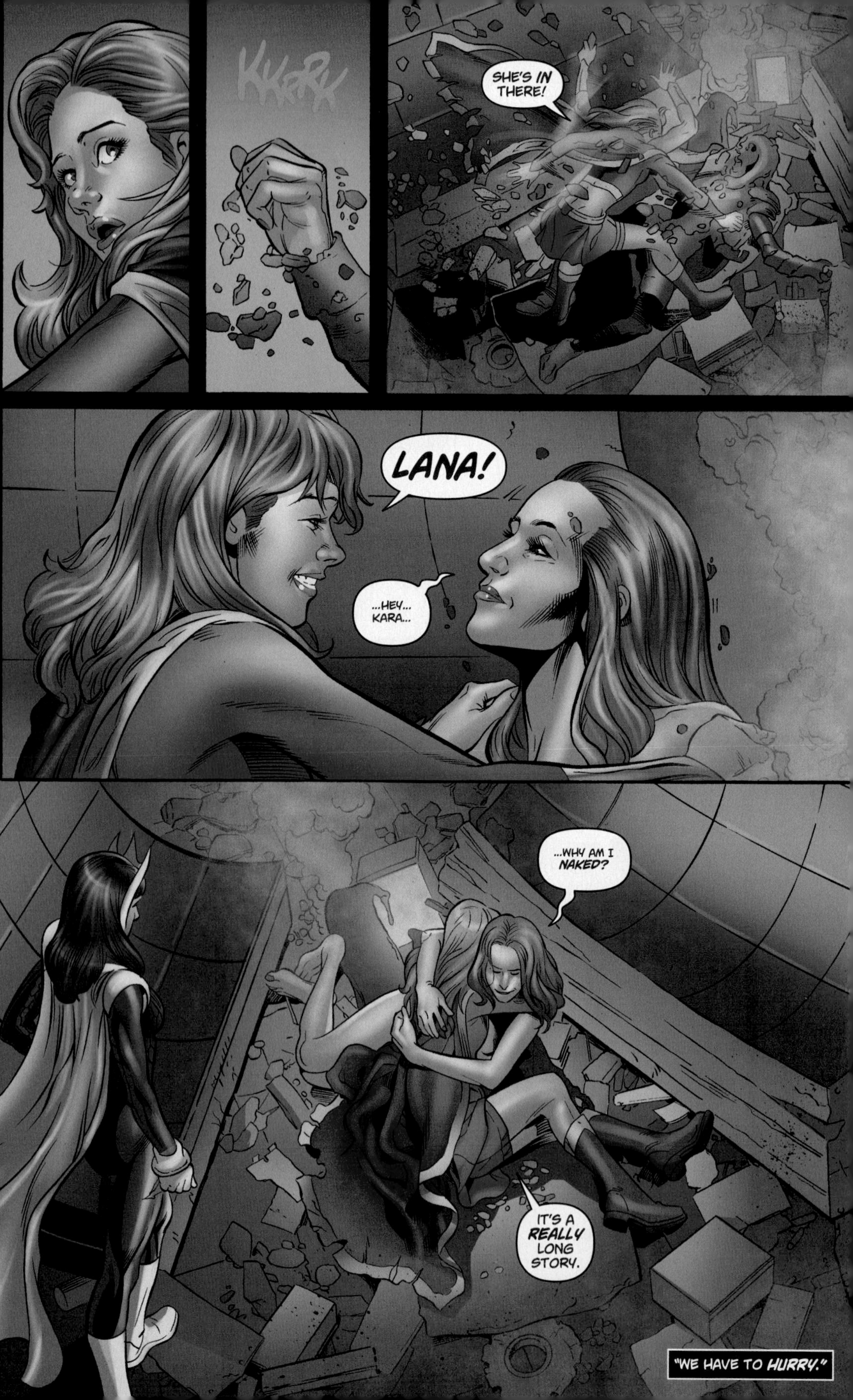
KKRRK
SHE'S IN THERE!
LANA!
...HEY... KARA...
...WHY AM I NAKED?
IT'S A REALLY LONG STORY.
"WE HAVE TO HURRY."

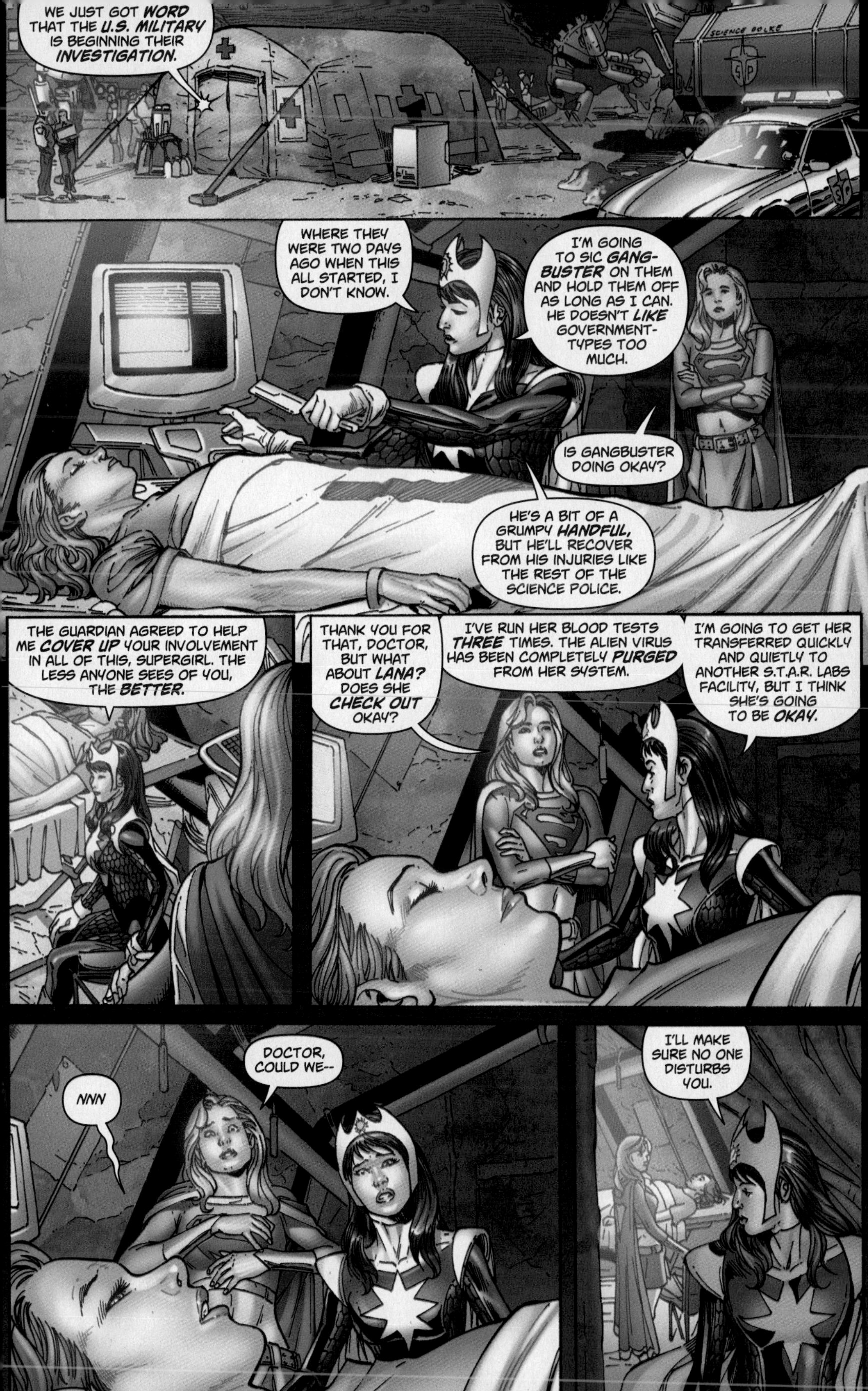
WE JUST GOT WORD THAT THE U.S. MILITARY IS BEGINNING THEIR INVESTIGATION.
SCIENCE POLICE
WHERE THEY WERE TWO DAYS AGO WHEN THIS ALL STARTED, I DON'T KNOW.
I'M GOING TO SIC GANG-BUSTER ON THEM AND HOLD THEM OFF AS LONG AS I CAN. HE DOESN'T LIKE GOVERNMENT-TYPES TOO MUCH.
IS GANGBUSTER DOING OKAY?
HE'S A BIT OF A GRUMPY HANDFUL, BUT HE'LL RECOVER FROM HIS INJURIES LIKE THE REST OF THE SCIENCE POLICE.
THE GUARDIAN AGREED TO HELP ME COVER UP YOUR INVOLVEMENT IN ALL OF THIS, SUPERGIRL. THE LESS ANYONE SEES OF YOU, THE BETTER.
THANK YOU FOR THAT, DOCTOR, BUT WHAT ABOUT LANA? DOES SHE CHECK OUT OKAY?
I'VE RUN HER BLOOD TESTS THREE TIMES. THE ALIEN VIRUS HAS BEEN COMPLETELY PURGED FROM HER SYSTEM.
I'M GOING TO GET HER TRANSFERRED QUICKLY AND QUIETLY TO ANOTHER S.T.A.R. LABS FACILITY, BUT I THINK SHE'S GOING TO BE OKAY.
NNN
DOCTOR, COULD WE--
I'LL MAKE SURE NO ONE DISTURBS YOU.

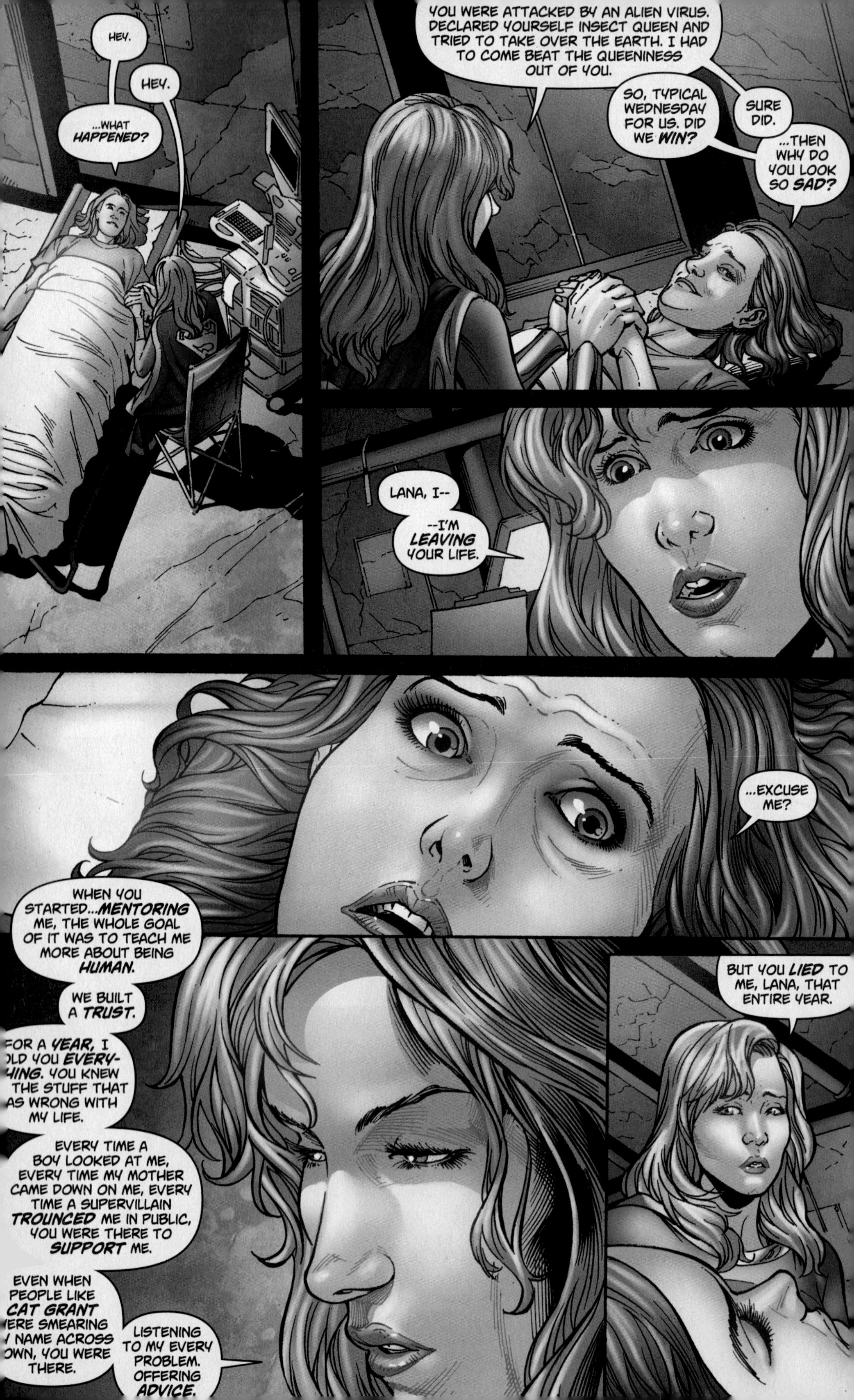

HEY.
HEY.
...WHAT HAPPENED?
YOU WERE ATTACKED BY AN ALIEN VIRUS. DECLARED YOURSELF INSECT QUEEN AND TRIED TO TAKE OVER THE EARTH. I HAD TO COME BEAT THE QUEENINESS OUT OF YOU.
SO, TYPICAL WEDNESDAY FOR US. DID WE WIN?
SURE DID.
...THEN WHY DO YOU LOOK SO SAD?
LANA, I--
--I'M LEAVING YOUR LIFE.
...EXCUSE ME?
WHEN YOU STARTED...MENTORING ME, THE WHOLE GOAL OF IT WAS TO TEACH ME MORE ABOUT BEING HUMAN.
WE BUILT A TRUST.
FOR A YEAR, I OLD YOU EVERY-HING. YOU KNEW THE STUFF THAT AS WRONG WITH MY LIFE.
EVERY TIME A BOY LOOKED AT ME, EVERY TIME MY MOTHER CAME DOWN ON ME, EVERY TIME A SUPERVILLAIN TROUNCED ME IN PUBLIC, YOU WERE THERE TO SUPPORT ME.
EVEN WHEN PEOPLE LIKE CAT GRANT ERE SMEARING NAME ACROSS OWN, YOU WERE THERE.
LISTENING TO MY EVERY PROBLEM. OFFERING ADVICE.
BUT YOU LIED TO ME, LANA, THAT ENTIRE YEAR.

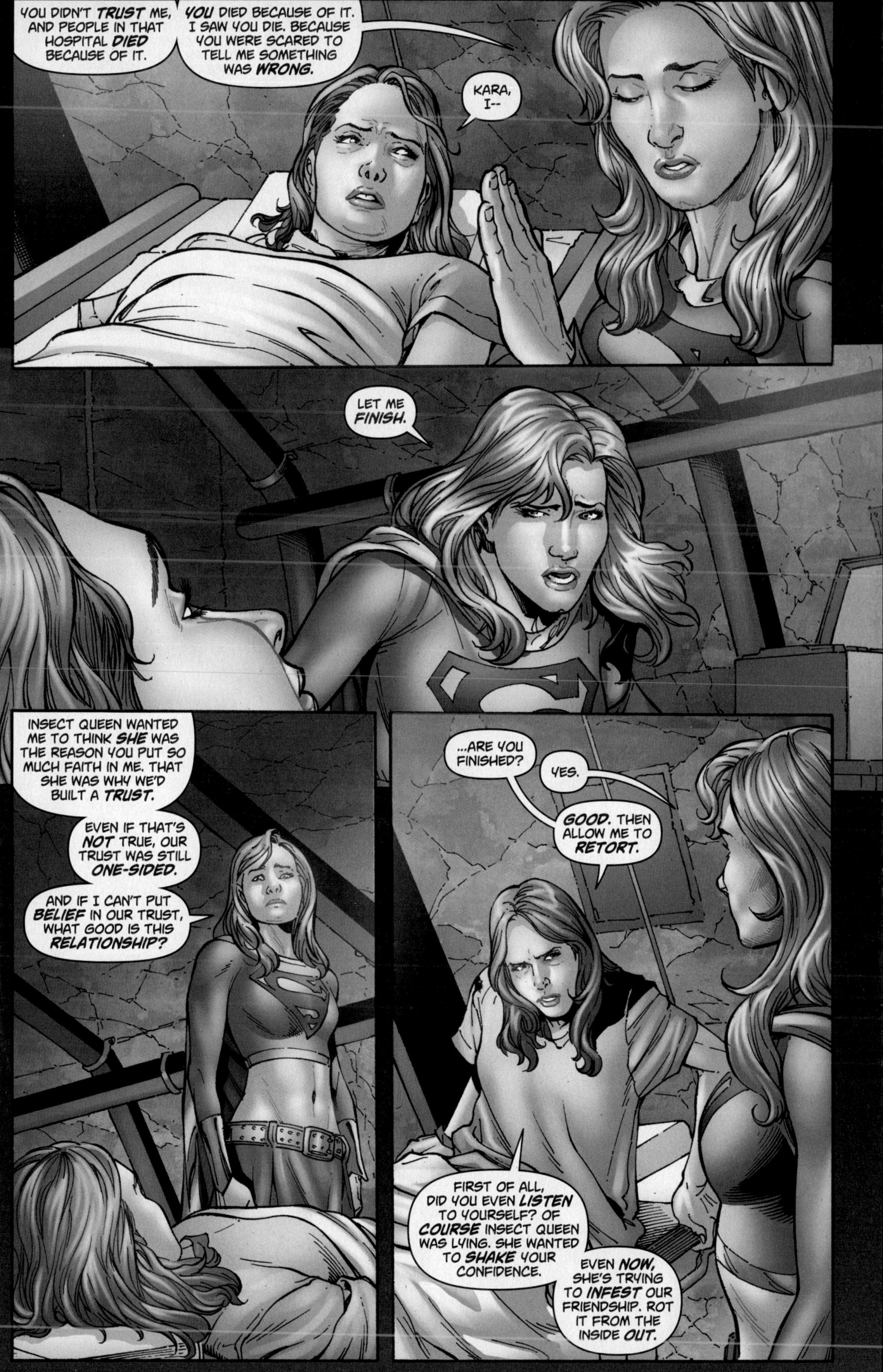
YOU DIDN'T TRUST ME, AND PEOPLE IN THAT HOSPITAL DIED BECAUSE OF IT.
YOU DIED BECAUSE OF IT. I SAW YOU DIE. BECAUSE YOU WERE SCARED TO TELL ME SOMETHING WAS WRONG.
KARA, I--
LET ME FINISH.
INSECT QUEEN WANTED ME TO THINK SHE WAS THE REASON YOU PUT SO MUCH FAITH IN ME. THAT SHE WAS WHY WE'D BUILT A TRUST.
EVEN IF THAT'S NOT TRUE, OUR TRUST WAS STILL ONE-SIDED.
AND IF I CAN'T PUT BELIEF IN OUR TRUST, WHAT GOOD IS THIS RELATIONSHIP?
...ARE YOU FINISHED?
YES.
GOOD. THEN ALLOW ME TO RETORT.
FIRST OF ALL, DID YOU EVEN LISTEN TO YOURSELF? OF COURSE INSECT QUEEN WAS LYING. SHE WANTED TO SHAKE YOUR CONFIDENCE.
EVEN NOW, SHE'S TRYING TO INFEST OUR FRIENDSHIP. ROT IT FROM THE INSIDE OUT.

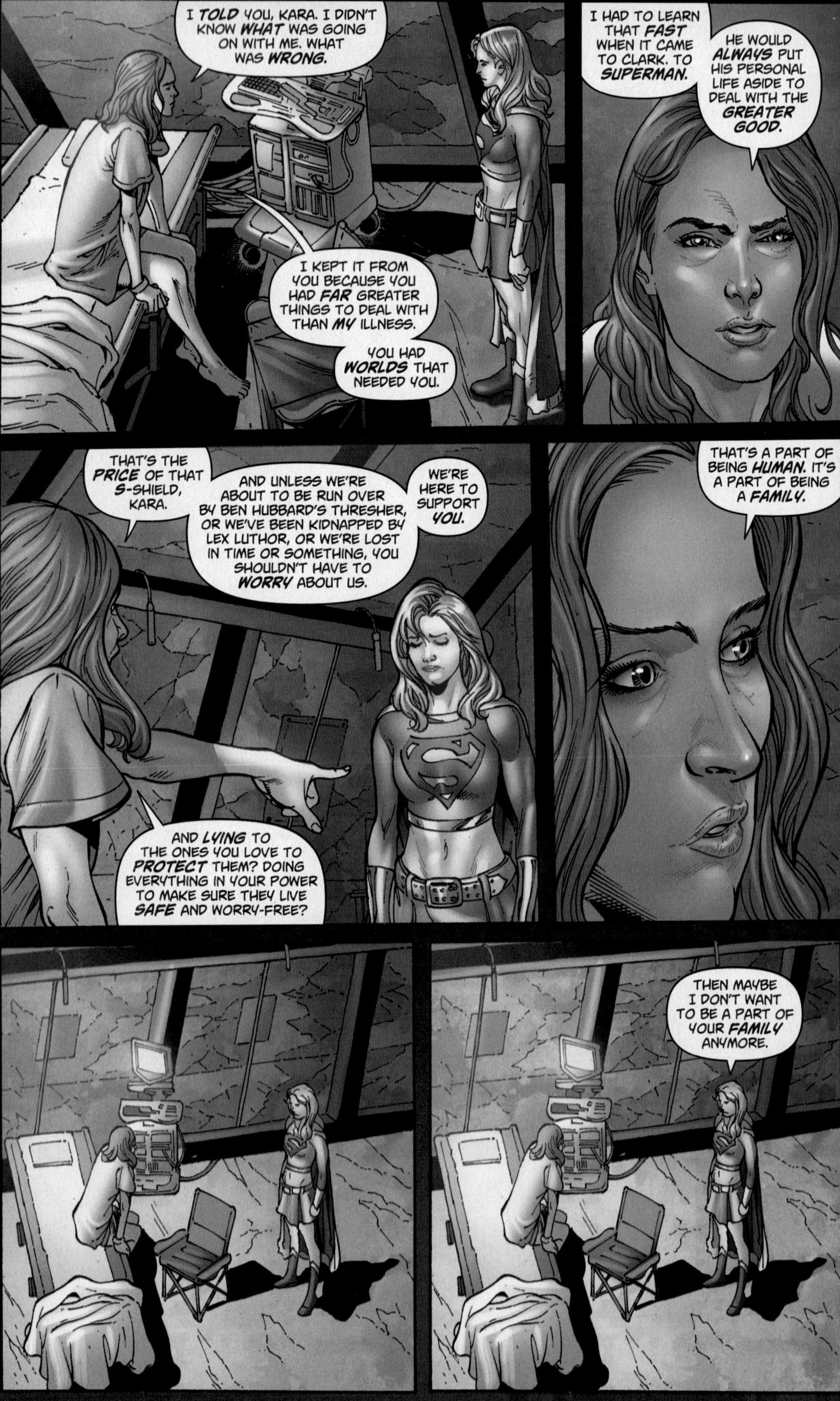

I TOLD YOU, KARA. I DIDN'T KNOW WHAT WAS GOING ON WITH ME. WHAT WAS WRONG.
I KEPT IT FROM YOU BECAUSE YOU HAD FAR GREATER THINGS TO DEAL WITH THAN MY ILLNESS.
YOU HAD WORLDS THAT NEEDED YOU.
I HAD TO LEARN THAT FAST WHEN IT CAME TO CLARK. TO SUPERMAN.
HE WOULD ALWAYS PUT HIS PERSONAL LIFE ASIDE TO DEAL WITH THE GREATER GOOD.
THAT'S THE PRICE OF THAT S-SHIELD, KARA.
AND UNLESS WE'RE ABOUT TO BE RUN OVER BY BEN HUBBARD'S THRESHER, OR WE'VE BEEN KIDNAPPED BY LEX LUTHOR, OR WE'RE LOST IN TIME OR SOMETHING, YOU SHOULDN'T HAVE TO WORRY ABOUT US.
WE'RE HERE TO SUPPORT YOU.
AND LYING TO THE ONES YOU LOVE TO PROTECT THEM? DOING EVERYTHING IN YOUR POWER TO MAKE SURE THEY LIVE SAFE AND WORRY-FREE?
THAT'S A PART OF BEING HUMAN. IT'S A PART OF BEING A FAMILY.
THEN MAYBE I DON'T WANT TO BE A PART OF YOUR FAMILY ANYMORE.

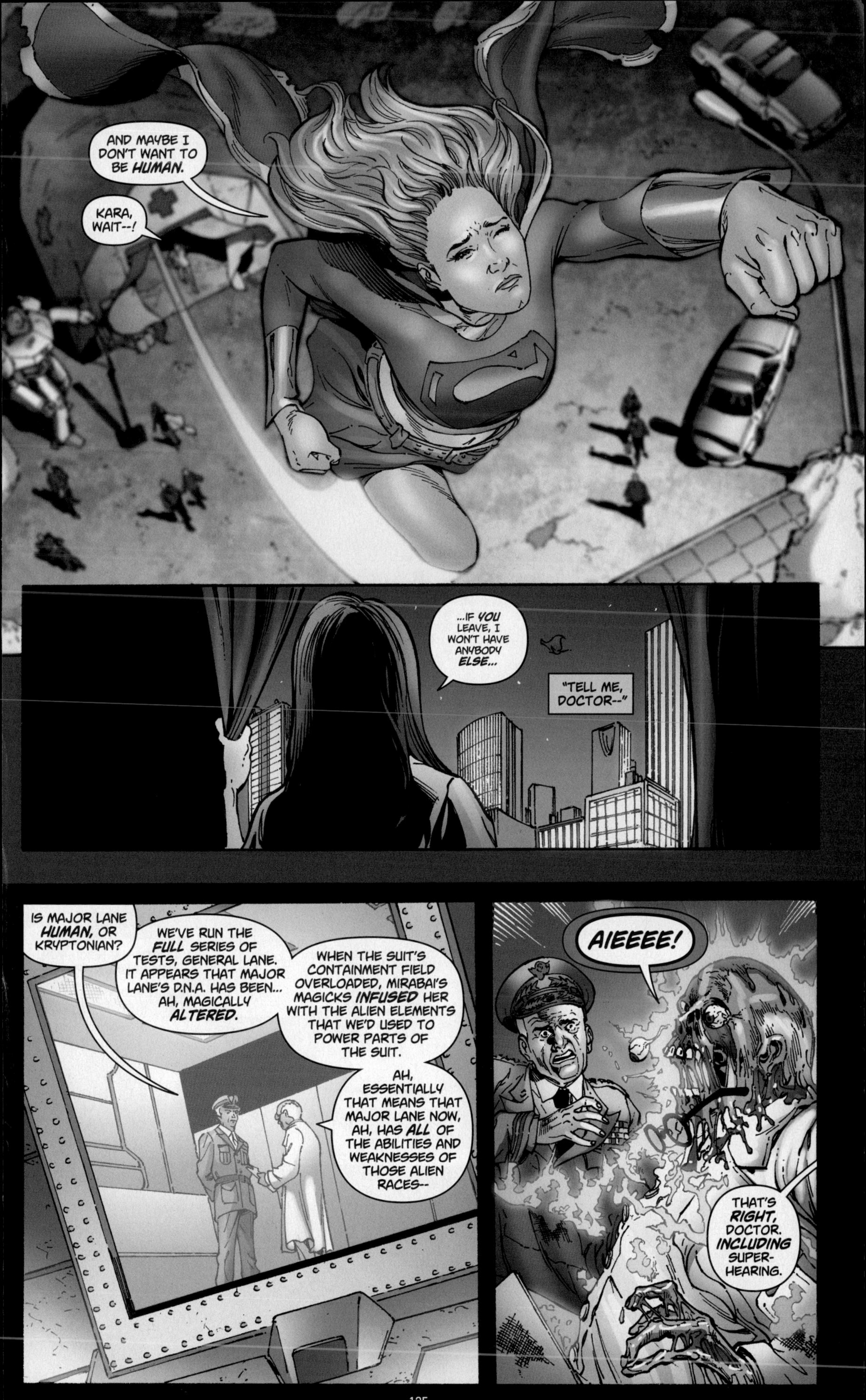

AND MAYBE I DON'T WANT TO BE HUMAN.
KARA, WAIT--!
...IF YOU LEAVE, I WON'T HAVE ANYBODY ELSE...
"TELL ME, DOCTOR--"
IS MAJOR LANE HUMAN, OR KRYPTONIAN?
WE'VE RUN THE FULL SERIES OF TESTS, GENERAL LANE. IT APPEARS THAT MAJOR LANE'S D.N.A. HAS BEEN... AH, MAGICALLY ALTERED.
WHEN THE SUIT'S CONTAINMENT FIELD OVERLOADED, MIRABAI'S MAGICKS INFUSED HER WITH THE ALIEN ELEMENTS THAT WE'D USED TO POWER PARTS OF THE SUIT.
AH, ESSENTIALLY THAT MEANS THAT MAJOR LANE NOW, AH, HAS ALL OF THE ABILITIES AND WEAKNESSES OF THOSE ALIEN RACES--
AIEEEE!
THAT'S RIGHT, DOCTOR. INCLUDING SUPER-HEARING.

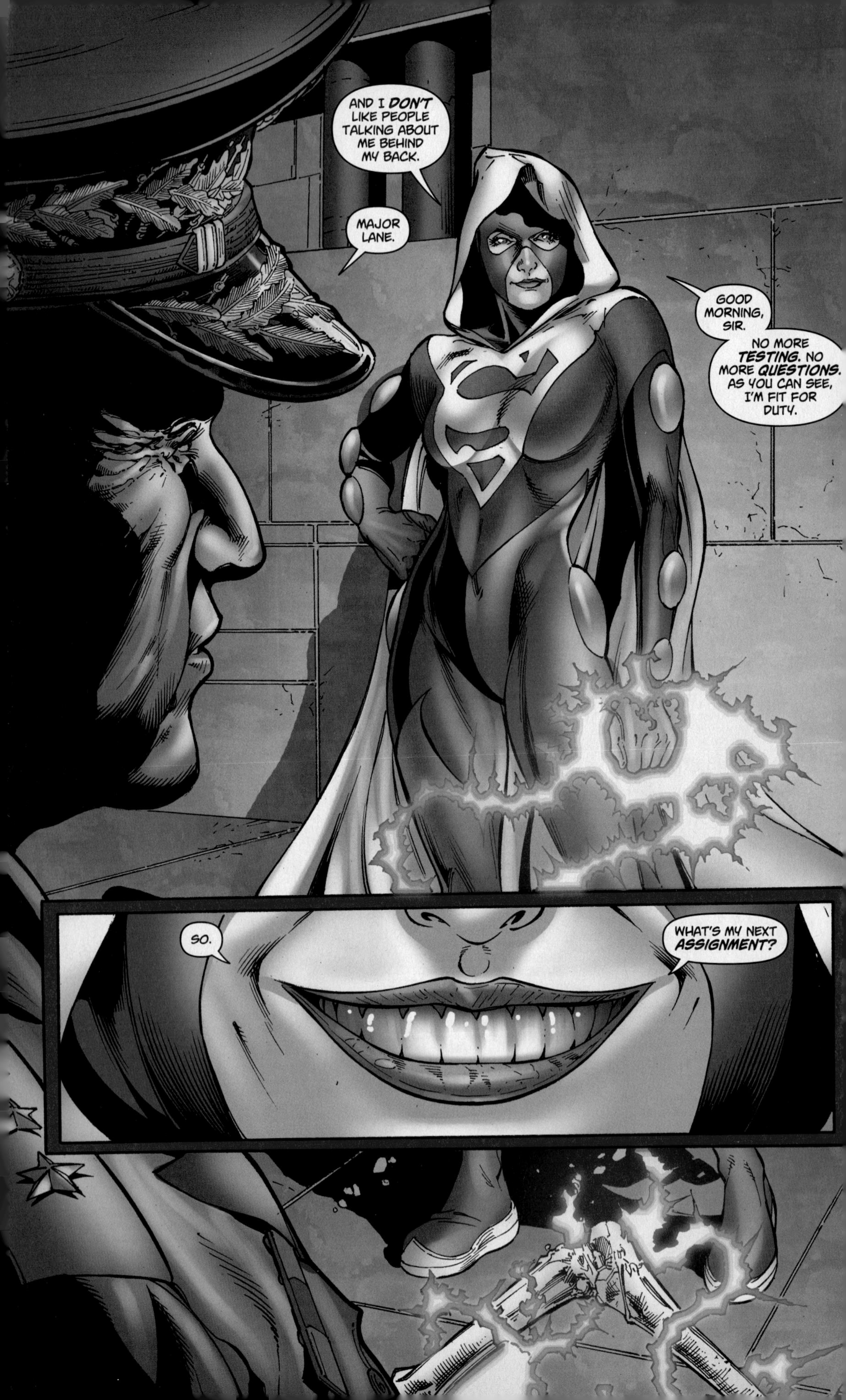
AND I DON'T LIKE PEOPLE TALKING ABOUT ME BEHIND MY BACK.
MAJOR LANE.
GOOD MORNING, SIR.
NO MORE TESTING. NO MORE QUESTIONS. AS YOU CAN SEE, I'M FIT FOR DUTY.
SO.
WHAT'S MY NEXT ASSIGNMENT?

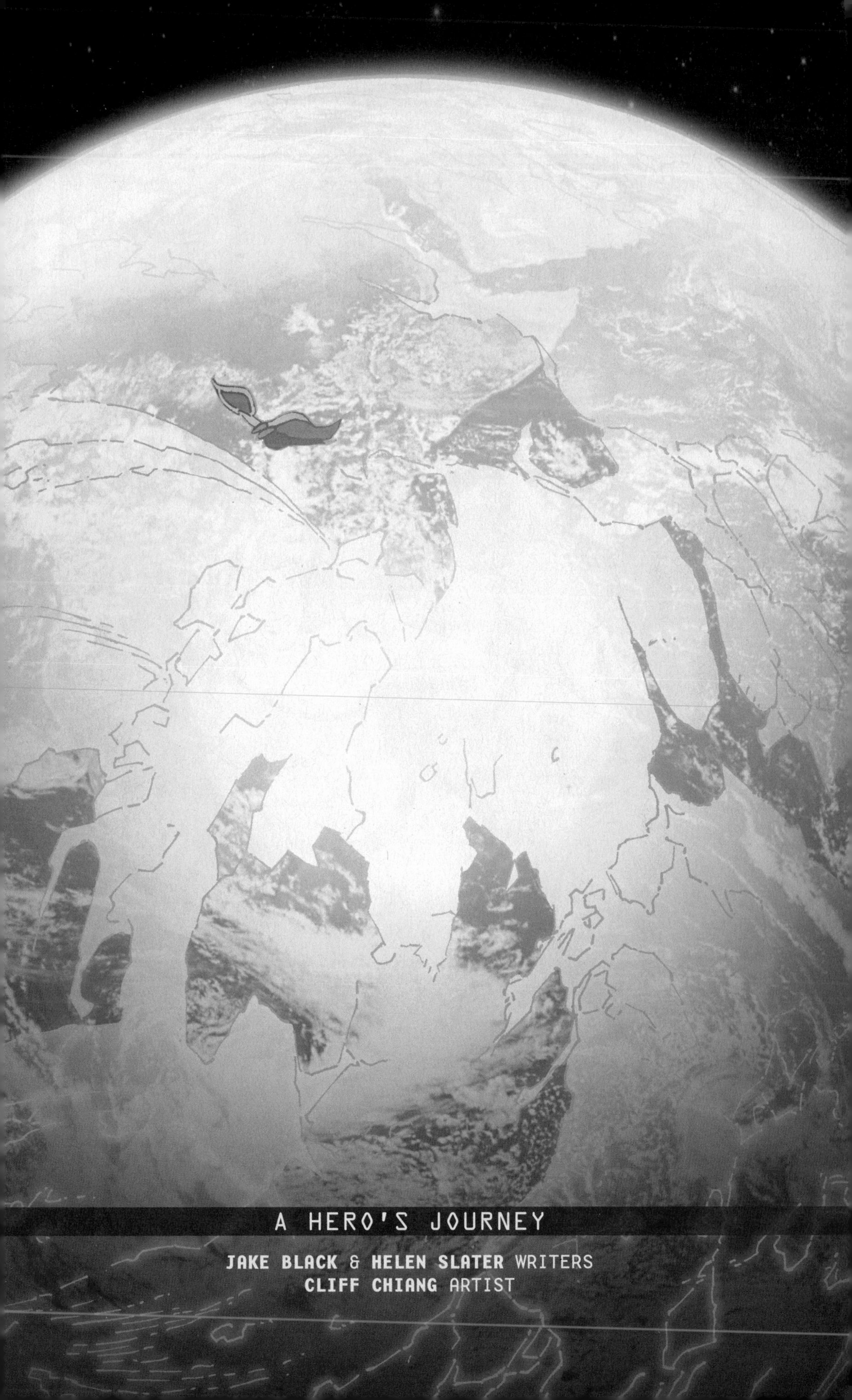
A HERO'S JOURNEY
JAKE BLACK & HELEN SLATER WRITERS
CLIFF CHIANG ARTIST

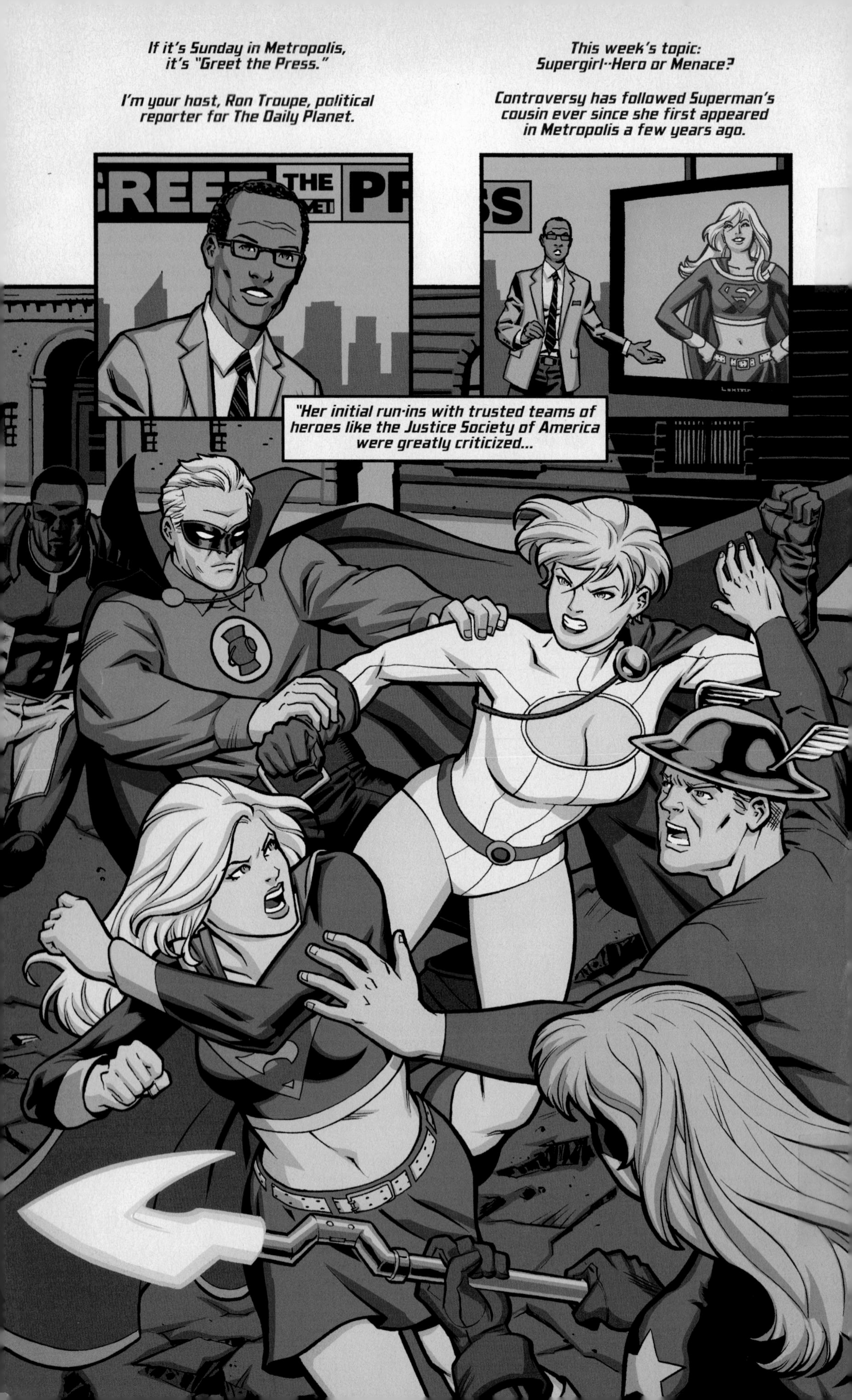
If it's Sunday in Metropolis, it's "Greet the Press."
I'm your host, Ron Troupe, political reporter for The Daily Planet.
This week's topic: Supergirl--Hero or Menace?
Controversy has followed Superman's cousin ever since she first appeared in Metropolis a few years ago.
GREET THE PRESS
"Her initial run-ins with trusted teams of heroes like the Justice Society of America were greatly criticized...

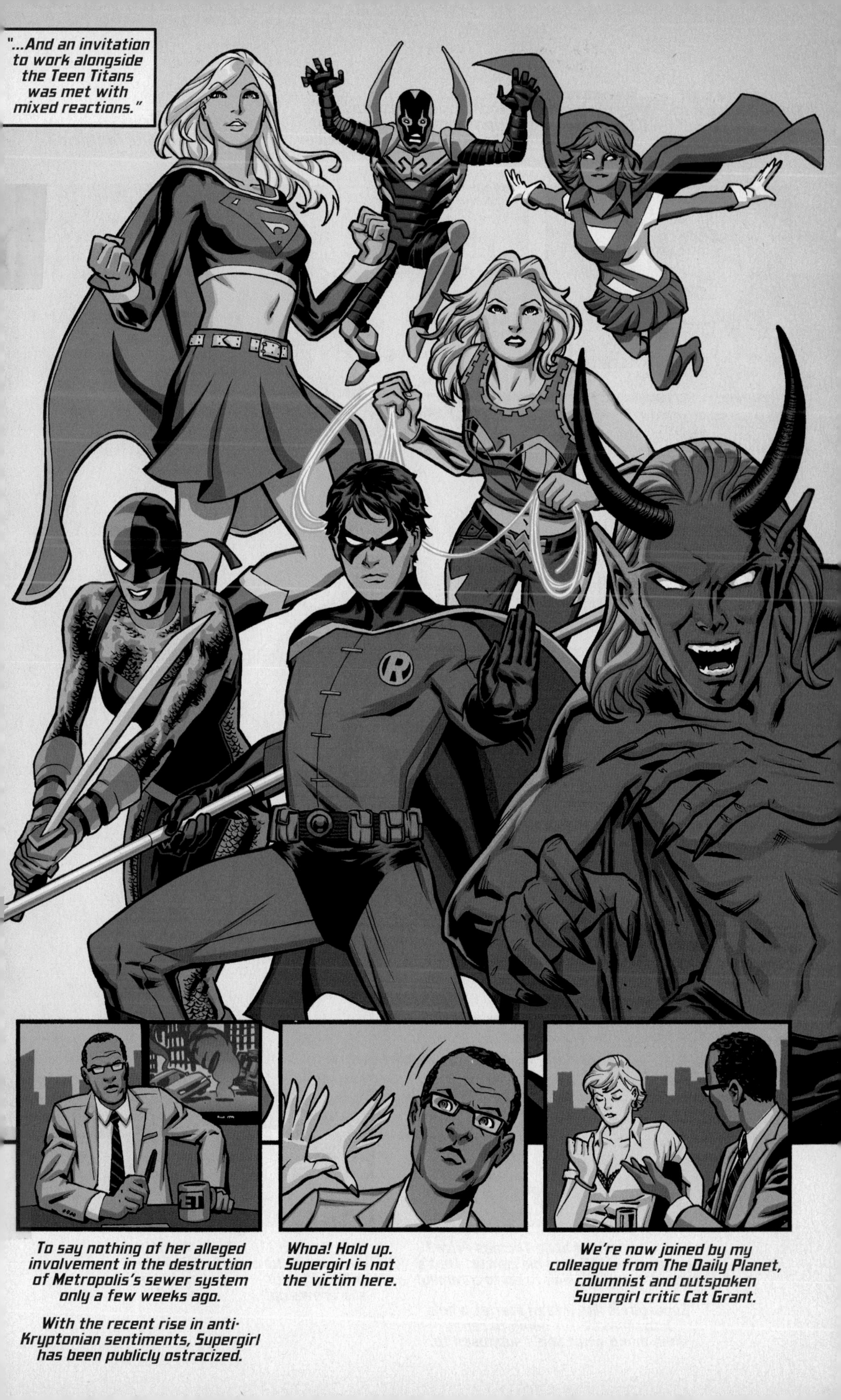
"...And an invitation to work alongside the Teen Titans was met with mixed reactions."
To say nothing of her alleged involvement in the destruction of Metropolis's sewer system only a few weeks ago.
With the recent rise in anti-Kryptonian sentiments, Supergirl has been publicly ostracized.
Whoa! Hold up. Supergirl is not the victim here.
We're now joined by my colleague from The Daily Planet, columnist and outspoken Supergirl critic Cat Grant.

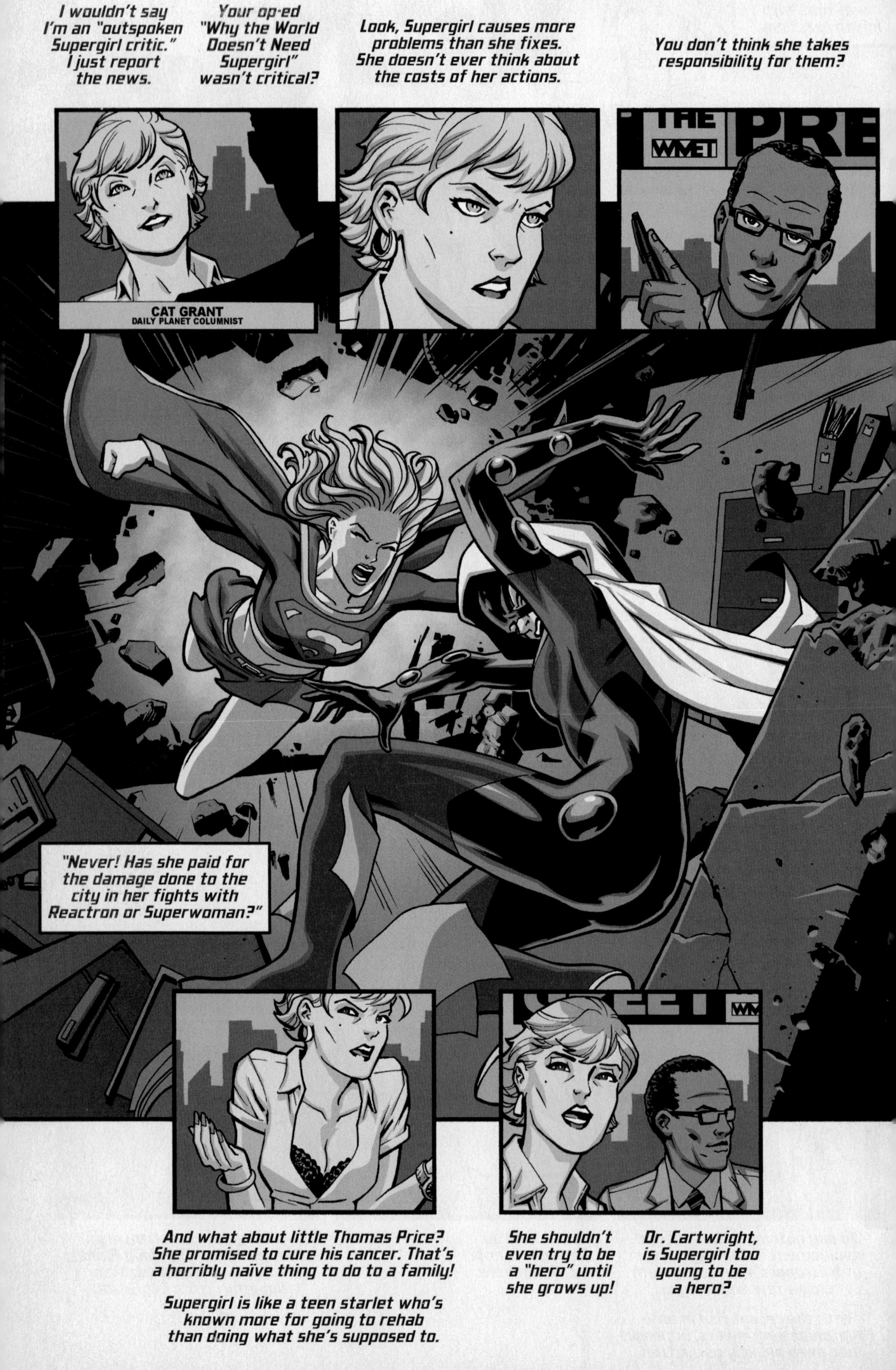
I wouldn't say I'm an "outspoken Supergirl critic." I just report the news.
Your op-ed "Why the World Doesn't Need Supergirl" wasn't critical?
Look, Supergirl causes more problems than she fixes. She doesn't ever think about the costs of her actions.
You don't think she takes responsibility for them?
CAT GRANT
DAILY PLANET COLUMNIST
THE
WMET
PRE
"Never! Has she paid for the damage done to the city in her fights with Reactron or Superwoman?"
And what about little Thomas Price? She promised to cure his cancer. That's a horribly naïve thing to do to a family!
Supergirl is like a teen starlet who's known more for going to rehab than doing what she's supposed to.
Dr. Cartwright, is Supergirl too young to be a hero?
She shouldn't even try to be a "hero" until she grows up!

She is heroic in her wish to do good in the world, and she is struggling to balance her power with her intention.

I would say she is perhaps too young to be so exposed to the scrutiny of society. Clearly she has the "call to adventure."

And from the "Hero's Journey" perspective, now may be the time for a teacher. Someone who could provide discipline, guidance and training.

Shouldn't that person be Superman?

DR. JOSEPH CARTWRIGHT
PROF. OF ANTHROPOLOGY - METROPOLIS UNIVERSITY

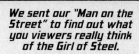

It's possible. However, many times the people who light our path are not the ones we are related to.

Just because she wears his costume, that doesn't automatically make him her guide.

Fascinating stuff.

We sent our "Man on the Street" to find out what you viewers really think of the Girl of Steel.

Here's what he found.

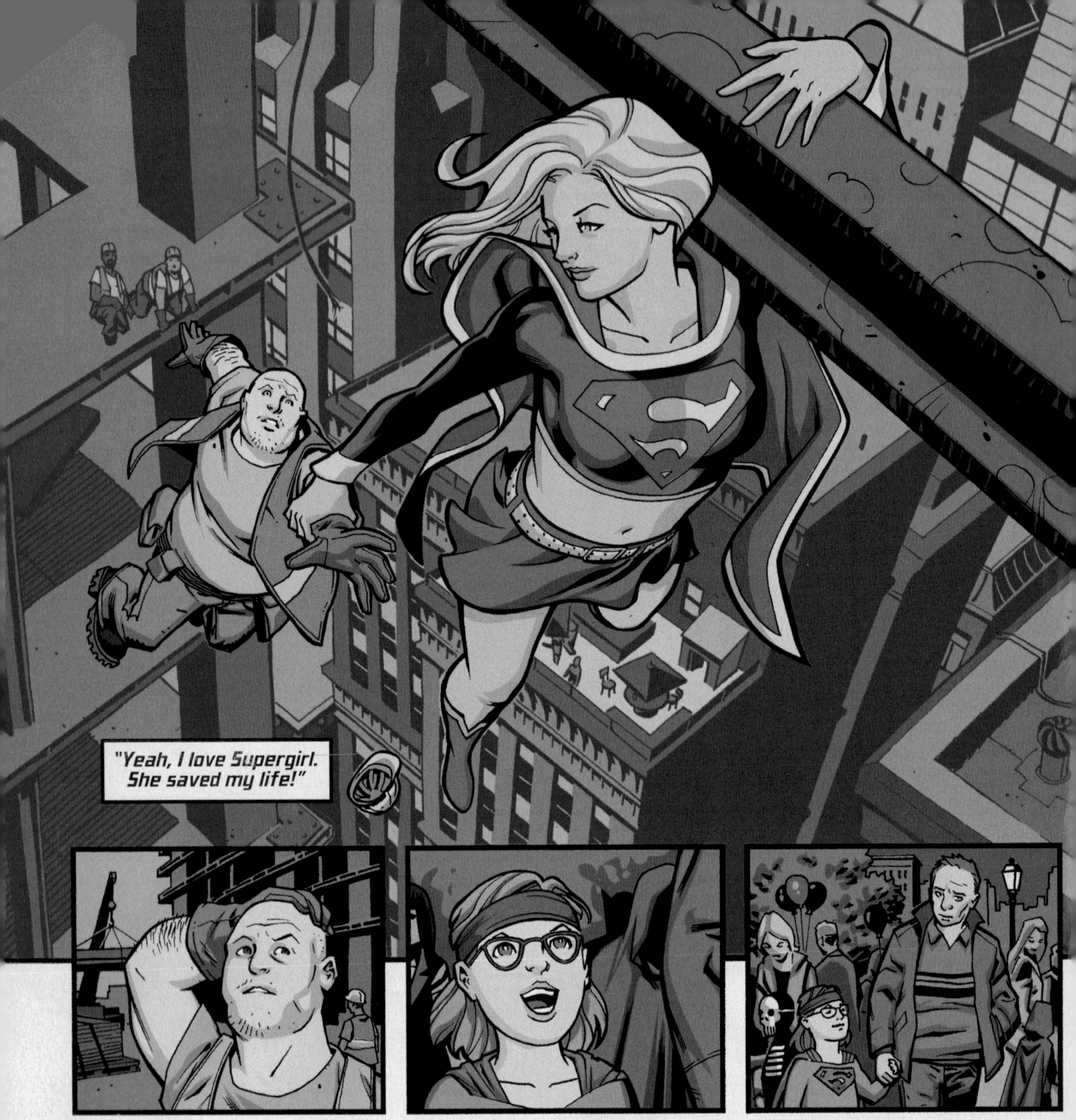
"Yeah, I love Supergirl. She saved my life!"

I don't like the Kryptonians any more than the next guy, but you can't judge a person only because of her race!

Supergirl brought my daddy back home to my family! She's my hero!

Yeah. She, uh, gave me a new way of looking at life when I'd pretty much hit rock bottom.

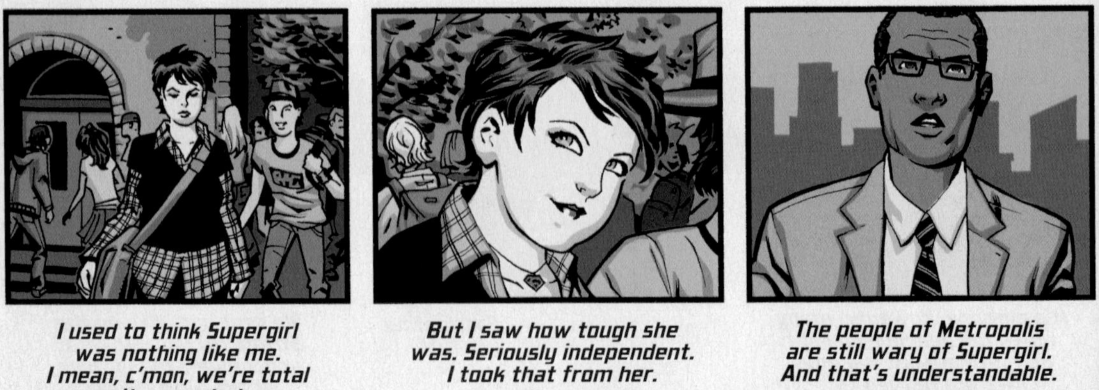

I used to think Supergirl was nothing like me. I mean, c'mon, we're total opposites or whatever.

She's all bright and happy. And I'm not.

But I saw how tough she was. Seriously independent. I took that from her.

Supergirl made me stronger.

The people of Metropolis are still wary of Supergirl. And that's understandable.

She is, after all, an inexperienced and perhaps undisciplined Kryptonian girl.

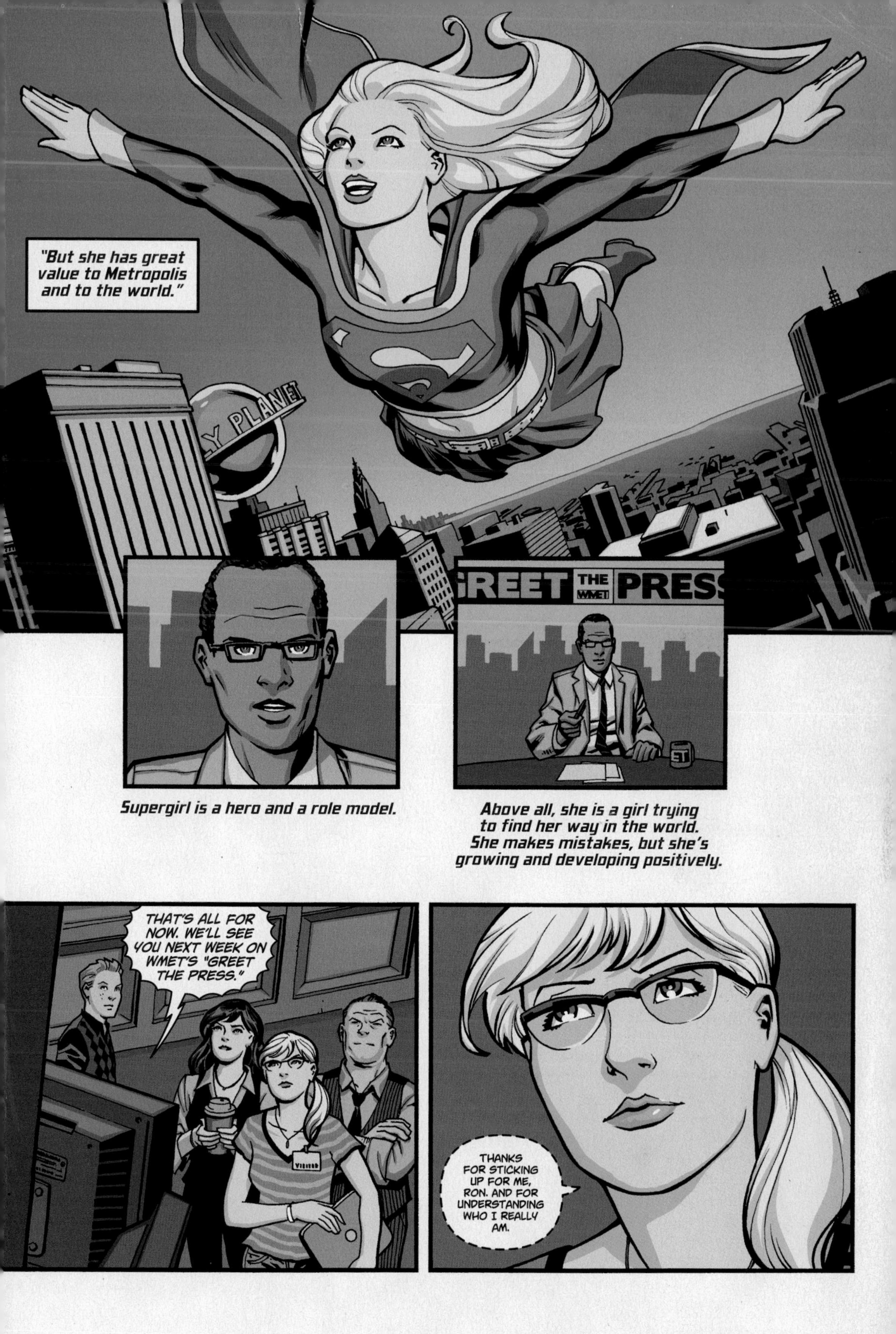
"But she has great value to Metropolis and to the world."
DAILY PLANET
GREET THE WMET PRESS
Supergirl is a hero and a role model.
Above all, she is a girl trying to find her way in the world. She makes mistakes, but she's growing and developing positively.
THAT'S ALL FOR NOW. WE'LL SEE YOU NEXT WEEK ON WMET'S "GREET THE PRESS."
VISITOR
THANKS FOR STICKING UP FOR ME, RON. AND FOR UNDERSTANDING WHO I REALLY AM.

SUPERGIRL #50 VARIANT COVER BY **JOSHUA MIDDLETON**

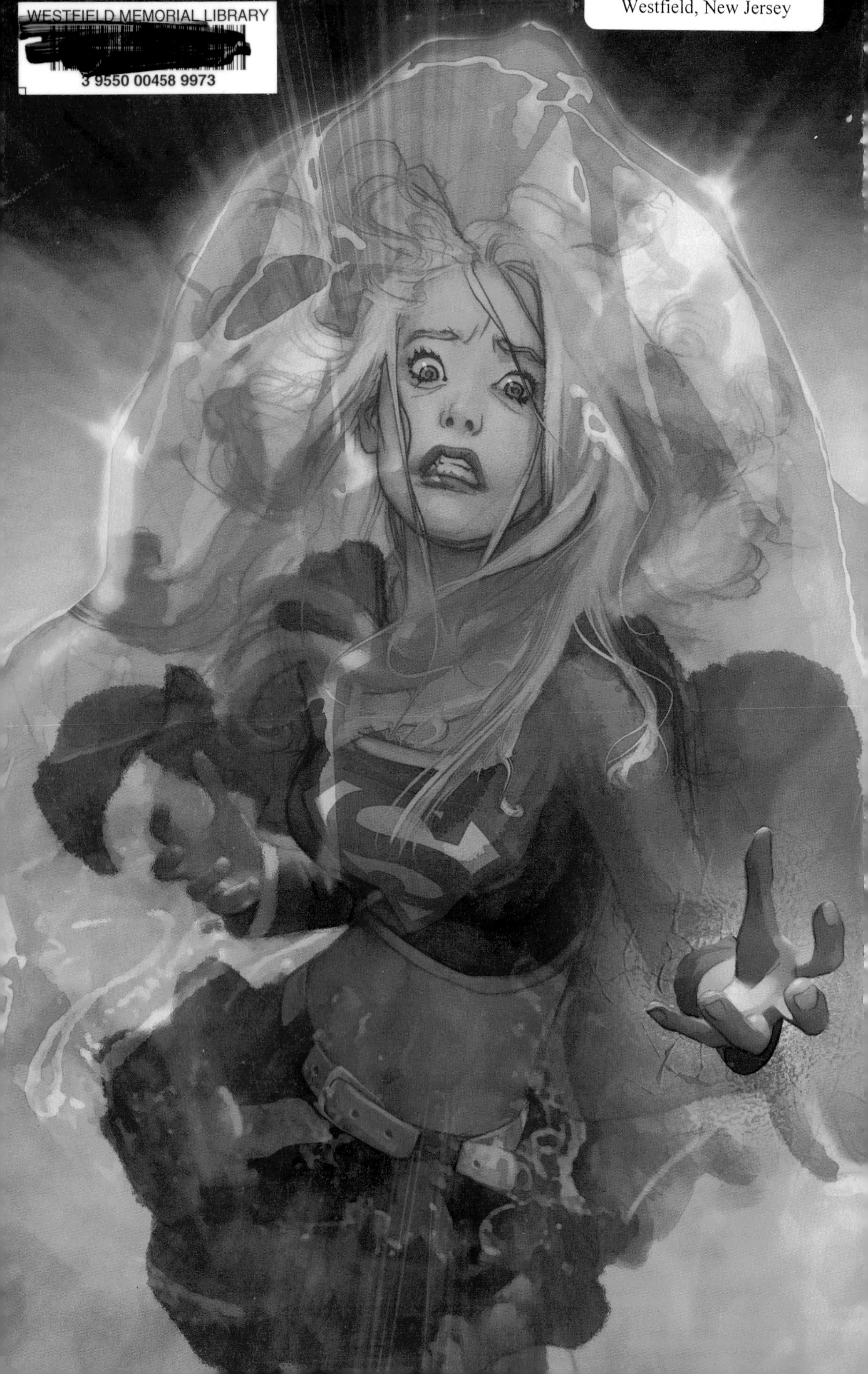